Chamberlain Association of America

Report of the Meetings for Organization and of the ... General Meeting

Together with the President's Address, and a List of Members

Chamberlain Association of America

Report of the Meetings for Organization and of the ... General Meeting
Together with the President's Address, and a List of Members

ISBN/EAN: 9783744729628

Printed in Europe, USA, Canada, Australia, Japan

Cover: Foto ©Suzi / pixelio.de

More available books at **www.hansebooks.com**

THE CHAMBERLAIN ASSOCIATION OF AMERICA

REPORT OF ANNUAL MEETINGS HELD IN BOSTON, MASSACHUSETTS, IN 1908, 1909 AND 1910

WITH

MEMORIAL SKETCHES OF MEMBERS OF THE ASSOCIATION

FOUR GENERATIONS OF THE DESCENDANTS OF WILLIAM CHAMBERLAIN OF WOBURN AND BILLERICA, MASSACHUSETTS.
AND OTHER PAPERS CONCERNING THE CHAMBERLAIN FAMILY

CHAMBERLAIN ASSOCIATION OF AMERICA

ANNUAL MEETING OF 1908

THE scene of the annual gathering of 1908, the eleventh, was again the Parker House, Boston. The Executive Committee met at ten o'clock. At noon the President of the Association, General Joshua L. Chamberlain, held a reception; and later the company adjourned to the Crystal Dining Room for luncheon.

After the good things provided by "mine host" had been discussed and secluded, the President introduced Rev. E. E. Strong, D. D., who spoke briefly of the life-work of Rev. Dr. Jacob Chamberlain, physician, explorer, scholar, and preacher. Jacob Chamberlain went in 1859, to India, where he labored as a missionary for nearly fifty years. Being able to speak in several of the native dialects, he was equipped for work of wide extent, which included a revision of the Bible in the Telugu language. He was the father of Jacob Chester Chamberlain, who died some two years ago.

At the conclusion of Dr. Strong's address, the President spoke of the absence from the meeting of General Samuel E. Chamberlain, who is ill at his home in Barre. This is the first annual meeting of the Association from which he has been absent. On motion, a telegram of sympathy was sent to him.

Following this came an interesting speech by Mr. J. H. Walling, whose mother was a Chamberlain. He has but recently joined the Association, but evinced all the enthusiasm of a veteran. He read a paper prepared by his father, which gave a sketch of the life of his grandfather Chamberlain.

Eugene Chamberlin of New York, began a picturesque and eloquent address with the dictum: "As by the grace of Providence we meet again, each one present should offer something in honor of the name we bear." He was proud of his name and of his descent, for it was becoming more and more of an honor to trace descent from a grandfather who was born in this country. In the great city of New York with its millions of people, there were barely eighty thousand whose fathers were natives of this land. One of his ancestors, John by name, was scourged nine times because he would not forego his faith, and another, William of Connecticut, proved his virility by raising so many children they were never counted. The speaker's great grandfather was one of the party who helped Washington cross the Delaware. His father served through the Civil War in the 25th Ohio. He finished his address with an eloquent tribute to the strong sterling qualities of the men who had borne the name of Chamberlain.

Mr. Kendall extended an invitation to the members to visit his home at

Holden on the morrow. "The calf has not fatted worth a cent, but two young pigs have offered themselves, and we hope that all of you will try their flavor."

Mr. George W. Adams of Dorchester, was proud of the sweet-natured little woman who had been by his side for forty-three years, and who had made him feel it an honor to be a member of this Association.

Vice President Emerson Chamberlin was next called upon. He thanked the assemblage for conferring upon him the honor of his election, and expressed his pride in being connected with a family which had produced so many strong, purposeful men and women. His descendants would be proud of the honor.

Mrs. Austin sang several songs, and Dr. George M. Chamberlin of Chicago, and Dr. George M. Chamberlain of Brookline, added their quota of speechmaking. Miss Jessie Chamberlin of Texas, gave an interesting sketch of a four years' tour through Europe and Egypt. In Germany she happened upon a Chamberlain who was a scholar of note, his specialty being history.

Hon. Milton Reed said he was a stranger within our gates, a trespasser, who had been helped over the fence by his old friend, Dr. George M. Chamberlin of Chicago. His witty sallies brought hearty applause.

After Miss Ella Chamberlin had delighted the assemblage with music, the business of the Association was disposed of,—chiefly matters of routine and the election of officers for the year.

The Association adjourned.

MONTAGUE CHAMBERLAIN,
Recording Secretary.

SOCIAL GATHERINGS OF 1908

THIS year we followed the advice of our President to be social, and after the annual meeting most of the members adjourned in the evening to the home of the Misses Chamberlain on Exeter Park, in Cambridge, for an informal reception and social time, with vocal and instrumental music interspersed. Miss Alice M. Raymond opened with a brilliant piano solo; two of our well-known members, Mrs. M. E. Austin and Miss Jessie Chamberlin, favored us with sweet old-time songs; and after refreshments, Miss Ella Chamberlin delighted all with her wonderful bird-like warblings. All were much pleased because the President, Gen. Joshua L. Chamberlain, and his daughter, Mrs. Allen, were able to be present. The next day found a large and merry party ready for the delightful trolley ride from Park Square, Boston, to Worcester and Paradise Hill, Holden, where they were met by members of the Kendall family with carriages and automobiles to take them up the hill to the family home. Tables were set on the spacious lawn in the rear of the house, in the form of a square. With appetites sharpened by the long ride, all were ready to do justice to the bountiful dinner. The vegetables

SUMMER HOME OF MR. AND MRS. J. H. KENDALL

and the fruits were the products of the farm, and were most deliciously cooked, and served to the enjoyment of all. Appetites being appeased, Mr. James Kendall asked Dr. George M. Chamberlin of Chicago, to take charge of the program. Judge Wm. T. Forbes of Worcester, referred to the severe illness of General Robert Chamberlain, and of Gen. S. E. Chamberlain, and moved that an expression of sympathy be sent to them, which motion was unanimously carried. Dr. E. E. Strong and Mr. James H. Walling of Brooklyn, N. Y., made a few brief remarks. Mrs. Anna E. Smiley read an interesting letter and poem from Mrs. Jane Moore of Ohio, one of our members. Dr. George M. Chamberlin indulged in a few facetious remarks, and introduced his old-time friend and fellow-traveller, Hon. Milton Reed of Fall River, Mass., who entertained the company with witty anecdotes and brilliant remarks, producing much merriment. After these pleasantries, it was voted to adjourn to a pine grove, called the "Pine Parlor", where Mr. and Mrs. James H. Walling of Brooklyn, N. Y., received the congratulations of the members on the twenty-sixth anniversary of their marriage. Mrs. Walling's maiden name being Pine, the guests, in appreciation of his great admiration for the Pine family, decked themselves with a sprig from the trees, and formed in line to greet them. Later Mr. Kendall, Senior, conducted the party over the estate and showed the points of interest. His robust form and the healthful glow on his face spoke well for the climate of Paradise Hill, and you will not be surprised to hear that Mr. and Mrs. George B. Caswell have decided to build them a home there. All too soon the setting sun warned the party that it was time to bid good-by to Paradise Hill. All seemed to feel that the day had been a red-letter day in the history of the society; and with many kindly wishes and adieus, they turned their faces homeward, only regretting that all of our members could not have been there to enjoy the beautiful scenery, and the hospitality offered on this occasion. A. M. C.

REPORT OF THE CORRESPONDING SECRETARY

THE eleventh annual meeting finds us assembled again in the Parker House, which has now become almost a Boston home for this organization. Our Report has been so recently issued, and our Recording Secretary has given so full an account of the meeting last year that I will only refer to two or three items. We enjoyed the pleasure of having invited guests with us, which added to the interest of the occasion. One family represented three generations of the name of Chamberlin, from sweet sixteen to over eighty years of age. We refer to the twin brothers, Hon. Albert and Augustus Chamberlin of North Abington, Mass., and their descendants. Miss Lila A. Chamberlin, the granddaughter, favored us with music.

We have added twenty-three names to our membership, so we are verging toward four hundred names on our record book. Only three deaths have been recorded the past year, but we have lost our Honorary Life Member, Rev. Jacob Chamberlain of India, who died with the harness on. Although partially paralyzed, he continued working on his Telugu Bible Dictionary, hoping to complete it during his life-time. After the death of the venerable Dr. Paton, it was stated that Dr. Chamberlain, with his forty-seven years of service, had the longest record of any living missionary in the foreign field. He had a varied experience as a physician as well as a missionary. Colonel Simon E. Chamberlin, one of our Vice Presidents, died last spring; he had a remarkably brilliant and patriotic record during the Civil War, being one of the leading factors in saving the city of Washington, D. C., at the time that the Confederate General, Jubal Early, made his raid in 1864, followed by the battle of Fort Stevens. An interesting account of the part that he took in helping to save the Nation's Capital, was written by Captain Henry A. Castle of Minnesota, and published in the *National Tribune Repository*, November, 1907. I wish that we had the space to print the article in full to do justice to the memory of such a brave man. We have received his photograph, taken twenty-five years before his death. He was a great sufferer from rheumatism, contracted during the war, the latter part of his life, but bore it with remarkable fortitude and patience. Mr. William Hayes of Minnesota, informs us of the death, in January, of his wife, Mrs. Charlotte Prentiss Hayes.

The Biennial Report seems to have given general satisfaction to our members. Our President writes that it is not only the largest but the finest that the society has published. Vice President Thomas Chamberlin said that it was the banner Report of the society. The illustrations are especially fine, and the Grafton Press is entitled to the thanks of the society. Several of our members loaned plates and photographs for this number, for which we return thanks. Prof. Paul M. Chamberlain of Chicago, sent generously 550 pictures of his late father, Hon. Henry Chamberlain of Michigan, to be bound in the Report. Last year it was suggested that fifty dollars be spent in preparing a genealogy of four or five generations of each of the five or six branches in the society. The Executive Committee selected the New England pioneer, Henry of Hingham, for the first branch, and they will, we trust, continue in the same line.

On account of services rendered during the Civil War, we learn, Mr. Roe Reisinger of Franklin, Penn., was awarded the Congressional Medal of Honor, February 2, 1907, by the unanimous vote of both Houses of Congress. His only son is a graduate of West Point, and a Lieutenant in the 27th U. S. Infantry.

Some of us received a pleasant call from President McKendree H. Chamberlin, when on a trip to the East. The Chase-Chace Family Reunion at the Vendome was a very fine affair; some Chamberlains are connected with that family.

The account printed of Col. Harding's search for his wife's ancestors is both interesting and stimulating, and may lead others to attempt the same

MR. HERBERT B. CHAMBERLAIN

thing. We need the coöperation of every member in finding "missing links". When all of the members of an organization spring from a common ancestor, the work of tracing the line of descent is usually an easy task; but with five or six branches, with several progenitors, who settled in different states at various times, with twenty-three variations of spelling the name, the work is more complicated. When the society was first formed there were comparatively few family genealogies published, nor were there many "Vital Records" of historic towns. Now that patriotic societies are printing such statistics year by year, let me urge you to consult the records of the towns where your forefathers lived; you may thus find valuable data or "missing links". The work is growing easier in many respects. Allow me to relate an incident to encourage and stimulate you to research. General William Chamberlain of Hopkinton, Mass., later of Vermont, wrote out for his descendants a sketch of what he had learned of his ancestors. In it he stated that John, the son of Jacob Chamberlain of Chelsea, Mass., had four sons; two went to western New York, then a wilderness, and two settled in Jaffrey, N. H. In after years frequent inquiries for those sons failed to find the lost tribe of Israel, until the year before this Association was organized, the clue that General Chamberlain left was followed in New Hampshire, and a connecting link was found in Oneida County, N. Y. After examining files of old letters, visiting cemeteries, consulting dates in family Bibles and in the Hopkinton and Chelsea records, it was found that dates and names harmonized, although all trace of the New York and the New Hampshire contingents had been lost for half a century or more. So many family ties have now been established, that it seems very possible that many New England Chamberlains may find they are connected. This society never seemed more hopeful than to-day. We begin to see some of the fruitage of our work; and if it proves as hopeful as our committee seem to believe it will, the day-dawn will soon overspread our horizon, and not many years need elapse before all will find their lost tribes of Israel.

Thanking you all again for the expressions of kind forbearance and patience, as well as for your hopefulness in the work for the future, we close with friendly greetings to all.

CAMBRIDGE, MASS., Faithfully submitted,
September 9, 1908. ABBIE MELLEN CHAMBERLAIN.

REPORT OF THE TREASURER

In account with the Chamberlain Association

FROM AUGUST 1, 1907, TO SEPTEMBER 9, 1908

		DR.	
1907.			
Aug.	1.	Balance on hand,	$281.44
		Yearly fees,	228.00
		New members,	23.00
		Exchange on check,	.10
		Sale of reports,	18.25
			$550.79

		CR.	
1907.			
Aug.	1.	Expenses of annual meeting,	$ 9.00
1908.			
March	6.	Paid Louis F. Weston, printing 1,000 application papers,	9.50
March	7.	Paid George W. Chamberlain, genealogical work,	50.00
April.		W. J. Dobinson Engraving Co., 12 plates for pictures for reports,	30.55
July	2.	Samuel Ward, envelopes for reports,	4.67
		Express on reports,	5.90
		Typewriting for reports,	4.00
		Grafton Press, New York, printing 550 reports,	176.25
		Exchange check,	.10
July	31.	Louis F. Weston, printing 450 notices of meeting September 9,	2.50
		Postage, envelopes, paper, etc.,	44.84
			$337.31
1907.			
Sept.	27.	Deposited in Quincy Savings Bank,	$150.00
1908.			
Sept.	9.	Balance in hands of Assistant Treasurer,	63.48
			$550.79
		Total sum in Quincy Savings Bank,	$710.70

SOPHIA A. CHAMBERLAIN CASWELL,
Assistant Treasurer.

Correct:
LEWIS J. BIRD.

ANNUAL MEETING OF 1909

The twelfth annual meeting of the Association was held at the Parker House, September 15, 1909. Fifty people from ten states gathered for the social hour from twelve to one. The two members who came from the greatest distances were found to be our genial Vice President, Dr. George M. Chamberlin of Chicago, and Mr. William C. Chamberlain of Louisville, Ky., who, though one of the earliest members of the Association, had never before attended one of the reunions.

At one o'clock the mirrors of the Crystal Room reflected a joyous company, who questioned the red and white roses strewn on the table, not knowing whether our English ancestors followed the house of Lancaster or of York. It was hoped that some day the Committee on English Ancestry might inform us whether the white or the red rose were the more appropriate decoration for a Chamberlain gathering, or at least enable us to divide the red and the white roses justly when the dinner ended.

Rev. E. E. Strong, D. D., called the company to order as the coffee was passed. He spoke of the illness of our President, Major-General Joshua L. Chamberlain, LL.D. A special delivery letter from Major-General Chamberlain was read wishing us all well and regretting that he had not, as he had hoped, recovered sufficiently from a severe illness to endure the journey from Portland to Boston. Dr. Strong referred to a fact worthy of note, that until this twelfth annual meeting, our President had never been absent but once. He spoke especially of his worth as a man, delivering an eulogy that was heartily applauded. He appointed Dr. George M. Chamberlin and Mr. P. M. Chamberlain a committee to prepare and dispatch a telegram expressive of our sorrow at his absence, and our hopes for his recovery.

The first speaker of the day was a guest, Hon. Milton Reed, who gave a most delightful account of his journey around the world through the northern half of the two hemispheres. He had but one regret,—that he had not known how easy it was to make a dash to the North Pole, so that he might have won for us the laurels that Dr. Cook was enjoying, instead of wandering as he did an ungarlanded stranger through the courts of the University at Copenhagen. When he ended his lively account of many lands and peoples, Miss Ella Chamberlin charmed us with her musical whistling.

Rev. Lewis Cornish of Hingham, Mass., explained the plan to erect at Hingham, at a cost of about $10,000, a tower with a chime of bells as a memorial to the first settlers of the town on the two hundred and seventy-fifth anniversary of the founding of the town. The name of Henry Chamberlin will appear on the tower on a tablet listing the first settlers, and Mr. Cornish wished that the name of every one of his descendants might appear in the

Book of Donors that will be preserved in the tower. He asked the Association to appoint a committee. The chair named Col. William J. Harding, Mr. Eugene Chamberlin of Brooklyn, and Miss J. C. Watts, with power to increase their number.

Mrs. M. E. Austin entertained the company with songs, accompanied on the piano by Mrs. Noah Curtis. Mrs. Anna E. Smiley of Holyoke, Mass., read a poem by Mr. William R. Chamberlain of Chicago, entitled "A Dream", a fond dream of a visit to historic Massachusetts and the Chamberlain reunion.

Dr. Strong was compelled to withdraw, and resigned the chair to Dr. George M. Chamberlin, who was compelled to accept the honor because a Crystal Room offers no hiding places. He charged his reverend brother with breach of promise, desertion, and other high crimes and misdemeanors, but the Association, though entertained by his complaint, refused to entertain it, and gave their departing officer a vote of thanks.

Chamberlain Brown, grandson of Gen. Samuel E. Chamberlain, contributed a brief item concerning Chamberlain Falls in Africa. Mr. Edwin M. Chamberlain of Albany, N. Y., told us briefly how he heard of the Chamberlain Association through Senator Chamberlain of Oregon. Mr. Pierson M. Chamberlain, one of our Vice Presidents, brought us news of the New Jersey Chamberlain Reunion Association. His speech was followed by a piano solo by Miss Elizabeth O. Chamberlain of Concord, N. H. Mr. George W. Adams of Dorchester, gave an interesting memorial sketch of the life and personality of his wife's brother, Dr. Albert H. Chamberlain of London, England,—also dentist to Queen Margarita of Italy. Brief remarks were made by Mr. James H. Walling of Brooklyn, N. Y., and by others.

Dr. George M. Chamberlin called the business meeting to order and, as he was chairman of the Nominating Committee, resigned the chair temporarily to Mr. Martin H. Chamberlin of Rutland, Vt. Miss Jenny Chamberlain Watts was appointed by the chair Secretary *pro tem.* Owing to the lateness of the hour the reading of the reports of the Secretaries and of the Treasurer was waived, and the reports were ordered placed on file and printed. Dr. George M. Chamberlin presented the report of the Nominating Committee, which was accepted. The officers so nominated were elected.

The Association voted: That the Executive Committee be authorized to appropriate money, if they deem it advisable, for the genealogical work outlined in the letter of Judge William T. Forbes, chairman of the special committee appointed to secure genealogical material to be printed with the annual reports.

The business meeting was declared adjourned *sine die.*

JENNY CHAMBERLAIN WATTS,

Secretary pro tem.

REPORT OF THE CORRESPONDING SECRETARY

SEPTEMBER finds many of our members here again surrounding the festal board, renewing old friendships, listening to each other's joys and sorrows, and learning something of the welfare and prosperity of the society. Our ambition is gratified by having over four hundred names recorded in our list of members since its formation. Year after year brings changes, but only fifty deaths have been reported during the past eleven years. We shall all miss from our annual meetings the kindly face and stalwart form of our Senior Vice President, Brigadier-General Samuel E. Chamberlain of Barre Plains, Mass. A grand, courageous kinsman and officer has gone home after his patriotic service for his country! Shall we ever forget his entertaining stories and anecdotes? Our sympathies have been extended to his beloved wife and family. Those who were privileged to attend his funeral at Mount Auburn Chapel will not soon forget the loving tribute paid by his soldier-comrades of the Mexican and Civil wars, nor the music by the quartette. One of our most esteemed charter members, Mrs. H. P. Kimball of Dubuque, Iowa, has passed away, followed soon after by her husband, leaving an only son, Mr. Elliot C. Kimball, whom we most cordially welcome as a new member. She was a superior woman, a niece of the well-known railroad and bridge contractor and builder, Mr. Selah Chamberlain of Cleveland, Ohio, and a cousin of Lady Naylor-Leyland of London. We have learned of the death of Mr. Edward W. Chamberlain, a lawyer in New York City, on January 18, 1908. Many may recall the presence of Mr. and Mrs. Chamberlain at our annual meeting three years since. We are happy to have had fifteen accessions to fill the vacancies by death in our Association.

Some of our members from a distance manifest much interest in the prosperity of this organization by their gifts, and others by striving to enlist their friends. Mr. Emerson Chamberlin of New York City, sent generously a type-written copy of his ancestry; also quite an account of Dr. Hugo Chamberlen of London, England, with a fine photograph of himself. General Frank Chamberlain of Albany, N. Y., has presented us with a copy of his interesting book, "The Hudson Tercentenary, an Historical Retrospect". Commissioner Eugene T. Chamberlain of Washington, D. C., and Mr. Charles A. Chamberlain of Detroit, Mich., have favored us with their photographs, and we have one from Mrs. H. P. Kimball. Mr. W. H. Chamberlin of Chicago, wrote one of his "Dreams" in verse for our annual meeting. Mr. William C. Chamberlain of Dubuque, Iowa, sent his copy of the favorite coat of arms of one branch of the Chamberlain family, which his cousin in Utica, N. Y., obtained when in England; also an autograph letter from Mr. Joseph Chamberlain, when Colonial Secretary of Great Britain. Mr. Sylvester

Chamberlain of Buffalo, N. Y., has deposited his genealogy with the Association, and been helpful in many ways. Mrs. Isabella W. Ball, Associate Editor of the *National Tribune* of Washington, D. C., has kindly presented two interesting books relating to the Civil War, "Washington during War Times" and "When and Where We Met Each Other," a list of battles and places from 1861 to 1866. By means of her photograph some of us have made the acquaintance of a new member, Miss S. Belle Chamberlain, State Superintendent of Education in Idaho. The Governor of Oregon has become a Senator of the United States and sends his greetings to all. Our worthy kinsman, Mr. Warren Chamberlain of Honolulu, has sent more of their historical literature, the Fifty-Seventh Report of the Hawaiian Missionary Children's Society for 1909. In it are letters from Mr. Levi Chamberlain, his father. Also two of their newspapers have arrived, showing that those distant possessions of the United States keep in touch with the central government and country. No doubt they are now discussing the North Pole, Cook or Peary?

In our next Chamberlain Biennial Report we expect to make the acquaintance of the William of Billerica Branch for the first four generations, and trust that some members will be able to connect themselves with that family. The Executive Board plan to continue the genealogy of the other branches, and hope to press the work to completion. We thank you all heartily for your helpfulness in so many ways, and trust you will not be disappointed in the Report. With best wishes for the coming year,

Very sincerely submitted,

ABBIE MELLEN CHAMBERLAIN.

MR. WILLIAM C. CHAMBERLAIN, DUBUQUE, IOWA

REPORT OF THE TREASURER

In account with the Chamberlain Association

FROM SEPTEMBER 9, 1908, TO SEPTEMBER 15, 1909

		Dr.	
1908.			
Sept.	9.	Balance on hand,	$ 63.48
		Yearly fees,	223.00
		New members,	20.00
		Exchange check,	.10
		Sale of reports,	26.55
			$333.13

		Cr.	
1908.			
Sept.	9.	Expenses of annual meeting,	$ 3.00
		Printing and sending notices,	8.75
		Postage, envelopes, etc.,	28.84
		Express on plates,	2.25
		Exchange check,	.10
			$42.94
1908.			
Dec.	8.	Deposited with Central Trust Co., Çambridge,	$ 30.00
1909.			
March.		Deposited with Central Trust Co.,	30.00
Sept.	15.	Balance in hands of Treasurer,	230.19
			$333.13
		Total sum in Quincy Savings Bank,	$781.70
		Total sum in Central Trust Co.,	61.07

SOPHIA A. CHAMBERLAIN CASWELL,
Assistant Treasurer.

March 8, 1910.
Correct: LEWIS J. BIRD.

ANNUAL MEETING OF 1910

THE thirteenth annual meeting of the Chamberlain Association was held at the Parker House, Boston, on Friday, July 8, 1910. Major-General Joshua L. Chamberlain and three Vice Presidents, Rev. E. E. Strong, D. D., of Auburndale, Dr. George M. Chamberlin of Chicago, and Mr. Emerson Chamberlin of New York City, met the members at an informal reception from twelve to one, when a march, played by Miss Alice M. Raymond of Cambridge, summoned the company to luncheon in the Crystal Room.

A telegram had been received from Washington, D. C., from Senator George E. Chamberlain, who was expected to deliver the address of the day, regretting that illness in his family prevented him from attending the gathering, and expressing a "hope that the occasion may be a most delightful one to the whole membership of the Association who may have the pleasure of being present, and profitable as well to them as to the absent ones." After the banquet, Major-General Joshua L. Chamberlain called on Judge William T. Forbes of Worcester, chairman of the Executive Committee, to begin the speechmaking. He had prepared, he said, no set speech for the occasion, but as Senator Hoar remarked of a politician, he could always speak,—he did it to rest his brain. There followed a witty address, which added to the merriment of the gathering, especially when Judge Forbes related a personal experiment on an Englishman who could see no fun in Mark Twain's writings. At the close he referred to the splendid services in the Civil War of two of our members who can meet with us no more, General Samuel E. Chamberlain of Barre, and General Robert H. Chamberlain of Worcester.

Rev. John Chamberlain of New York City, chaplain to the deaf and dumb, assured us that it was his intention to be brief lest his hearers regret that he did not belong to the class he served. His wife was the genealogist of his family. Her researches led him to feel that if he passed the name down as honored as he received it, he would do well. Miss Gertrude Chamberlin favored us with a selection from "Carmen" arranged for the piano. The pleasure of hearing her we have missed for several years. She brought with her, as one result of her wanderings in Europe, a stone from Tankerville Castle in Normandy, and a view of the castle. A scion of this noble house bore first the name of Chamberlain in England.

Rev. E. E. Strong, D. D., told of last summer's pilgrimage with his son to the homes of their ancestors among the green hills of Vermont, and of the pride and respect that he felt for his grandfather, General William Chamberlin. Dr. George M. Chamberlin of Chicago, complained that the only thing he had heard since he arrived in Boston was, "Where is your wife?" He sought to make us believe that he was of Irish descent by adding that his chagrin was so great that next year he would bring her and stay at home himself! He expressed his gratification over the honor accorded Mrs. Young of Chicago, in her election to the Presidency of the National Education Association, delivering quite an eulogy on this superior woman and great organizer, an old friend of his wife and himself. Dr. George M. Chamberlain of Brookline, confessed ingenuously that when he was a student in college he was delighted to speak on all occasions, adding that this desire had passed so completely that two years ago he married a wife to save him further effort in that direction. As she showed no inclination to relieve him on this occasion, he continued his entertaining talk, confessing toward the end that it was a new thing for him to interest himself in genealogy, and adding that he was willing to come forward in the Association and do what he could to take the place of those passing away. Miss Ella Chamberlin of Cambridge, delighted the company with her musical selections. Mr. Edwin Chamberlin of Albany, gave interesting data that he had discovered this year concerning the Wisconsin Regiments in the Civil War. It will be remembered that he himself served in the war from Wisconsin.

Mr. Emerson Chamberlin wished the work on English ancestry could be revived. He felt that certain traits in his character might be accounted for if he could trace his descent from the physician, Hugh Chamberlen of London, or from the fighter who followed William the Conqueror to England, or from the traveller and scholar, John Chamberlain of the reign of Elizabeth, or from the Quaker John Chamberlin of the Massachusetts Bay Colony. He wished this confusion as to his own personality might be dispelled. He presented the report of the Nominating Committee recommending the reëlection of the present officers.

The Association, turning to the business of the day, listened to the reports of the Recording Secretary, the Corresponding Secretary and the Treasurer, accepted them and ordered them placed on file. The officers whose names appear on the last pages of this Report were duly elected.

Major-General Joshua L. Chamberlain spoke eloquently of the aims of this Association. Genealogy was the anatomy of our organization. He hoped this part of our work might be organized more carefully and so as to make the records we possess more accessible to all. The life blood of the Association was its social life. The interchange of thoughts and ideas draws forth the best that is in us. Who knows how far the influence of his personality extends? He wished we might have better opportunities for sociability, that we might plan again a day out-of-doors together. Dr. E. Melville Quinby of England, delighted the company by singing "The Admiral's Broom," "The Curfew," and "The Bandolera." Mr. Raymond Chamberlain of Brooklyn, N. Y., made a thoughtful address, closing with a reference to his pleasure in attending the meeting this year. His friends in the New Jersey branch of the family had expressed warmly their enjoyment of earlier gatherings.

It was voted to send by Mr. Raymond Chamberlain an expression of regard and congratulation to the Chamberlain Reunion Association of New Jersey. It was voted to send an expression of sympathy to Senator Chamberlain, and to Mr. and Mrs. George W. Adams. The Committee on Revolutionary Wars were authorized to continue compiling the list of soldiers in the War of the Revolution.

Mr. James H. Kendall, when he felt a little worried as to what his children might think concerning him, was always consoled by the thought that they would approve of at least one act—his choice of a Chamberlain for a wife. He made a witty speech, ending with the declaration that he could not make a speech and must end matters abruptly, as did the gentleman who slid down stairs from Brooklyn Bridge, catching by the way and carrying to the foot a fat lady. As she was too dazed to rise instantly, he reached up, tapped her on the shoulder, and said, "This is as far as I go this trip." Letters were read from Col. Thomas Chamberlin of Pennsylvania; from Mr. A. C. Allen Chamberlain, starting for Germany; and from other absent members. Miss Alice M. Raymond closed the entertainment of the day with a brilliant piano solo.

A vote of thanks was passed to all who had kindly contributed to our entertainment. The Association adjourned *sine die.*

JENNY CHAMBERLAIN WATTS.
Secretary pro tem.

REPORT OF THE CORRESPONDING SECRETARY

NEW members continue to join the Association, bringing new life and vigor. Mr. Charles A. Chamberlin of Detroit, Mich., has made his four sons members to take the place of his deceased brother, Mr. Henry L. Chamberlin of Buffalo, N. Y.,—a worthy example to follow. His portrait will appear in our printed report, and also that of his brother.

The experiment of holding the thirteenth annual meeting in July was made at the suggestion of a few distant members, who could not attend a gathering in September and wished one at the time that the National Education Association held its forty-eighth convention in Boston. We see some of the name who have never been here before. There are responses either by letter or in person from our noble band of Vice Presidents, who continue as loyal and true to the society as ever. We trust that, in course of time, you will see the pictures of all of them, as well as of our life members, in our printed reports, and learn what genuine representative Americans they are. We all feel the death of our senior Vice President, General Samuel E. Chamberlain,

MR. CHARLES A. CHAMBERLIN

and of his sweet and gentle wife as a personal loss, but their daughter, Mrs. George M. Brown, is still with us. Col. Thomas Chamberlin of Philadelphia, never fails to send a message of cheer, although a great sufferer. He is rejoicing in having as a visitor a brother who has been absent twenty-seven years. All will be pleased to know that one of our western Vice Presidents rendered such excellent service as a Governor in Oregon, that the people sent him to the Congress of the United States to serve as their Senator; we anticipated welcoming him to this thirteenth annual gathering, but a telegram informs us that he is in quarantine on account of the illness of his daughter. President McKendree H. Chamberlin writes from Los Angeles, Cal., that he has found nearly fifty of the name of Chamberlain or Chamberlin in the City Directory, and he hopes to make the acquaintance of some of them. When Dr. and Mrs. George M. Chamberlin of Chicago, wrote that they did not expect to attend this meeting, there was great disappointment, for they have done much to enliven our meetings by their western hospitality and kindnesses. But at the last moment the Doctor walked in and received quite an ovation. Mr. Richard H. Chamberlain of Oakland, Cal., has never been able to attend a meeting, but you will see his portrait in our next printed report, as well as that of Mr. Herbert B. Chamberlain of Brattleboro, Vt., one of our helpful charter members. We have some charter members who make it a point to attend every annual meeting, and the President calls them his "stand-bys"; we are much gratified to find that they do not fail to come in July. We have received many letters sending kindly greetings to all. Some were on the eve of departure for Europe, others planning a western tour, or a trip to the mountains or the sea. If the "sky-pilots" succeed in establishing air-routes, who can tell what may occur within the next ten years!

Our kinsman in Honolulu has not forgotten to send his greeting and the Report of the Hawaiian Missionary Children's Society for 1910, which is interesting historically. Mrs. Follett, Regent of the St. Paul Chapter, D. A. R., of Minnesota, has sent a booklet on the "Old Sibley House and the Celebration of Flag Day." Dr. Alice Burritt of Washington, D. C., has a wonderful chart that she has evolved; she hopes soon to attend our meeting, and feels proud to claim descent from Edmund Chamberlain (born January 31, 1676). We fear that we may lose from our meetings one of our favorite songstresses, Mrs. Martha E. Austin of Roxbury, Mass., for she expects to remove her home to New York City. Great sympathy is felt for Mr. and Mrs. George W. Adams of Dorchester, Mass., on account of the death of their only daughter, who had been recently married in Berkeley, California. Mrs. Adams lost her brother, Dr. Chamberlain, a dentist in Rome, Italy, the previous year. We find sixty deaths recorded in the list of four hundred twenty-three names on our books. As our older members pass away from the field of action, we hope that the younger ones will come forward to help bear some of the responsibilities and burdens of the Association. We are glad to welcome new members.

Faithfully submitted,
ABBIE MELLEN CHAMBERLAIN.

REPORT OF THE TREASURER

In account with the Chamberlain Association

FROM SEPTEMBER 15, 1909 TO JULY 8, 1910

1909.	DR.	
Sept. 15.	Balance on hand,	$230.19
	Yearly fees,	215.00
	New members,	15.00
	Exchange on checks,	.20
	Sale of reports,	6.35
		$466.74
1909.	CR.	
Sept. 15.	Expenses of annual meeting,	$ 6.00
	Collection charges on checks,	.20
	Paid W. J. Dobinson, plates for the report,	30.60
	Paid Louis F. Weston, printing,	2.00
	Paid L. F. Weston, printing notices of meeting, 1910,	2.00
	Paper, envelopes, postage,	16.54
		$57.34
1909.		
Oct. 4.	Deposited with Central Trust Co., Cambridge,	$130.00
1910.		
July 8.	Balance in hands of Assistant Treasurer,	279.40
		$466.74
	Total sum in Quincy Savings Bank,	781.38
	Total sum in Central Trust Co.,	191.07

SOPHIA A. CHAMBERLAIN CASWELL,
Assistant Treasurer.

Approved:
LEWIS J. BIRD, *Auditor.*

NECROLOGY

The Association has lost by death the following members not before reported:

Mr. Edward Wilmot Chamberlain, LL.B., of New York City, d. Jan. 18, 1908.

Mrs. William Hayes d. Jan. 31, 1908, at Winona, Minn.

Rev. Jacob Chamberlain, M. D., D. D., LL.D., d. Mar. 2, 1908, at Madanapalle, India.

Col. Simon Elliot Chamberlin of Washington, D. C., d. at Waterford, Va., April 20, 1908.

Mrs. Lucinda Chamberlin Ragan of Ohio, d. May 29, 1908.

Mr. Charles W. Chamberlain d. at Dayton, Ohio, Oct. 31, 1908.

Gen. Samuel E. Chamberlain of Barre, Mass., d. Nov. 10, 1908.

Miss Clarissa A. Chamberlin d. at Lebanon, N. H., Nov. 9, 1908.

Mrs. Harriet P. Kimball d. at Dubuque, Iowa, Feb. 7, 1909.

Dr. Albert H. Chamberlain d. at Rome, Italy, Feb. 19, 1909.

Mr. Albert Chamberlin of No. Abington, Mass., d. April 17, 1909.

Mr. Henry L. Chamberlin of Buffalo, N. Y., d. Sept. 13, 1909.

Mrs. Charles A. Jewell of Hartford, Ct., d. Oct. 7, 1909.

Miss Elizabeth E. Chamberlain of Roxbury, d. Nov. 19, 1909.

Mr. James Dale Chamberlin of Toledo, Ohio, d. Jan. 4, 1910.

Mrs. Samuel E. Chamberlain d. at Cambridge, Mass., Feb. 11, 1910.

Mr. Edward Wilmot Chamberlain of New York City, passed away January 18, 1908, after a two weeks' illness. He was born in New York City April 23, 1842, of good American stock, the seventh generation from Edmund Chamberlain, and a descendant of the Dudley, Lyman and Phelps families. Two of his great-grandfathers served in the War of the American Revolution, Capt. Moses Chamberlain and Col. Samuel Williams. Moses Chamberlain was first mustered into the service May 26, 1775, in Captain Walker's company; was Lieutenant in Colonel Bedell's New Hampshire Regiment in 1779; and as Capt. Moses Chamberlain represented the town of Winchester, N. H., in the convention which ratified the Federal Constitution, June 21, 1788, voting for the ratification. The mother of Edward Wilmot Chamberlain, Julia Wilmot, descended from the Phelps family of Connecticut, was a woman of unusual intellectual ability. Contrary to the wishes of both his parents, Mr. Chamberlain refused a university training, a step he regretted during his whole life, and which he endeavored to amend by constant reading and study. In 1872, he was admitted to the New York Bar. Throughout his years of practice his work was directed more towards reforms and helpfulness to others than towards material wealth. He was always willing to put his professional knowledge at the service of every one, and inheriting ample means, he was able to devote much time to the help of the needy and oppressed. He enjoyed excellent health and had a remarkably sunny and equable disposition. His sister misses a close comrade, and his wife a devoted and affectionate husband. He was a member of the Medico-Legal Society, the Bar Association, the Social Reform Club, the Manhattan Liberal Club, the Twilight Club, the Sunset Club, and the National Defense Association. He received the degree of LL.B. from Columbia University, class 1873.

MRS. CHARLOTTE PRENTISS HAYES, wife of William Hayes, died of pneumonia at Winona, Minn., January 31, 1908. She was born in Montpelier, Vt., May 10, 1854, the eldest child of Joseph Addison and Rebecca Dodge (Loomis) Prentiss, and granddaughter of Hon. Samuel Prentiss, a member of the Senate of the United States from Vermont from 1830 to 1842 and U. S. District Judge for Vermont from 1842 to 1857. Her maternal grandmother was descended from William Chamberlain of Woburn and Billerica, immigrant. In 1869, her parents moved to Winona, which was her home during the remainder of her life. Her mother and her husband survive her. She was a woman of kindly heart, gracious manners, vigorous mind, and great force of character. She was active in the regeneration of the Winona Library Association in 1877, and in its development into the Winona Free Public Library, which owes much of its success to her earnest efforts, her sound culture, broad range of interests, and tolerant spirit. She had a share in the library administration from 1877 until a few years before her death. She was a member of the First Congregational Church of Winona, but after her marriage attended the First Presbyterian Church, retaining an active interest in both organizations and giving freely of her time and strength, especially to the missionary work. She was a Regent of the Wenonah Chapter of the Daughters of the American Revolution, and was deeply interested in its patriotic purposes.

COLONEL SIMON ELLIOT CHAMBERLIN was born in Northfield, Vt., June 8, 1834. August 21, 1862, he was mustered into service as Second Lieutenant in Company A of the 118th New York Volunteer Infantry, himself enrolling twenty-six of the eighty-three men in his company. May 16, 1864, he was promoted to be Captain of Company K of the 25th New York Volunteer Cavalry. July 11, 1864, he rendered gallant and critical service in the defense of Washington, D. C., against the forces of Gen. Jubal Early, as an article by Capt. Henry A. Castle in the *National Tribune Repository* shows at length, (Vol. 1, pp. 34–40, November, 1907). He was given the brevet rank of Colonel by the Governor of New York for gallantry in the field. After the war ended he was commissioned First Lieutenant in the 8th Cavalry of the regular army. While serving in Washington Territory, in 1867, he contracted rheumatism, from which he suffered much during his life, and by which he was confined to his room during the last three years. He resigned from the army in 1867, and married Miss Edith Dawson Matthews of Waterford, Loudoun County, Virginia, whom he had met when provost marshal at Point

COLONEL SIMON ELLIOT CHAMBERLIN

of Rocks, Md., toward the close of the Civil War. She belonged to a "Quaker family well known throughout Loudoun County for their loyalty during the war." He became active in politics and interested in agriculture; was at one time chairman of the Virginia State Republican Committee and first President of the Cotoctin Farmers' Club. He was a special agent of the U. S. Treasury Department, stationed at Baltimore. Later, until 1905, he held a responsible post in the Treasury Department at Washington, D. C. He was a member of the Loyal Legion and of the Grand Army of the Republic. The National Cemetery, Arlington, was his burial place. He left behind him his wife and the following children: Justin Morrill Chamberlin, a lawyer in Washington, D. C., Capt. Paul E. Chamberlin of the U. S. Marine Corps, Edward M. Chamberlin, Leroy Chamberlin of Philadelphia, Eleanor M. Chamberlin, and Mrs. William H. Clendenin, wife of Lieut. Clendenin of the 17th Infantry, U. S. A.

Mrs. Lucinda Chamberlin Ragan was born November 7, 1838, at Lisbon, Clark County, Ohio, daughter of Stephen Harriman Chamberlin, who migrated from Strafford, Vt., to Ohio, by his wife Esther Robb, daughter of Joseph and Esther (Lafferty) Robb of Mercer County, Penn. Her line of descent has been traced to Henry Chamberlin of Hingham, immigrant. She belonged to a patriotic family. Two great-grandfathers, Elias Chamberlin (1753–1835) and Stephen Harriman, Jr., served in the War of the American Revolution; her grandfather, Isaac Chamberlin, (1782–1863) in the War of 1812; eight cousins and an uncle in the Civil War, and a nephew in the Spanish-American War. Her family has been largely an agricultural people, farmers and breeders of stock, and, as became New Englanders, gave their children the best educational advantages possible. Her father, in his youth, was one of the early schoolmasters of Ohio, and she was a teacher until her marriage to William H. Ragan of Springfield, Ohio. She was much interested in floriculture, exhibiting successfully as an amateur florist at State and County fairs. During the last two years of her life she was blind and a great sufferer. One sister, Mrs. Adeline C. Hamilton, is a member of this Association.

Miss Clarissa A. Chamberlin was born December 27, 1840, at Newbury, Vt., and died at Lebanon, New Hampshire, November 9, 1908. She was the daughter of Abiel and Eunice (Wetherbee) Chamberlin, and granddaughter of Charles and Rachel (Varnum) Chamberlin. Her great-grandfather, Abiel Chamberlin (born November 22, 1739, died at Newbury, Vt., May 14, 1787,) when seventeen years of age, was captured by the Indians and held in captivity many months. Later he served in the War of the Revolution. Her brother, Charles Chamberlin, served in the Ninth New Hampshire Regiment in the Civil War, was in the battle of Antietam, and died the night before the battle of Fredericksburg. She was a sweet and gentle spirit, ministering as a nurse to the bodies and souls of her friends. She was warmly interested in this Association, and came frequently from Worcester to our annual gatherings. We shall miss her winsome face.

Mrs. Harriet P. Kimball, one of the earliest and most interested members of the Chamberlain Association, was the daughter of Reuben and Olive (Chamberlain) Taft, a granddaughter of Selah and Abigail (Burnett) Chamberlain, and a descendant of Henry Chamberlin of Hingham, immigrant. Born in Newfane, Vt., in 1833, she received an academic education in Vermont, supplemented by instruction from private tutors in the home of her uncle, the late Selah Chamberlain of Cleveland, Ohio. She was a cousin of Jenny Wilson Chamberlain, daughter of William Selah Chamberlain of Cleveland, a famous American beauty who married Capt. Sir Herbert Scarisbrick Naylor-Leyland, baronet. As a favorite niece of her two uncles, Selah and Joseph Chamberlain, Mrs. Kimball was throughout life a frequent guest in their beautiful homes in Cleveland. In September, 1864, she was married in her Vermont home to Nelson W. Kimball and went to Dubuque, Iowa, to reside, dispensing there in her stately home a charming hospitality. Mrs. Kimball possessed a rare personality, great force of character, blended with sweetness of temper and a vivacious temperament. She won a foremost place in the literary circles of the city. She was admitted to the Conversational Club, became a charter member of the Dubuque Woman's Club and of the Dubuque Chapter of the Daughters of the American Revolution, of which she was at one time Regent. She was ever a peacemaker, and esteemed and beloved by all as a Christian woman. At a memorial service in the Dubuque Woman's Club the following tribute was paid by the first President of the club: "* * * Her intellectual ability, her tender grace, courtesy and kindness won hearts to her, and once gained she held them by the strong cords of an abiding, unselfish love. She was one who wrought life's work with a fervent heart, and life's duties were performed with fidelity and integrity. She has gone from our presence but not from our hearts." Her only child, Mr. Elliot C. Kimball, is a member of this Association.

Dr. Albert Henry Chamberlain, eldest son of Henry M. and Martha A. (Soper) Chamberlain, was born in Auburn, Me., October 5, 1844. He went to the school in Auburn and for a few months to Lewiston Falls Academy. When seventeen years of age, he enlisted in the 23rd Maine Regiment. He served the nine months for which the regiment was enlisted, returned home, and enlisted again in the 29th Maine Regiment for three years. The regiment was ordered to New Orleans, joining the forces of General Banks. Albert was small but energetic and ambitious, and became a general favorite with both officers and men. They thought him small to carry a musket, and made him Regimental Bugler, in which position he gave satisfaction to Colonel

ALBERT HENRY CHAMBERLAIN, D.D.S.

Virgen and the regiment. While in New Orleans he contracted malaria and other ailments, and was taken to the hospital, where he hovered between life and death for six weeks. When his regiment was ordered north, he begged to be taken, believing that if he were left there he would surely die. His request was granted, his comrades carrying him in their arms to the steamer. He was placed in a hospital in Washington, D. C. It was there that he conceived the idea of studying dental surgery and began the study. He received an honorable discharge with his regiment when the three years for which he had enlisted had expired, and returned home. His health was so far improved that he was able to go to Augusta, Me., and continue his studies in dentistry. Later he studied in Boston, Mass. Receiving his diploma, he returned to Augusta and opened an office, with flattering results. He applied his whole energy with the determination, not only to succeed, but to surmount every difficulty and stand at the head of his profession. Ultimately he accomplished this. He married Miss Nellie Holcomb in Augusta. To escape the effects of chronic disease, he followed the advice of his physician and friends and went to Europe to regain his health. He opened an office in Nice in partnership with another dentist, but soon sold out to his partner and journeyed to Florence, Italy. Opening an office alone, his practice grew far beyond his expectations, and his health improved. At the end of three years he opened an office in Rome, still retaining that in Florence. The report of his skill and success at Florence preceded him to Rome. Soon after his arrival he was called to the palace to do professional work for Queen Margherita. His work gave satisfaction, and he was given permission to place upon his business cards, "Dentist to the Queen and Prince Victor of Naples," now King of Italy. He was the Queen's dentist as long as he lived. Several years later he opened an office in London, England, spending six months of the year in each country. In February, 1909, Dr. Chamberlain left London for Florence at the request of the Dowager-Queen Margherita. After completing professional work for her, he went to Rome to visit his son, who was associated with the father in the office at Rome. He was exceedingly fatigued on his arrival and retired early. In the morning the young man charged the servants to let the father sleep as long as he pleased. Shortly before noon the son left his office, went to his house and to his father's room and found him lying on the bed unconscious. Physicians were at once summoned, but no hope was given. He died February 19, 1909, and was buried in the English Cemetery in Rome, beside his wife, who had died five years before. His only son, Edward, succeeds to his father's business. A sister, Mrs. George W. Adams, is a member of this Association. One brother, Arthur K. Chamberlain, is living in Marlboro, Mass. Dr. Chamberlain was of a lovable and genial nature. He won hosts of friends and kept them. His success in life illustrates what energy, determination and high resolves will accomplish. He will be missed by a large circle of friends in London, Florence and Rome.

Hon. Albert Chamberlin was born in Abington, Mass., February 27, 1826, the son of Deacon John and Mary Porter (Norton) Chamberlin. He had five brothers and two sisters, who all lived to an advanced age, retaining their vigor of mind and body to a remarkable degree. He died in the eighty-fourth year of his age. A sister and two brothers survive, one of whom, Augustus, is his twin. For several years Albert and Augustus Chamberlin were distinguished as the oldest twins living in this section of the country. Albert Chamberlin married in 1852 Matilda M. Cobb of East Sumner, Me. To them were born two sons and two daughters, one of whom died in infancy. The surviving children are Horace A. Chamberlin of West Somerville, Mass., Isetta M. Wales of Hyde Park, Mass., and Everett F. Chamberlin of Abington, Mass. Enjoying very meagre educational advantages he became, by reading and study, a well educated man, and won by his integrity the respect of all his acquaintances. For many years he was one of the largest shoe manufacturers in the town of Abington, his principal product being buffalo overshoes. The last years of his life were spent in agricultural pursuits, and, although during the last two years his strength was declining, he held to his occupation until one month before his decease. He joined the Baptist Church at South Abington (now Whitman) when a young man, and retained his membership until the formation of the Baptist Church at East Abington (now Rockland), where he served as Deacon and Superintendent of the Sabbath School many years until the formation of the Baptist Church at North Abington, where he held the same office. He was always engaged in religious and benevolent work, sparing neither time and strength nor money in carrying out what he considered was for the welfare of humanity. Although a non-combatant, he did much for the "Boys in Blue" during the Civil War, and has always been a guest of Post 73, G. A. R. He was a charter member of Winthrop Lodge, I. O. O. F., North Abington. He was a Director in the Abington Mutual Fire Insurance Co., and Vice President and Trustee of the Abington Public Library. He represented his district in the Massachusetts Legislature in 1869 and 1870. When the twin brothers, eighty-one years of age, attended the Chamberlain dinner at the Parker House in 1907, they were greeted by the President and given the Chatauqua salute by the Association.

Mr. Henry Lathrop Chamberlin was born October 10, 1853, the son of Charles E. Chamberlin. His mother, Mrs. Eliza Chamberlin of Port Washington, Wisconsin, is a member of this Association, as is also his brother, Charles A. Chamberlin of Detroit, Mich. A sister, Mrs. Alexander Wood of Spring Lake, Mich.; his wife, who was Miss Eliza J. Anthony of Spring Lake, Mich., and three children, Royal H., Gertrude and Hazel Chamberlin, survive him. Mr. Chamberlin began work as a purser on one of the Engelman boats in 1871, and was rescued by the life-saving crew from the *Amazon*, wrecked

HON. ALBERT AND AUGUSTUS CHAMBERLIN

MR. HENRY LATHROP CHAMBERLIN

at Grand Haven in 1881. Later he was agent for the Ward line of steamers with headquarters at Buffalo; was associated with his brother-in-law, Alexander Wood, in the control of a line of freight boats on the Erie Canal; and assumed the position of freight agent for a number of companies. He was a member of the Transportation Club of Buffalo and of the Sons of the American Revolution. His grandfather, Aaron Chamberlin, aroused his interest in military history when a boy by telling how he was wounded in the knee at the engagement of Lundy's Lane in the War of 1812. His great-grandfather, Aaron Chamberlin (1758–1825), served with the Connecticut troops during the War of the Revolution from May 21, 1777, to May 21, 1880, and from September to December of the latter year; and later in New York State was an officer in the militia, first of Otsego and later of Delaware County, holding various ranks from that of Ensign in 1792 to that of Brigadier-General in 1805. Henry L. Chamberlin was an attendant at the Universalist Church, a firm believer in the Great Creator, a man of exemplary habits and of a genial and sympathetic nature, ever willing to listen to the pleadings of the unfortunate and lend a helping hand by word or deed, ofttimes beyond his financial ability. One of his fellow-townsmen writes: "Mr. Chamberlin was conspicuously identified with the railroad and steamboat interests for more than twenty-five years in this State and particularly in the region of the Great Lakes. He was a thorough business man of the highest character, and left behind him a beautiful memory among the friends in fraternal organizations as well as those in the ordinary walks of life. He was regarded as one of the best in his particularly chosen line of life."

Mrs. Julia W. Jewell, wife of the late Col. Charles A. Jewell, and an associate member of this Association, died at her home in Hartford, Conn., October 7, 1909, after a lingering illness. She was either Treasurer or President of the Hartford Branch of the Woman's Board of Foreign Missions of the Congregational Church for twenty-eight years, and gathered about her exceptionally fine women as officers and helpers. Her interest in mission work never wavered, her faith in it never faltered, her effort never weakened, and her beautiful service was a source of strength and courage to those associated with her. On May 5, 1910, a "Memorial Gift Service" was held at the semi-annual meeting of the Hartford Branch. Loving tributes were paid to the character and influence of Mrs. Jewell in two addresses entitled, "The Purpose of the Gift" and "The Story of the Gift." Then the presidents of the auxiliaries formed in procession, and singing "Jerusalem the Golden", brought forward in memorial envelopes pledges and gifts amounting to over $4,000. A memorial building will be erected for the girls' boarding school at Van, in Asia Minor, to be called probably the "Julia W. Jewell Hall". Her name will be honored in distant parts of the earth. The memory of her gracious presence will long linger in the hearts of those who knew her.

Mr. James Dale Chamberlin was born in Union Co., Pennsylvania, April 12, 1814. He removed with his wife and family to Toledo, Ohio, in 1859, and in November, 1860, located on the East Side on a high bluff, at a bend in the river, commanding a magnificent view up stream. Here, on what is now Miami Street, he lived for fifty years. His death, in his ninety-sixth year, was hastened by a fall on December 15, 1909, by which his right limb was broken near the hip. He was interred in Willow Cemetery, Toledo. A son, Frank Chamberlin, Infirmary Director at Toledo, and two daughters, Mrs. Elijah Whitmore and Mrs. Warren Whitmore, both of Toledo, survive him. He was a successful gardener and manager of a fruit preserving industry until forced by the infirmities of age to give up active employment. While still living in Pennsylvania he conceived the idea of hermetically sealing fruit to preserve it, from reading about the fruits discovered in excavating Pompeii. His first success was with tomatoes, marketing the fruit in Philadelphia and nearer markets in three-quart tin cans. In 1877, he began the preserving of rhubarb or pie plant, and this industry has been continued by himself and his son to the present day, thousands of barrels having been marketed, Evaporated fruit was, it is said, also first introduced to the market by him.

VETERANS OF THE ARCOT MISSION

Dr. and Mrs. Chamberlain are at the left of the group

THE REV. JACOB CHAMBERLAIN, M. D., D. D., LL.D.

"YOURS for Christ and India" was the favorite signature of our honorary life member, Jacob Chamberlain, M. D., D. D., LL.D. He was born in Sharon, Conn., April 13, 1835. Both his parents were of fine New England stock reaching back to the middle of the seventeenth century. He described his father, Jacob Chamberlain, as "a man of strong faith and active Christian character, a consistent member of the Church for seventy years, thirty-one in Sharon, and thirty-nine at Hudson, Ohio. He was always one of the active working members, and, according to his means, one of the most liberal supporters of the Gospel at home and abroad. He died in 1878, at the age of eighty-six."

"His mother, Anna Nutting Chamberlain, belonged to a family which for several generations, down to the present time, has furnished many inventors, teachers, lawyers, college professors, ministers and missionaries. She was a woman of earnest faith, deep piety and much prayer, and intensely interested in missions."

Three years after his birth his parents journeyed west to Hudson, Ohio, buying a farm within half a mile of Western Reserve University, in which his mother's brother was professor of Greek. The boy expected to become a scientific farmer, the assistant of his father, who from the birth of the son had been an invalid. But before he entered college, several remarkable escapes from death by accident led him to consider seriously what his life-work ought to be, and reconciled the father to his decision to be a missionary in India. A sister and her betrothed, who had intended to go to India, had both died. He wished to take their place. Later, another sister expected to go to the foreign field with her betrothed, but died. His eldest sister married Rev. Joseph Scudder and went to India in 1853. For many years the parents had welcomed missionaries to their home, so that, Dr. Chamberlain writes, "when I graduated from the college there was scarcely a land to which I could be sent as a missionary where I had not personal acquaintances and friends already at work to greet me." After passage had been engaged to India in 1860, the mother told the son that at his birth, "her first-born son, her first act on rising from her bed had been to carry me to her closet and laying me on God's altar consecrated me to His service as a foreign missionary, if He would accept the gift and Himself call me to the work, and she had yearly renewed the consecration, asking Him in His own time and way to present His call to my soul." During the twenty-four years of his life till then, he had never suspected this. Yet the mother did not neglect to prepare the way for the call by telling missionary stories to her children, praying with them "for those who sat in darkness", taking them to the monthly missionary concert at the church, and aiding them to earn pennies to give to the cause.

Dr. Chamberlain told the moving story of his mother's life and influence to a gathering of women at the Ecumenical Conference on Foreign Missions in New York City in 1900, and wrote it for the *Missionary Review of the World*, in which it appeared under the title, "The Making of Missionaries: The Mothers' Influence," in May, 1908 (vol. XXXI pp. 352–356).

"If ever a man were foreordained to be a missionary," his life-long friend, Dr. Cobb writes, "Jacob Chamberlain evidently was. His boyhood days afforded abundant evidence of the possession of those traits and capacities which were afterwards so signally exhibited and which so eminently fitted him for the life and work on which he ultimately entered: Mental and physical power and alertness, intense earnestness of purpose, an indomitable determination to overcome obstacles and achieve the best possible results, unfaltering courage under all conditions, a scorn of everything low and mean, keenness and sweetness of humour, cheerfulness always, with the desire to know and willingness to do the will of God."

Entering Western Reserve College in 1851, but absenting himself for one year because of ill health, he graduated in 1856, valedictorian of his class. He spent a month in the autumn of 1856 at Union Seminary in New York City, but was graduated in 1859 from the Theological Seminary at New Brunswick, New Jersey, being attracted to this institution by the course in Hebrew under Dr. Campbell. "By his insistence on 'the best' in Hebrew, he was thus unconsciously preparing himself for the important and influential part he afterwards took in the revision of the Telugu Bible." During this period he took, also, some medical studies, chiefly in the College of Physicians and Surgeons in New York, and received later the degree of M. D. from the Western University Medical College at Cleveland, Ohio. He had remarkable success in medicine and surgery in India. Three summers he served as colporteur in Ohio and Illinois, for the American Tract Society and the Presbyterian Board of Publication, thus meeting "all sorts and conditions of men." A year before his graduation from the Seminary, he had an opportunity to study Tamil with some members of the Arcot Mission then in America, and hence applied for appointment as a missionary to India of the Reformed Protestant Dutch Church, now denominated the Reformed Church in America. He was ordained in May, 1859, in the Marble Collegiate Church, Fifth Avenue and Twenty-ninth Street, New York. For several months thereafter he labored in the Reformed Churches in the Western Synod, of Chicago, by assignment of the Board of Foreign Missions. This varied training and service helped to develop in him "that rare faculty of meeting men, answering their arguments and objections and pressing home upon them the truths of the Gospel which was so remarkably displayed in after years" in India and in his work for the cause of missions among the churches in America.

September 7, 1859, he married at Hudson, Ohio, Charlotte Close Birge, daughter of Rev. Chester Birge, at one time settled over the Presbyterian Church at Vienna, Ohio. December 21, 1859, they sailed from Boston in the ship *Goddess*, arriving in India April 12, 1860.

The Arcot Mission, south-west of Madras, was founded in 1853, by three sons of Dr. John Scudder, the pioneer medical missionary. Dr. Chamberlain studied the Tamil language first, but in 1861 was sent to Palmaner to begin work among the Telugus. Two years later he journeyed thirty-five miles further north and opened a station at Madanapalle, about one hundred and fifty miles inland from Madras. The story of these beginnings, with the little house and school-house church thatched with rushes and with mud walls, is told in the seventh chapter of "In the Tiger Jungle." This was his station from 1863 to 1901, when his health compelled him to withdraw to the hills,—to Coonoor.

In this same year, 1863, he made what was probably the longest evangelistic tour of his life, and the most dangerous. He took with him two cart-loads of Gospels, Bibles, and tracts in Telugu,—including also a small supply in four or five other languages of the region,—and four native helpers, each able to preach in two or three of these languages. Starting in June they were absent between four and five months journeying through Hyderabad and the Upper Godavery, where no missionary had ever been before. Incidents of this tour of nearly 2,000 miles are related by Dr. Chamberlain in the first and second chapters of "In the Tiger Jungle," and in the third chapter of "The Cobra's Den." On this journey Dr. Chamberlain contracted the jungle-fever, from which he was never able to free his system, in spite, as he said, of "barrels of quinine," sojourns in the hill country, and voyages to Australia and the United States. But because of his vigorous constitution the fever could not destroy his vital energy. Note this record in his report for the year 1871: "I have been out on six preaching tours during the year. Three of these were five weeks long each. I have spent on tours 125 days. * * * * My native helpers were out 293 days and we together preached 739 times, to 538 different audiences in 351 towns and villages, to 18,730 people. We have also sold on these tours 2,403 Scriptures. Besides this we have preached systematically in Madanapalle and the surrounding villages 527 times, to 13,661 people, and sold 1,030 books and tracts." Dr. Chamberlain had the utmost faith in such tours, and made them every year. In 1902 he wrote: "It is safe to say that of the 10,060 converts now on the rolls of the Arcot Mission, more than eighty per cent have been brought in by this 'public proclamation' of the Gospel in the vernaculars. These have, indeed, come mostly from the lower classes, but a large percentage of our high caste converts have also thus been brought to the knowledge of Christ."

Dr. Chamberlain's interest in the early Hindu literature, and the readiness with which he quoted (or chanted) the ancient Vedas and poets (an example of which may be seen in our "Report for 1900") was of special value in approaching the higher castes enabling him to disarm prejudices and enforce the truth.

Throughout his life in India he strove to make his medical work reënforce his evangelistic labors, and not usurp the chief share of his time and attention. His medical and surgical work was so successful that this was sometimes difficult. Soon after his arrival in Madanapalle a man, Ramanna, had his right hand and forearm crushed accidentally under the wheels of the great idol car of the town. Dr. Chamberlain set the ten fractures so successfully that the man was able to use his arm again in ploughing and reaping. This won for him a friend in one of the strongest and most numerous castes in Madanapalle. Seventy-five miles from any surgeon or physician, crowds came to him till he was treating over one hundred patients a day, preaching also to those who gathered at his dispensary before he treated their ailments. At length, in July, 1869, he appealed to the Madras Government, which supported thenceforth at Madanapalle a hospital and dispensary. Dr. Chamberlain organized next a travelling dispensary, which won to friendliness many unknown and many hostile villages. In 1873 he treated about 30,000 patients. Some patients he sent to Madanapalle, riding in many miles for serious operations, especially in opthalmic surgery, but all operations he could he performed in a tent. In 1871 the people of Palmaner appealed to him so strongly that he established a hospital there with a Christian staff, supported by the local government, but under his supervision. Until 1874, when ill health drove him to America, he visited it frequently for critical operations and a monthly inspection. From 1879 to 1884 he supervised again the three dispensaries and the medical work of the region. This responsibility he resigned when he started on his second journey to America in 1884. He did some medical work in his tent on his later evangelistic tours. This side of his life-work is especially described in the ninth chapter of "The Cobra's Den," and in the sixth and seventh chapters of "The Kingdom in India," and references to it are frequent throughout his writings.

One other talent of value to the missionary pioneer deserves mention. He possessed an inventive mind and mechanical skill. At one time the ceiling of his library in India fell and smashed his typewriter. In putting it in repair unaided, certain improvements occurred to him. These he submitted later to the manufacturer, who offered him a large salary if he would leave the mission field, and serve the firm as an inventor. This inventive skill was inherited by his son, Jacob Chester Chamberlain, well known to the members of this Association.

From 1873, to 1896, he represented the Arcot Mission on the committee for the revision of the Telugu Bible, and was chairman of the committee. He compiled also a Telugu Hymn Book, five editions of which have been sold, the last edition containing 11,500 copies. It is in general use among the Telugus of India and Burma. These beautiful hymns were sung at his burial. Some he translated, others he composed in this, to him, "mellifluous and beautiful language." During the last six years of his life, in Coonoor, in the Nilgiri Hills, he labored to prepare a Telugu Bible Dictionary. To translate one of our western dictionaries would have been useless, as the oriental mind grasps swiftly much that puzzles the occidental, but needs a careful elucidation of other points. Stricken by paralysis in May, 1902, the work was interrupted for months, but in 1906, the first volume was printed,—one-fourth of the work he had planned.

He wrote often to the papers of America, England and Australia to awaken and sustain interest in missions, and prepared many graphic leaflets, sundry of which were reprinted and circulated by the mission boards of other denominations than his own. Many thousands of copies of his two books,—"In the Tiger Jungle," issued in 1896, and "The Cobra's Den," issued in 1900,—have been sold. To rest his "Telugu brain cells" he prepared at Coonoor his last book,—"The Kingdom in India," which was in the press when the news arrived of his death.

He rendered distinguished service to the cause of church union in India, advocating it in the United States in 1885, in Scotland in 1887, and in India for many years. He had a principal share in the final plans which brought about the South India United Church,—a union of the native churches planted by the Reformed Church and by the United Free Church of Scotland. He was the Moderator of the first Synod of South India in 1902. His counsel was sought by those who secured, in 1905, the union of all the Presbyterian and Reformed Churches of India in the Presbyterian Church in India.

Four times the jungle-fever, which he contracted in 1863, and other serious and complicated ailments, from which he suffered often great pain, drove him to America, compelling him to spend in all ten years here on furlough, and also several months in Australia. The years were not wasted. During his first visit in 1874, he began wonderful missionary addresses, to which many generous friends of foreign missions ascribe their first interest in the cause. They were marked "by great intellectual force, breadth of vision, wide knowledge," a "clearness alike of perception and of statement," an "intense earnestness," and "a wonderful fertility and aptness of illustration,"—"convulsing at times even the General Synod with merriment and again almost melting it to tears." One writer has said: "We have seldom heard any missionary speak whose tongue burned with such genuine fire." (*Missionary Review of the World*, August, 1908, p. 578.) The degree of Doctor of Divinity was conferred on him by three colleges,—Rutgers, Western Reserve, and Union,—in the same year, 1878. He was the first foreign missionary to serve as President of the General Synod of the Reformed Church (1878). He visited missions in Japan and China on his way to India in 1878. On his way from India in 1874, he journeyed at a friend's invitation through Palestine and the peninsula of Mount Sinai. His careful study of the land was of great value to him in preparing the Telugu Bible Dictionary. In 1881, he spent several months in Australia to escape the hot season in India, made many addresses, and won an interest by which his mission profited for many years. During his second furlough in America, from 1884 to 1887, he raised $45,000 for the establishment of a theological seminary,—later securing the increase of this sum to $70,000. This was the first endowed school of the kind in India. His third visit, from 1894 to 1896, was marked by the publication of his first book, "In the Tiger Jungle." In 1900, he attended the Ecumenical Conference on Foreign Missions in New York City. His name was then "known throughout the Church universal, and perhaps no figures were more marked and noticed in that great missionary congregation of 1900, than those of Jacob Chamberlain and John G. Paton." He was honored by being chosen the one missionary to speak at the opening session in Carnegie Hall on April 21, and made a thrilling address in response to the welcome to the missionaries. (Condensed report in *Missionary Review of the World*, XXIII, 411–413, June, 1900.) He spoke also at the Students' Conference at Northfield. The degree of Doctor of Laws was conferred on him by Hope College in 1900, and by Western Reserve University in 1901. This was his fourth and last visit to America.

His forty-eight years of service for India were closed in 1908. He is buried on the spot where he pitched his tent first in Madanapalle. In October, 1907, he was compelled to cease work. He went from Coonoor, where, an invalid, he had borne the care of the Church and mission, while working also on the Telugu Bible Dictionary, to the physicians at Vellore, who could not restore him. He longed so for his beloved Madanapalle that he was finally carried there, and lingered a few weeks among his Telugu people until March 2, 1908. Four of the six sons born to him in India,—William Isaac, Lewis Birge, Rufus Nutting, and Charles Starr Chamberlain,—and also his wife, survive him. "To her who for thirty-seven years has shared my labours and my joys and shares them still," Dr. Chamberlain dedicated, in 1896, his first book. Dr. Chamberlain and his wife appear at the left of the picture accompanying this sketch, the "Veterans of the Arcot Mission." One of the sons, Mr. Jacob Chester Chamberlain, was well known to the members of this Association. Another son, Prof. William I. Chamberlain of Rutgers College, is a member.

April 13, 1908, a memorial service was held in the Marble Collegiate Church, Fifth Avenue and Twenty-ninth Street, New York City,—the church in which he was ordained and in which a farewell service was held when he left for the mission field over forty-eight years before. Those who took part in the service were Rev. Edward B. Coe, D. D., LL.D.; Rev. A. E. Kittredge, D. D.; Rev. Mancius H. Hutton, D. D., President of the Board of Foreign Missions of the Reformed Church; Rev. Arthur J. Brown, D. D., Secretary of the Presbyterian Board of Foreign Missions; Rev. J. C. R. Ewing, D. D., President of Lahore College, India; and Rev. Henry N. Cobb, D. D., Secretary of the Board of Foreign Missions of the Reformed Church.

Dr. Cobb writes: "Throughout all India he was recognized as one of the leading missionaries in that country. As one who has recently visited India has said since his death, 'I heard his fame spoken of all over Southern India, and I did not hear one single reference to him that was not highly appreciative of his splendid qualities of mind and heart and of the admirably successful work which he has done during his long period of service in connection with your board.'" He might have attained eminence in many fields of endeavor. He was an inventor and mechanical genius, an explorer, a great evangelist, a skillful doctor and surgeon, a linguist, a "sagacious, far-sighted, broad-minded, constructive missionary statesman," a delightful companion. "Perhaps no trait was more characteristic of him than his abounding joy. Joy in his work and in its fruits. Joy in his associations and fellowships. Joy in his plans and hopes, and joy in God even when those plans and hopes seemed frustrated and disappointed." His genial face can be seen in our "Report for 1902." "No man did more with his life than did Jacob Chamberlain," a writer in the *Independent* says: "A great preacher, an accomplished scholar, a business man of ability, a medical practitioner of no mean skill, all his talents were devoted with tremendous enthusiasm to the evangelization of India."

Biographical sketches by Rev. Henry N. Cobb, D. D., have been printed in the *Christian Intelligencer*, March 11, 1908; the *Missionary Review of the World*, April, 1908; and as an Introduction to "The Kingdom in India." (Fleming H. Revell Company.)

BREVET BRIGADIER-GENERAL SAMUEL E. CHAMBERLAIN, U. S. VOLS.

By Major-General William A. Bancroft, M. V. M. (Retired), Late Brigadier-General, U. S. Vols.

This address was delivered at a banquet given by the First Volunteers Citizens' Association in April, 1909, in honor of Company C, Third Regiment, M. V. M., the first company (not militia) to respond to President Lincoln's call for volunteers at the outbreak of the Civil War. Of this company General Chamberlain was first lieutenant. After the address a portrait of General Chamberlain was presented to the city of Cambridge and was accepted by the mayor, William F. Brooks. It hangs in the mayor's office.

Samuel Emery Chamberlain, the fifth and youngest child of Ephraim and Lydia (Leonard) Chamberlain, was born at Centre Harbor, in the state of New Hampshire, on November 28, 1829. When he was seven years old, the family moved to Boston. The boy attended the public schools, and had begun a business career, but, when he was about fifteen, his father died, and young Samuel went to Illinois to the home of an uncle, with whom he lived until May, 1846. The Mexican War had begun, and the government was raising volunteers to augment the forces of the regular army. The makeup of the boy, then sixteen years old, showed itself when he enlisted as a private in Company A of the Second Illinois Volunteers, Colonel Bissell commanding. The regiment was raised for a year's service, and proceeded to San Antonio, Texas. General Wool, commanding the troops there, issued an order which provided that any twelve months' man who would reënlist in the regular army should be transferred to such arm of the service as he might elect. We can imagine that young Chamberlain had perceived the difference between the requirements of the foot and those of the mounted arms. He might have transferred to the light artillery, of which there were some excellent batteries, but he chose to transfer to the cavalry. His fondness for a horse had already been developed. He very likely had had experience with those belonging to his uncle, and had, no doubt, learned to ride fairly well. He was relieved of locomotion and the burden of carrying his musket and accoutrements, but he took on, besides the care of a cavalryman's belongings and the chief preparation of his own food, the care, also, of his horse, though he felt, no doubt, as the Englishman felt who said: "I never walk when I can ride." So, having served barely a month in the volunteer infantry, on June 16, into the First Dragoons, Troop E, he went, and became initiated into that arm of service with which he was to serve in both the Mexican and Civil wars—not only to see hard service, but to gain distinction.

The regular army of the United States at the time of the Mexican War was not only one of the best equipped, but, also, for its size, one of the most efficient fighting machines which the modern world has seen. It was officered almost wholly by graduates of West Point, then, as now, a school without superior, and the men had become seasoned by such service as they had already done. In drill, in discipline, and in leadership, it stood on the very highest plane. The discipline of the "Old Army," as the regular service before the Civil War was called, was rigorous. In our time it might be called brutal. Objections were made to some phases of it by the volunteers, at least, in our Civil War, but the officers, with the qualification of the personal element, administered it, and the enlisted men accepted it because they found it there, and, being recruited either individually or in small squads, they knew no other, and thought of no other. Conditions were quite different from those when a regiment of volunteers, unaccustomed to military methods, entered the military service. Chamberlain was taught this system of discipline, and flourished under it, as did his fellows. It may not be true, but one cannot help feeling that the regular soldiers of sixty years or more ago were of a hardier, tougher, and more enduring character than those of to-day. Their drill was more precise and exacting; their clothing was not intended for ease of body; the infantry wore leather stocks about their necks; their food was poorer; they were inured to heat and cold—to all kinds of hardship—and they met them with equanimity, even if not with indifference. Certainly, if our hero was representative, they were rugged men, indeed; but, harsh discipline and endurance aside, they were most capably led, and they responded with spirit. Scott and Taylor were men of consummate ability, and soldiers of a lifetime; both of them without scholastic military training, but with the severest and most instructive training of active service. The subordinates were composed largely of the brilliant galaxy of officers who, scarcely more than a dozen years later, were to lead both the Federal and Confederate armies in the most terrible struggle of modern times. Among them were Grant, an infantry subaltern; Lee, older and more accomplished, already of high reputation, and one of Scott's engineers; Sherman and Longstreet, Thomas and Jackson, Meade and Hood, Hancock and Pickett and Armistead, and the bearers of other famous names. Always greatly outnumbered, but taking advantage of every opportunity which the highest military skill could recognize, this army moved on, conquering and resistless, at first under Taylor, and later under Scott, to the end of the conflict.

In this potent school of military knowledge and experience, young Chamberlain served for two years. The foundation of his military attainment was laid and was laid securely. Any youth of native capacity, both physical and mental, and of fearless disposition, who had passed through this school, had received a military education which would carry him far, without the training of any military academy.

I have dwelt upon his environment at that time because I conceive that his whole life thereafter was shaped by it. However kind-hearted as a friend, however considerate and affectionate as husband and father, however sympathetic as a man; as a soldier Chamberlain showed that he was trained in a school of stern, hard and successful service. This training was not fully appreciated at first by his comrades of a later day, but it stood him in good stead when the exacting requirements of Civil War fighting had to be met.

There is not time to recite many incidents of his Mexican service. Detailed with an escort carrying dispatches from Wool to Taylor, after a tedious march of five days the party joined Taylor's army, thirty miles from Monterey. Chamberlain was attached to Troop H, of the Second Dragoons, with which he served in the attack upon Monterey. His horse was killed on the Saltillo Road, and he was then ordered to join the stormers of the Obispado. He took part in the fighting of the second day, and witnessed the surrender from the Black Fort, on September 25th. At Mont Clova he rejoined Wool's division and was present at the battle of Buena Vista, February 22 and 23, 1847. It sounds strange to recall that he joined in cheering Jefferson Davis, when the latter, at the head of a Mississippi regiment of volunteers, repulsed the dashing charge of Minon's Lancers. Later he was made a corporal for some special service to his commanding officer, which showed quickness of apprehension, of decision and of action—a high soldierly trait.

After he left the army, at the close of the Mexican War in 1848, his enterprising spirit started him upon a life of adventure. He boarded a government wagon as wagon master, and started for California with an expedition under the charge of General Lawrence P. Graham. Upon reaching Chihuahua, inducements were offered him by the governor to join a party of rangers just moving against the Apache Indians This he did and engaged in a campaign rife with the horrors of warfare. Of the forty survivors of this campaign, Chamberlain was the last. He next went to California and remained there until 1853, when he joined Walker's filibustering expedition for lower California and New Mexico. He took part in the engagements at Lopez, Encenada and Saint Thomas. In 1854, he left for the East Indies by way of the Sandwich and Philippine Islands. From there, he proceeded to China, and then to India, where he journeyed to the foot hills of the Himalayas in quest of game.

In the autumn of 1854, he returned to Boston, and in the following year he was married, taking up his residence in Cambridge. Some of you who hear my voice knew him from then. A few brief years, and the "Wide-Awakes" were parading these streets. Now, the first volunteers were drilling with Prentiss Richardson's old musket in his law office yonder, and then came that showery April morning, forty-eight years ago—and how many times we have heard General Chamberlain tell the story in this hall—when you and he and the drummer, with Prentiss Richardson at your head, marched to the State

MRS. SAMUEL E. CHAMBERLAIN

House, with ranks steadily increasing until there was nearly a full company of one hundred men; the assignment as Company C to the Third Regiment of the Volunteer Militia, the muster into the United States service, with Chamberlain as first lieutenant, and then the three months of honorable service at Fortress Munroe and at Hampton, followed by the muster out of the company on July 22.

But, like most of you, Lieutenant Chamberlain did not stay out of service. Not receiving a commission, he enlisted, on September 6, in the First Massachusetts Cavalry, for which, of course, his youthful service had eminently fitted him. He was now nearly thirty-two years of age, mature in mind, but still young and vigorous in body, of commanding figure, erect and soldierly, standing six feet, three inches, in his boots, of courtly manners and a perfect horseman. Naturally, Chamberlain felt that he ought to have a commission. There were but few other men in the regiment who had had any military training whatever, and fewer still a cavalry training, and he, a veteran dragoon, had already been more times under fire than most soldiers, even in war, ever are, and had had, besides, years of military service, during which he had been a private and a non-commissioned officer in the regulars, and a first lieutenant in the volunteers. Why, under the circumstances, should he not receive a captain's commission? He ought to, and he did. This came to him on November 25, and at last he had the responsibility of a command.

The First Massachusetts Cavalry was highly favored in its roster. Originally commanded by Robert Williams, a capable and energetic officer of the regular army, there were Horace Binney Sargent, and his brother, L. M. Sargent, Jr., Charles Francis Adams, the Higginsons—Henry Lee and James Jackson, Arnold Rand, the Crowinshields—Casper and Benjamin, Charles G. Davis, Louis Cabot, Lawrence Motley, the Bowditches—H. P. and Nathaniel, Charles A. Longfellow, Atherton H. Stevens, Jr., and others of high character. To be associated with these men meant to be with the best of our community then, as to-day, and it goes without saying that Chamberlain did not lose the opportunities which four years of daily intercourse with these Boston gentlemen and gallant officers gave him. But we cannot stop to dwell upon his services and the services of this famous regiment in the Civil War. They are a part of the history of our country, and the glorious deeds need not be recited here.

Chamberlain was taken prisoner and also severely wounded. It is said that, in his career, he participated in more than one hundred battles. In extent, as well as in intensity, some of these battles were among the fiercest that the world has ever known. Their importance is measured only by the importance of their results. General Chamberlain, it is said, had fourteen horses shot under him in action, and was wounded seven times.

Chamberlain was promoted. He deserved to be. Only a few days ago,

I asked an officer of distinction, who was a captain with Chamberlain in the First, and later commanded another Massachusetts cavalry regiment, if General Chamberlain was brave and if he was capable. "He was both," said he, "and the men had confidence in him in action. He deserved his promotion." Of a military officer, this is the final word.

On October 3, 1862, he was promoted major, and was for a period division inspector. On March 5, 1864, he was promoted lieutenant-colonel. On September 30, 1864, he was promoted colonel and regimental commander. He was breveted brigadier-general, United States Volunteers, on February 24, 1865, for "gallant and meritorious service in covering the retreat of Gregg's division of cavalry at the disastrous battle of Saint Mary's Church, Virginia, on June 25, 1864." Transferred to the command of the Fifth Massachusetts Cavalry on July 26, 1865, he was mustered out on November 28, 1865, his 36th birthday.

Major-General Joseph Hooker commended him in a report, for "distinguished gallantry at Kelley's Ford, and for heroic services, commanding the applause of his companions, until he fell severely wounded."

After the Civil War, he returned to Massachusetts, where he served on the staffs of Governors Bullock and Claflin, and for ten years—from 1871 to 1881—he was warden of the State Prison at Charlestown, and at Concord, and for over eight years—from 1885 to 1893—he was warden of the Connecticut State Prison at Wethersfield. He held other positions of responsibility and trust, and his comrades, both in the Mexican War and in the Civil War, recognized his distinguished services. In 1893, he withdrew from the activities of public life, and lived quietly upon his estate, Maple Hill, at Barre, Mass. There, for fifteen years, with the wife of his young manhood, and with visits from his children and grandchildren, in a home of comfort, filled with reminiscent collections of his public service and his travels, in the delightful environment of a New England countryside, he lived over his stirring career, conspicuous among Massachusetts' fighting officers and patriotic citizens.

Last November we laid him at rest in Mount Auburn, among the illustrious dead. The last page of his life book has been written, but the book will be opened many times, not only by those nearest and dearest to him, but by you whose first lieutenant he was, and by others, his countrymen, in whose country's service he never faltered. To him and to you, his comrades of Company C, wherever you may be, we shall not cease to do honor. Your roll in enduring bronze is inscribed upon the Cambridge city hall. Your services in gratitude will be remembered by the people of Cambridge forever.

ART GALLERY, HYDE PARK HOUSE, LONDON, ENGLAND

HYDE PARK HOUSE, LONDON, ENGLAND

A FRIEND sent recently a sketch of Hyde Park House, and a picture of its art gallery, both from a New York press. This is of interest to the Association, as it is the home of Lady Naylor-Leyland, better known as the beautiful Jennie Chamberlain of Cleveland, Ohio. Some of her connections were, and are still, members of this society. It is one of the most stately houses in the West End of London; a veritable treasure-house of art! Its magnificence is largely due to the father of Sir Herbert Naylor-Leyland, who brought together the nucleus of this fine collection over forty years ago. Possessing as he did a remarkable taste and love for fine art, everything seems unique. Built in a regal style, it possesses a home-charm and does not seem a private museum. The outer hall is typical of the house. Passing up a flight of marble steps, flanked on each side by huge crouching lions, the visitor reaches the central hall, whence rises a great staircase lighted from above. Statues, tapestries, bas-reliefs and pictures are on every side. The balustrades of the staircase and balcony are finely wrought bronze, with hand-rails of burnished brass. Near the entrance to the picture gallery is the world-renowned "Crucifixion" by Pisano, 1243 A. D. Leaving this gallery with its marble floors and pillars, the centre archway is reached, flanked by other rooms, each filled with gems of art of the 16th and 17th centuries.

The picture gallery contains "The Graces" by Rubens; a remarkable triptych with scenes from the miracles by Memling; "The Day of Judgment," with Christ seated on a rainbow throne; a painting of the Veronese school; a canvas by Guido Reni; and many other paintings. Near the entrance are two beautiful dishes of Italian design, for rose water; also the "Triumph of Hercules," an exceptionally large composition in Dresden china. A buhl table near the entrance to the four drawing-rooms is called the finest example of Boule's work in England, if not in Europe. It is of elaborate design with the arms of Louis XIV emblazoned in the center, and was doubtless made for him. At each end of the gallery stand four great candelabra of Oriental china, mounted in ormolu, branching eight or ten feet from the ground. Passing between two of these the ball-room is reached, the finest in London.

Lady Naylor-Leyland's portrait by Edward Hughes is in the farther drawing-room. Her marriage to the son of the art-loving millionaire was on September 5, 1889. She is the daughter of William Selah Chamberlain, formerly of Cleveland, Ohio, and grand-niece of the late Selah Chamberlain, the noted multi-millionaire of Cleveland, builder of railways and bridges. Her sister Josephine married, in 1895, Sir Tom Talbot Leyland Scarisbrick, created a Baronet in 1909, only son of Sir Charles Scarisbrick, and a member of Parliament since 1906. Lady Naylor-Leyland has two sons, Sir Albert

Edward Herbert Naylor-Leyland, born in 1890, and George, born in 1892. Their country estate is Nautclwyd Hall, Ruthin, North Wales. Her husband died in 1899. It is reported that Queen Victoria said that she was as good as she was beautiful, and was as simple as a child. She has always been a favorite with Queen Alexandra and the late king of England.

SELAH CHAMBERLAIN OF CLEVELAND

Selah Chamberlain of Cleveland, Ohio, the well-known builder of canals, railways and bridges, was born in Brattleboro, Vt., May 4, 1812. After attaining his majority, he journeyed to Boston, and served for two years as a clerk in a wholesale grocery; then journeyed to western Pennsylvania, where he began his life-work by engaging in the construction of the Erie extension of the Pennsylvania Canal. Acquiring some capital in this venture, and in a similar service for the Ohio and Pennsylvania Canal, he took a large contract on the Wabash and Erie Canal that occupied him until 1845. In 1844 he married Miss Arabella Cochran of Crawford Co., Pa. In 1845, he went to Canada, entering into extensive contracts for constructing canals along the St. Lawrence River. Two years later he returned to Vermont and assumed complete control of the construction of the Rutland and Burlington Railway to connect the Great Lakes with the sea-board, and became interested, also, in the construction of the Ogdensburg and Rouse's Point road, later called the Lake Champlain road.

When Selah Chamberlain removed to Cleveland, Ohio, in 1849, he was already, though less than forty years of age, a man of wealth, but was still full of ardor and energy. He contracted to construct the entire line of a railway to connect Cleveland and Pittsburg, and pushed the work so rapidly that the road was opened for business in 1851. During the next quarter of a century, he was constantly employed building or managing railroads, chiefly in Wisconsin, Minnesota and Iowa. He extended the Hastings and Dakota Railroad from the central part of Minnesota to Big Stone Lake near the western boundary of the state. He built the La Crosse and Milwaukee Railroad, and operated it under a mortgage lease until his claims for construction were satisfied. He built the Minnesota Central, and was for many years its president; and built also the Southern Minnesota Railroad, losing by Minnesota's repudiation of its railroad bonds till the Legislature of 1882 redeemed the good faith of the state. He built in Iowa several roads, which form a part now of the Chicago, Milwaukee and St. Paul system, becoming a director, a member of the executive committee and a heavy stockholder of this line, in the consolidating and strengthening of which he was active for some twenty years, until two years before his death, the mileage increasing during this period from 800 to 5,000 miles.

In 1871, he built the Lake Shore and Tuscarawas Valley Railroad. When it was reorganized as the Cleveland, Lorain and Wheeling Railroad, he became by purchase its chief stockholder and was president of the line until his death. This road gave an outlet to the Lakes at Cleveland and Lorain for the coal of West Virginia and southern Ohio. In 1871, he established the banking-house of Chamberlain, Gorham & Perkins, which was considered for nearly a decade one of the most trustworthy financial institutions in the state, and was then merged, in 1880, in the Merchants' National Bank, later the Mercantile National Bank, of which he was a director until his death. He was a director, also, of the Iron Cliff Co., of the Minnesota and North-western Railroad, and of the Commercial National Bank of Cleveland. He was president, at some period of his life, of the Cleveland Transportation Co., of the Cleveland Iron Mining Co.; and was, at the time of his death, president of the Pittsburg and Lake Angeline Iron Co. He was one of the owners of the waterworks of Dubuque, Iowa.

He died at his home on Euclid Avenue, Cleveland, December 30, 1890. His wife died March 25, 1887, and his two children died in childhood. His country estate was at Wickliffe in the Lake Country. By his will the chief heirs of his estate, approximately $10,000,000, were three of the children of his nephew, Robert Chamberlain, who died at Santa Barbara, California, August 11, 1888, and who was the son of Joseph Chamberlain, who died at Cleveland, Ohio, December 6, 1864, aged sixty-three. Joseph Chamberlain had three sons, the other two being William Selah Chamberlain, now living in England, where his daughters live, as the preceding sketch shows, and the late Joseph Chamberlain of Cherry Valley, New York. Two sisters of Selah Chamberlain have passed away since his death,—Mrs. Holbrook of Cambridge, Mass., and Mrs. Olive Chamberlain Taft of Dubuque, Iowa, mother of Mrs. Harriet P. Kimball, whose death is recorded in this Report.

For thirty-eight years Selah Chamberlain was a member of the Second Presbyterian Church of Cleveland, and for some years was president of the Congregation. There is not room to repeat the high eulogy delivered at his funeral by his pastor. "During the war for the Union Mr. Lincoln's administration had no more zealous supporter", writes E. R. Perkins, a business associate, "and he contributed freely of his means and in every other practicable way lent the government his aid". He was a Republican until 1872, when he ran for Congress in Cleveland on a Greeley ticket. Later he was an independent voter. Mr. E. R. Perkins wrote of him a few years before his death: "In person Mr. Chamberlain is tall and spare. His manner is modest and retiring. * * * * * His judgment of character is almost absolutely perfect, so that in all the positions of trust in which he has placed men he has in no single instance been deceived. In his friendship he is warm-hearted and sincere and commands in return the affectionate respect of all who share his confidence. Young men always find in him a prudent adviser and friend, and more than one successful business man owes his success to his timely assistance, generously and considerately bestowed."

Notwithstanding great pressure of business he "acquired a high degree of culture", Mr. J. H. Kennedy writes in the *Magazine of Western History*, October, 1885 (vol. II, pp. 613–615). To this article we acknowledge hereby indebtedness, as well as to friends of the family. As Mr. Kennedy remarks, a complete story of Selah Chamberlain's railway interests would fill a volume.

Wm Chamberlin

HON. WILLIAM CHAMBERLIN OF VERMONT

By Jenny Chamberlain Watts

William Chamberlain was born in Hopkinton, Mass., April 27, 1755, and was baptised May 4th. He was the son of Samuel and Martha (Mellen)

Samuel Chamberlain

Chamberlain. His grandfather, Deacon Henry Mellen, is said to have "built the first house in what is now Hopkinton", more probably the first house on land leased for ninety-nine years from the trustees of Edward Hopkins' estate for the benefit of Harvard College. He was a member of the town's first Board of Selectmen, chosen March 25, 1725; and a deacon of the church from 1732 to 1767. (Hurd, Hist. of Middlesex Co., iii 800, 801.) William spent much of his early boyhood in the home of this grandfather. (2 Proc. Mass. Hist. Soc., x. 491.) His uncles and aunts intermarried with the leading families of the town,—Wood, Burnap, Jones, Nutt. Rev. John Mellen, a graduate of Harvard College in 1741, pastor at Sterling and later at Hanover, was his uncle. Prentice Mellen, later the first Chief Justice of Maine, was a first cousin. (Drake, Middlesex Co., i 495; N. E. Hist. and Gen. Reg. VII., 75, 167.) His uncle, Thomas Mellen, married Elizabeth Wood, and his aunt, Martha Chamberlain, married Benjamin Wood, both children of John Wood, who received in 1714, from his wife's father, Joseph Buckminster, a deed of half of Whitehall Farm, and with Elnathan Allen owned what was probably the first saw mill in Hopkinton, standing as early as July, 1717, at the outlet of Whitehall Pond. Wood was a member of the first Board of Selectmen of Hopkinton (1725) and one of the original members of the church gathered there. When he died in August, 1725, his seven children were all minors, but they retained his estate and were prominent in town affairs when William Chamberlain was a boy. His uncle, John Chamberlain, married Mary Wood. The settlement of Woodville in the western part of Hopkinton near the Whitehall Reservoir of the Boston Water Works keeps alive the memory of this family. William's aunt, Mary Mellen, married in 1749, John Jones, son of Capt. John Jones, who owned a tract of 631 acres by the Sudbury River, where the village of Ashland stands now, and who represented Hopkinton in the General Court of Massachusetts from 1735 to 1767, when he was succeeded by Capt. Joseph Mellen, uncle of William Chamberlain. In the thirty years from 1744 to 1773, there were only six years in which, apparently, his father, his grandfather, or an uncle did not serve on the Board of Selectmen; and for ten years of this period both a Chamberlain and a Mellen were on the Board.

Hopkinton was a farming community, and William enjoyed only about two months' schooling in a year. Yet he was fond of books, was possessed of a quick apprehension and an uncommonly tenacious memory, and hoped for a college education, borrowing Latin books and committing them to memory in preparation for the longed-for opportunity. His hopes were defeated by sickness in his father's family, by the death of an uncle, by the removal of the family to New Hampshire, and finally by the outbreak of the War of the Revolution. His father, Samuel Chamberlain, "though not poor, was not in very affluent circumstances, & was able by dint of industry to bring up a large family in a reputable manner". This sentence and the facts which follow are from a sketch of his early life written by General Chamberlin to his son, Mellen, in 1827, and published in the "Proceedings of the Massachusetts Historical Society", March, 1896, (pp. 491–502). In September, 1767, his elder brother, Samuel, was taken ill of a terrible fever of a typhus kind; and this fever continued in the family until March of the following year. Four children and both parents were ill, one child died, and the mother's health was permanently impaired. The expense of doctor, nurses and hired help left the family in debt, and for two or three years William and his father worked from sunrise to sunset cutting cedar shingles on the lots which the father owned in swamps two or three miles from home, while his younger and older brothers managed the farm except in haytime and harvest. On a visit to Capt. Joseph Eastman of Concord in 1772, his father was persuaded by this brother-in-law to purchase a tract of 600 acres in the adjoining town of Loudon, N. H. This he did in partnership with John Chamberlain. In the summer of 1772, William and his brother, Samuel, went with this uncle John, to Loudon, and cleared and sowed a field of wheat. William is said to have taught school that winter,—when seventeen years of age. The father and uncle entered into an agreement, by which the uncle took the father's farm in Hopkinton, and the father the land in Loudon. In March, 1774, the family moved to New Hampshire.

Two days after the battle of Lexington, in the middle of the night, a horseman knocked violently on the door of the isolated farmhouse in Loudon, and summoned William Chamberlain to appear the next morning at the place of parade prepared to march south to check the British advance. The courage and determination of the lad of nineteen stood the test of a march of two miles alone through a dark pine woods with the thought of a possible death in battle or execution for treason; and two days later the news of the British retreat permitted the minute-men to return home. He had "read with deep interest and feeling all the essays in newspapers and pamphlets in which the natural rights and dutys of man in society were explained and vindicated, and in which the act of the British Parliament de[c]laring their right to bind the Colonies by their legislative acts in all cases whatsoever were denounced as arbitrary & tyranical, repugnant to every principle of natural or civil liberty," and had "imbibed the most enthusiastic ideas of liberty and the rights of man". Thus not only the sentiments, but much of the language of the speeches and writings of Hancock, Otis, Quincy and Adams were almost indelibly impressed upon his memory.

Samuel Chamberlain, his elder brother, enlisted as Orderly Sergeant in Capt. Jeremiah Clough's company of Col. Enoch Poor's regiment for eight months. He entered the service May 27, 1775, but was released at the end of six weeks to return to his young wife in Loudon, on William's enlisting as a private with exemption "from other duty to do the writing for the company." As Captain Clough had promised to receive him in his brother's place as sergeant, William Chamberlain was duly indignant. His account of his trials in this company encamped at Winter Hill, Somerville, is interesting reading. When his term of service expired, he enlisted six or seven men out of this company and marched off in triumph to join as sergeant Capt. Joshua Abbott's company in Colonel Stark's regiment. (See in confirmation N. H. State Papers, XIV, 303–305, 465.)

Immediately after the evacuation of Boston, on March 19 or 20, 1776, he marched with his regiment to Norwich, Conn.; rested two days, marched to New London, spent several days very distressingly on Long Island Sound buffeted by adverse winds, and arrived finally in New York City for an enjoyable month, March 29th to April 29th. Seven days were then passed on a journey from New York to Albany, struggling against adverse winds on the Hudson and marching the last of the way on foot. After a few days in Albany, they marched to Lake George and proceeded by boat to Ticonderoga. Continuing their journey north in sail boats, they landed for an hour at Crown Point; were forced a few hours later, by high waves and winds, to camp for two days on the western shore of Lake Champlain; arrived at St. Johns May 29, 1776. Immediately volunteers were called for to relieve the fort at the Cedars on the St. Lawrence. Marching the next morning they met the capitulated American forces at La Prairie. They were ordered to Montreal, and were forced to spend two weeks in that smallpox-infested city. Then the troops marched to Sorell, whence, two days after their arrival, they were driven, by the advance of Burgoyne's army, in precipitate retreat, travelling day and night. Arriving at Fort Chambly they loaded their boats deeply with ammunition and, destroying the fort, towed the boats up the falls. Every commissioned officer in his company had been inoculated for smallpox and preceded the company to the Island Aux (Isle aux Noix), so William Chamberlain, Sergeant, directed himself and his men and boats in this retreat without supervision. Arriving at St. Johns at sunset, he was ordered immediately to Isle aux Noix, spending by the way a foggy night on shore without a fire, so great was the fear of the enemy. The island was covered with soldiers sick with the smallpox. William Chamberlain inoculated himself with a jack-knife and continued his journey south in the same boat with smallpox patients, several of whom died. About five days of hard rowing brought them to Crown Point. He was afraid to touch salt pork, which was supposed to increase the danger from smallpox, and lived for these five days of hard labor on clear tea, boiled in an open tin dish, and flour cakes, for as no one lived then on the shores of the lake, it was impossible to get other supplies than those furnished to the troops by the poverty-stricken Continental Congress. The tea he bought in Montreal. At Chimney Point, across Lake Champlain from Crown Point, they encamped "in a tow tent on the cold ground". All but two of his company were ill with the smallpox before their arrival there, and these two succumbed to the disease. They had neither medicines nor nurses. Although he had lived on a starving regimen for over a month, he was the most capable man in his company and crossed the lake every other day to draw and distribute provisions. Several times he fell in a swoon, and when the Declaration of Independence arrived, he could read it for only two minutes at a time, his eyes were so seriously affected. From seventy-six men in his company at St. Johns on May 29th, twenty-three were dead before November 16th. For six or seven weeks at Fort Independence (Ticonderoga) during the later months of this period, he and Sergeant Seth Spring (later Capt. Seth Spring of Saco, Me.) were actively engaged making spruce beer for the troops. The first barrel they drank themselves and gave away; the second, they sold by the mug, and soon were making and selling from three to five barrels a day. They improved their health and the health of the troops. William Chamberlain believed that he would never have reached home alive, if he had not had money to spend on the march through New York and New Jersey, and to purchase a horse to carry him back to New Hampshire.

November 16, 1776, they resumed the march south, first to Fort George, where a week was spent; thence to Albany, where they received two months' pay. As the time for which they had enlisted expired on the first day of January, the order to march farther south was a surprise and disappointment. The night of December 3rd was, he thought, the most uncomfortable of his life, spent between Albany and Kingston in the hold of a boat so crowded that he could not escape to the storm-beaten deck from its ill odours, fighting and cursing. A day or two were passed pleasantly among the people of Dutch descent at Esopus. Then he suffered in a cold and dreary march through West Jersey to Newtowne, Pa., where he arrived on December 20th, or 21st, being one of nine officers and privates, out of a company of seventy, to survive the northern campaign and join the army of General Washington.

On Christmas morning they were paraded and kept the field until sunset, then marched for Trenton, eighteen miles distant. William Chamberlain shared in the famous crossing of the icy Delaware, the silent march through a snowstorm to surprise the Hessians at Trenton, and the quick, sharp engagement just before sunrise. He was near General Washington when the British standard was surrendered. Sent with the detachment that pursued the British, he returned drenched with rain, his shoes drinking in half melted snow and water at every step, and found that he must wait for the prisoners to be ferried across the river. He bent for half an hour over a fire, shaking with an attack of the ague. Recovering sufficiently to return to the river, he was again chilled by the keen northwest wind that had arisen, but was so fortunate as to discover a Miss Chamberlain in a house not far from the ferry and obtain for his name's sake a bowl of hot meat broth. Crossing with the rear guard, he returned to headquarters at Newtowne. There the men had to shift for themselves; only six or seven of the company remained; their time of service expired. William Chamberlain had seen enough of the war for the time being, and asked the discharge of himself and men from Colonel Stark. He and Seth Spring and a few others bought horses, visited Philadelphia, and on January 3rd rode north. In a biographical account, written at the time of his death, it is stated that he bore dispatches from Washington to Green, presumably en route to Philadelphia.

In the spring of 1777, William Chamberlain purchased one hundred acres of land, and worked on it until July, when he was persuaded by Capt. Benjamin Sias of Canterbury to join his company as orderly sergeant. July 20, he marched in Col. Thomas Stickney's regiment in General Stark's Brigade into Vermont to defend the frontier threatened by the retreat of St. Clair from Ticonderoga. (See also N. H. State Papers, XIV, 179.) During a week's delay at Manchester, he did duty as adjutant to Colonel Stickney's regiment till the adjutant arrived, and was then appointed sergeant major. He took part in the Battle of Bennington, for the militia of the northernmost states, the most splendid victory of the war, as amateurs withstood through a long day's fight professionals trained in the Prussian army, and, though the attacking party, won the victory. He brought away, his biographer stated, "as trophies a stand of arms wrested from a Hessian soldier in personal contest and the Book of General Orders for Baum's detachment describing the route and objects of the expedition". (See also Proc. Mass. Hist. Soc., April 1896, pp. 503–506.) For the rest of that brief campaign he served as Quarter Master, the Quarter Master having been wounded in the battle. He was not commissioned. His time of service was from July 20 to September 27, and the allowance for travel was for 180 miles. He declined, he said, further service. An interesting confirmation of this statement is the following: June 23, 1779, the House of Representatives of New Hampshire voted to raise 300 men for the defense of Rhode Island in six companies, etc., "William Chamberlain of Concord to be a Lieutenant to command the Major's company," etc. William Chamberlain did not go to the field, presumably because in June, 1779, he was in Peacham, Vermont; during that month he "pitched a lot" on a right which he had purchased.

With the Battle of Bennington General Chamberlin's autobiography ends abruptly. A few facts concerning his later life have been gleaned from such family papers as the mice have spared and from printed records. It is possible that a young woman in Concord was partly responsible for the waning interest in military affairs noted above, as some months later he married (March 15, 1781) Jenny Eastman, daughter of Captain Joseph and Abigail (Mellen) Eastman. She was born in Concord, N. H., September 12, 1762, and died October 23, 1830, in Peacham, Vt. Capt. Joseph Eastman (born June 10, 1715; died in 1803) commanded a company at Crown Point in 1775, and later was with Colonel Gerrish at Ticonderoga. His father, Capt. Ebenezer Eastman (born February 17, 1681; died July 28, 1748) was one of the original grantees and the first settler of Concord, N. H., and was one of its most prominent citizens. He served in the expedition against Port Royal, was a Captain of Infantry in the expedition of 1711 against Quebec, was present as a Captain at the surrender of Louisburg, June 16, 1745, and went a second time to Cape Breton in 1746. Ebenezer was the grandson of Roger Eastman, who was christened April 4, 1610, in the church of St. Lawrence at Downton near Salisbury, England; sailed in the ship *Confidence* in April, 1638; and settled in Salisbury, Mass. This Roger was the third son of Nicholas Eastman of Charlton, on the Avon River two miles above Downton, and grandson of "Roger Eastman of Charleton", whose will was executed Jan. 11, and probated Feb. 21, 1604. (Bouton, *Hist. of Concord, N. H.;* Guy S. Rix, *Hist. and Gen. of the Eastman Family in America*, i 20–26, 74, 154; *Granite Monthly*, Dec., 1910, pp. 391–396.)

As early as 1779, William Chamberlain became interested in the settling of Peacham, Vermont, a township chartered in 1763 by Benning Wentworth, Governor of New Hampshire. May 13, 1779, William Chamberlain of Concord, N. H., purchased of Phineas Lyman, of Hadley, Mass., for £300, "one whole Reight or Share of land" in Peacham. The conveyance included a warranty against all "Persons whomsoever if Wm. Chamberlain or his assigns shall settle said Right in such a Manner as was Originally Requird by the Charter by the first day of January next, otherwise said warranty to extend to all persons claiming from by or under" Phineas Lyman or Wiseman Clagget. the original grantee. On the foot of the deed is the writing: "This deed to be delivered to the Grantee if ye consideration be paid in three Weeks from the Date." On the same day Peter Blanchard of Concord received a similar deed of a share in Peacham from Benjamin Colt of Hadley, Mass., William Chamberlain being one of the witnesses.

Wm Chamberlain
Elisha Porter
Hampshire ss May 13th 1779

It is interesting to note that the signature was *Chamberlain.* In the years which followed Chamber*lain* and Chamber*lin* both appear in his handwriting, sometimes on the same page. In later life he spelt it uniformly Chamber*lin.* So far as is known his father and grandfather always wrote Chamber*lain.* His brothers seem to have drifted into his habit of abbreviating the name. His two eldest sons reverted to the older form. In this paper the form Chamberlain will be used for the earlier years and Chamberlin for the later years of his life.

William Chamberlain did not fulfill this condition as to settlement in person. Though one-half of the lot drawn on the right of Wiseman Clagget in the second division of lands in Peacham is included in William Chamberlain's list for the direct tax of 1798, Captain Ephraim Foster "pitched" lot No. 50 in the "Square" on this right in June, 1779; and, in a list of grantees and lot owners drawn by William Chamberlain in 1785, appears as the owner of the lot. Also, in this month of June, 1779, William Chamberlain "pitched" lot Number 47 in the "Square" on the right of Oliver Smith. Lot No. 47 was west of the mountain road between Foster's Pond and the road. Two lots lay between it and the Farrow farm, which stands where the road to Cabot and the old road to Marshfield diverge. (Lot located by Miss Jennie Cowles.) Other men who made pitches in this month were Colonel Thomas Johnson, James Bayley, Benony Thayer, Moses Bayley, Robert Ambrose, Peter Blanchard and Joel Blanchard.

In April, 1779, Colonel Moses Hazen was ordered to move his military stores to Peacham in order to continue building the military road, which General Bayley had carried six miles beyond Peacham in 1776. A portion of Bedel's regiment was sent to Peacham to construct the road, and build blockhouses there and at points farther north. The road was extended that summer about fifty miles beyond Peacham through what are now Cabot, Walden, Hardwick, Greensboro, Craftsbury, Etc. The work on the road was discontinued late in August (N. H. State Papers, xvii, 329, 331, 343, 345, etc.; Frederic P. Wells, Hist. of Newbury, Vt., 86, 87; Records of the Governor and Council of Vermont, i. 218.)

The charter of Peacham was granted in December, 1763, and the first meeting of the proprietors was held at Hadley, Mass., Jan. 18, 1764. But an order of King George III in 1764, assigning all lands west of the Connecticut River to the Province of New York, compromised the titles received from the Governor of New Hampshire, and led to an irregular warfare in what is now Vermont between the settlers and the agents of the Provincial Government of New York. The outbreak of the War of the Revolution increased the insecurity of life and property in this region, hence the normal development of the township was checked. (Vt. Hist. Soc. Proc. 1908–1909, pp. 119, 145, 148, etc.) Shortly before William Chamberlain purchased a right to land in Peacham, Ira Allen, agent of Vermont. became convinced that the leading men in the Legislature of New Hampshire wished to extend the jurisdiction of New Hampshire over the lands west of the Connecticut River. William Chamberlain's father, Samuel Chamberlain, was a member of the Legislature in the autumn of 1778. Later, in the year 1779, New Hampshire laid its claims openly before the Congress of the Confederation. (Vt. Hist. Soc. Proc. 1908–1909, pp. 142–149.)

Presumably the ordering of troops to Peacham, and New Hampshire's decision to claim jurisdiction over what is now Vermont, led to a revival of interest in Peacham lands in 1779. At least two requests for a proprietors' meeting came to Elisha Porter of Hadley, the clerk chosen by the proprietors in 1764. One application was dated Newbury (Vt.), August 27, 1779; the other was signed at Hadley by Benj. Colt, Daniel White and Phineas Lyman October 13, 1779. According to a vote in 1764, meetings might be called by the clerk on the application of proprietors owning one sixteenth of the township by posting a notice in some public place in Hadley at least fourteen days previous to the day appointed. A meeting was thus called for Oct. 27th at Hadley. It met, adjourned twice, and dissolved on Nov. 3rd without transacting any business, because too few proprietors were present. A few months later, on March 17, 1780, Elisha Porter posted a call for a meeting at Hadley on March 30th. Benjamin Colt was chosen moderator; then the meeting adjourned, without transacting business, to April 20, at the home of Mr. Thomas Johnson in Newbury in the "New Hampshire Grants", now Vermont. The adjourned meeting "fell through", because the moderator did not appear with necessary papers. William Chamberlain, according to an account which he kept, made "a Journey from Concord to Coos to bring Papers and attend a Meeting in April 1780", hence he was one of the men disappointed by Benjamin Colt's failure to appear. (This northern region was commonly known as the Coos Country.) On the day on which Benj. Colt was expected as moderator at Newbury, he, Jonathan Child, Samuel Hopkins and Gen. Jacob Bayley signed at Hadley a demand upon Elisha Porter, Clerk, for the calling of a meeting at Hadley as soon as might be. Meanwhile, two days later, April 22, Benj. Whetcomb, Thomas Johnson, Samuel Merrill, Samuel Young, Samuel Atkinson, Asher Chamberlain and others, owners they claimed of more than one sixth of the township, signed at Haverhill,

N. H., just across the Connecticut River from Newbury, a demand for a meeting at the house of Mr. Thomas Johnson in "Newbury in Coos", May 25. William Chamberlain journeyed south with this paper to Hadley, for on May 11th the Proprietors voted "to pay William Chamberlain for a Journey from Coos to Hadley in order to get a Proprietor's meeting notified three pounds twelve shillings and ten pence making the money Equal to what it was in the Year 1774". When he arrived in Hadley, he found that Elisha Porter, in response to the earlier demand made April 20, had posted a call for a meeting at Hadley, May 4. The Proprietors met, chose Benjamin Colt moderator, and adjourned without transacting other business to May 10, at the house of Mr. Thomas Johnson at Newbury in the New Hampshire Grants. Thus the men who intended to settle in Peacham, won a victory over those whose only interest was financial. A two days' session was held at Newbury on May 10th and 11th, the first item of business being the choice of William Chamberlain as Clerk of the Proprietors to succeed Elisha Porter, who had resigned that office.

The Proprietors voted secondly, on May 10th, "that those lots which were laid out and sold by Jacob Bayley Esq., which are now settled to the Acceptance of a Committee that shall hereafter be appointed for that purpose be Confirm'd and Recorded to the present Inhabitants or Posessors On Condition of their paying six pounds making the Money Equal to what it was in the Year 1774 for Each hundred acre lot to the proprietors treasury if not already paid to General Bayley (and if Paid to said Bayley his Refunding the Money to the Proprietors)". The clause included in the parentheses was added when this vote was confirmed in September, 1782. Gen. Jacob Bayley had laid out seventy-five lots containing one hundred acres each, and had sold some lands to settlers under the authority of Phineas Lyman, who was given a power of attorney for that express purpose by six or more of the proprietors on June 1, 1773. (See also Vt. Hist. Soc. Proc., 1908–9, p. 119.) Also other proprietors or their assignees had, for instance in June, 1779, "pitched" upon one or more of these seventy-five lots, which were known collectively as the "Square". May 11th, it was, "Voted that Thomas Johnson, William Chamberlain, Joshua Bayley, Asher Chamberlain & Abial Blanchard be a Committee to Determine how many of those lots that are now pitch'd upon are properly settled and to order such as they shall accept to be (Confirmed and) Recorded to the present Inhabitants or Possessors." September 4, 1782, this vote was confirmed, the words included in parentheses being added. September 6, 1782, Jacob Bayley signed a promise "to Pay or account unto William Chamberlin, Clerk for the Proprietors of Peacham, Twenty Silver Dollers Per Lot for Sixteen Lots which the Proprietors have voted to me or the Present persesers." Thus this committee was able to settle one of the most vexed questions affecting the early settlement of the town.

May 11, 1780, the Proprietors voted to appoint a committee to lay out the rest of the township in accord with resolutions passed on the same day. For this committee the same men were chosen as for the committee just mentioned, but two changes were made later, so that the committee as confirmed September 4, 1782, was: William Chamberlain, Abial Blanchard, Asher Chamberlain, Ensign James Mitchell and Benoni Thayer. It is noticeable that three of these men, William Chamberlain, Blanchard and Mitchell, were from Concord, N. H.

A vote was passed to encourage the building of a grist mill, referring the matter to the committee, mentioned above, "appointed to settle the Pitches in the town". Sundry other votes of less permanent importance were passed. It was decided that, in the future, meetings should be notified by advertising in the weekly newspapers at Hartford for three successive weeks. The Proprietors adjourned to meet at Newbury on the first Thursday in July. William Chamberlain had been appointed on every committee chosen at this meeting.

During the following month, June, 1780, William Chamberlain spent seventeen and one-half days in Peacham as a surveyor running the line around the township and laying out lots, and four days in "viewing Pitches and Roads". (Account drawn by him August 18, 1783.) The proprietors were notified to meet at Newbury September 20, 1780. As few attended, those present adjourned to meet at Peacham October 24, but never met, because of the scare which accompanied the raid of the British to Royalton, Vermont.

When William Chamberlain became a land surveyor in this Vermont wilderness in June, 1780, the War of the Revolution was in progress, and as this was a frontier settlement it was in constant danger of a raid by the British from Canada or by the Indians. Though "the square", that is the central portion of the town, was plotted about 1774, and several pitches made, the first settlers spent their first winter there in 1776–7, and the first child was born within the limits of the township in October, 1777. In March, 1781, the first mill-stones were brought to town by Col. Thomas Johnson. He and his assistant, Jacob Page, and the son of his host were taken prisoners and carried captive to the British posts at the north. One of these captives, Jonathan Elkins, spent several months in Mill Prison, England. The other two returned to Newbury after several months of captivity in America. In 1782 others were carried captive to Canada from this region of country. (F. P. Wells, Hist. of Newbury, Vt., pp. 90–97, 384–393, 648.)

That the proprietors of Peacham were not eager to invest money in the development of the town, or journey to this northern frontier to attend Proprietors' meetings is not surprising, especially as New Hampshire, New York and Massachusetts had each laid before the Congress of the Confederation a claim to this region west of the Connecticut, against all of which claims the young government of Vermont had entered a "spirited remonstrance", requesting to be admitted as a fourteenth State into the Union, a request not granted until 1791. (Vt. Hist. Soc. Proc. 1908–1909, pp. 142–149.) An application for a meeting dated Concord, June 25, 1782, and addressed to William Chamberlain as Clerk of the Proprietors, an application signed by his friends, James Mitchel, Abiel and Benjamin Blanchard, and Thomas Johnson, contains this clause: "Whereas meetings formerly notified have failed we suppose for want of suitable Notification we desire you to take all possible pains to notify Every Proprietor." William Chamberlain notified the proprietors to meet at the Court House in Newbury in the New Hampshire Grants September 3, 1782. In addition to advertising this meeting for three weeks successively in the *Hartford Gazette*, he spent eleven and one-half days in a journey to Hadley, Roxbury, Haverhill, etc., in order to secure the attendance in person or by proxy of a sufficient number of proprietors for the transaction of business.

The meeting at Newbury in September, 1782, lasted four days, and at its close the Proprietors, warned by past difficulties, did not dissolve, but adjourned to meet at Haverhill, N. H., on the first Monday in June, 1783. The first business transacted was the drawing and signing of a bond binding the proprietors present to abide by the votes passed at this meeting. The bond recites that the township of Peacham

". . . . was granted by the late Governor Benning Wentworth as being under the Jurisdiction of said New Hampshire. But now it is doubtful to the Jurisdiction of which State it doth belong. By which means the transacting the necessary business of settling said Township is become very difficult. And many are doubtful whether the measures already taken by the proprietors of said Township for the Settlement and cultivation thereof are legal. And whether there are any legal ways of selling the Interest of any proprietor who may be delinquent in paying his proportion of such sum or sums of money as may be voted & assessed.

"And whereas much the greatest part of the proprietors of said Township of Peacham are now assembled together either personally or by proxy and desirous to confirm & establish such parts of the former proceedings & transactions of said proprietors as appear to them to be well calculated to Advance the Interest of said Township, for which purpose & to transact such other business as may appear necessary further to be done a meeting of said proprietors is now called.

"And whereas the said William Chamberlin is appointed an Agent for said proprietors & fully Authorized to carry into Execution all such former Votes & transactions of said proprietors as they at this present meeting, may think proper & order to be carried into execution & also such other votes & Resolves as they may think further necessary to be passed at the present meeting."

Therefore the proprietors present signed bonds aggregating £6,100, " at the rate of Silver at six shillings & Eight pence per Pound ", binding themselves and those from whom they held proxies to abide by the votes passed at this meeting. The names of those who signed, with the number of shares in the township which each controlled, are as follows: General Jacob Bayley (11),

Thomas Johnson (8), Asher Chamberlin (1), all of Newbury, Vt.; James Bayley (5) of Haverhill, William Child (5) of Lime, Benoni Thayer (1) of Orford, John Johnson (1) of Enfield, all of Grafton County, N. H.; Ensign James Mitchell (3), Abial Blanchard (2), both of Concord, N. H.; Samuel Atkinson (2) of Boscawen, N. H.; Col. Eleazer Weld (7) of Roxbury, Mass.; and Phineas Lyman (15) of Hadley, Mass. This bond was placed in the hands of William Chamberlin and is now in the possession of his descendants. He controlled four shares, and gave his bond to Thomas Johnson, moderator of the meeting.

Ten votes were passed confirming certain business transactions at the meeting in May, 1780. It was decided that "all lands in the Township of Peacham except one Hundred Acres to Each Right be divided by Draught among the Grantees". William Chamberlain, Abial Blanchard, Asher Chamberlain, Ensign James Mitchell and Benoni Thayer were confirmed as the committee "to lay out the Township", and were also appointed "to view those Lotts that are or may be pitched and make report to the Proprietors". They were also authorized, "to Extend the westwardly line so as to contain the full Complement of six miles square with the allowance which is given for rocks mountains ponds rivers highways & unimproveable lands". Thomas Johnson, William Chamberlain and Asher Chamberlain were appointed a committee "to settle and adjust all accompts that may be brought against the Proprietors". Votes were passed concerning grist and saw mills, the former of which was, apparently, already in use while the latter was not built until after August, 1783. Sixteen shillings were assessed against each proprietor's right for the clearing of roads, and £1. 4 sh. for the laying out of the township, James Bayley, Thomas Johnson and William Chamberlain being appointed assessors, and Capt. Samuel Atkinson, Collector.

In March, 1783, William Chamberlain spent twenty-four days as a surveyor in Peacham. During this month, apparently, the settlers in Peacham organized and chose town officers, though the first town meeting recorded in the town's book was that held in March, 1784.

When the Proprietors met at Haverhill, according to their adjournment of the preceding September, on June 2, 1783, they decided that each proprietor, who had not already "pitched" a lot, might have until August 20, 1783, to pitch the first one hundred acres on his right. Such proprietors as failed to do this were to have a hundred acre lot assigned to them by draught on August 20th. Thomas Johnson, Ashbel Martin, Abial Blanchard, James Mitchell and William Chamberlain were appointed a committee to "consult the Selectmen or a Committee Chosen by the Inhabitants" and "lay out Roads through said Township where it may best accommodate the Inhabitants and the Publick in General and make Report to the Proprietors in August next". The meeting was then adjourned to August 20, at Peacham.

In August, 1783, the Proprietors voted to "Accept the Plann & Survey of the Township as Exhibitted by William Chamberlain, Abiel Blanchard, James Mitchel and Asher Chamberlain a Committee Chosen by the Proprietors of said Town and signed by William Chamberlain as Surveyor". Lot 49 in "the square" was confirmed to William Chamberlain as his share in the second division of lots. Lot 49 was east of the road from Peacham to Cabot, next above Lot 40, which lay opposite Lot 47 "pitched" by William Chamberlain in June, 1779. (Located by Miss Jennie Cowles.) Other business was transacted. Colonel Thomas Johnson was directed to bring suit against John Goodwin if he did not fulfill the condition in his bond by building a saw mill. This was the first meeting of the proprietors within the limits of Peacham. It will not be possible to follow in detail their further proceedings. William Chamberlain continued as Clerk of the Proprietors, and in March 1785 was chosen by the inhabitants of Peacham as Town Clerk.

During this period, when William Chamberlain was actively surveying lands in Peacham and journeying through the unsettled regions of Massachusetts, New Hampshire and Vermont to notify and attend Proprietors' meetings, his young family remained in Concord, N. H. July 23, 1783, Nehemiah Abbot, as Treasurer of Phillips' Academy in Andover, appointed William Chamberlain of Concord, Gentleman, his "lawful attorney in all matters and things relating to the property which the said Academy has in two rights of land" in Peacham. Two of his children were born, apparently, in Concord. (According to the Concord records the second child, Betty, was born in Concord in September 1784.) Presumably the family removed to Peacham in the autumn of 1784, as William Chamberlain recorded on a slip of paper, — "clearing the South Road from my House to the Mill Brook, 1 Day of myself in October 1784 and four Days in 1787". Also a conveyance of land in Peacham, from Reuben Willmott of Peacham to William Chamberlin of Peacham, Gentleman, dated May 23, 1785, was witnessed by "Jenny Chamberlain", his wife.

Jenny Chamberlain

May 31, 1785, the Proprietors of Peacham passed a vote ratifying certain former votes and establishing on a firm basis the ownership of lands in Peacham. On the following day Eleazer Weld of Roxbury, Mass., who was attending this meeting in Peacham, conveyed to William Chamberlain, the consideration mentioned being £60, a one hundred acre lot (no. 28 in the Square). The conveyance was witnessed by Peter Blanchard and Samuel Miner of Peacham and acknowledged the same day before Alexander Harvey, J. P., in Barnet. This was the lot on which William Chamberlain's house was built and which became the nucleus of his home-farm, considered later the best farm in the town. November 10, 1787, he purchased of Jabez Bigelow of Westminster, Worcester County, Mass., for £91. 10 sh., the adjoining lot to the southeast, on which his mill was built. This farm was one mile west of the present village of Peacham.

William Chamberlin was active in town affairs, being Town Clerk for twelve years and serving on the most important committees. In 1785 he was sent as the Town's Representative to the State Legislature. Oct. 24, 1786, he was commissioned a Justice of the Peace for Orange County by Governor Chittenden. In 1787 he was again elected to the Legislature, and continued as the Town's Representative until he was chosen a member of the Governor's Council in 1796.

William Chamberlain surveyed lands in other Vermont towns. His descendants possess the original plan of the township of Barton, Vt., which he surveyed for the Proprietors, and several letters from Colonel William Barton of Providence, R. I., concerning the affairs of Barton. In 1792 he was collector of taxes for the Proprietors of Groton and Cabot. (Nov. 3, 1786, he received lot no. 60 in the first allotment of lands in Cabot.) His papers show that at some time in his life he was interested in lands in Barton, Cabot, Groton, Danville, Greensborough, Hardwick, Littleton (later Waterford), Lyndon, Walden, Cannaan, Lewis, Marshfield and Woodbury. How many of these towns he served as a surveyor is not known. A patent, signed by President Madison, protecting an improvement he devised in his surveying instruments, is still in existence, as are also his brass compass with its tripod.

The first church services in Peacham were held in the house of his nearest neighbor, Moody Morse, half a mile east of his home-farm. By 1791 the town was prepared to build a meeting-house, but its location proved a difficult problem. Those who lived on the west side of the town wished the meeting-house built near the house of Moody Morse, near which the minister's and the school lots had been located in the town survey. But apparently the east part of the town was not only increasing in size, but was also possessed by determined men. Unable to agree on a site, the town voted to choose as a committee to fix the stake Colonel Charles Johnson and Colonel Joseph Hutchins of Haverhill, N. H., and James Whitelaw, Esq., of Ryegate, Vt., and appointed four men to accompany them and point out the different sites desired. Ashbel Martin, brother-in-law of William Chamberlin and his nearest neighbor to the south, was chosen from the west side of the town. Thirty-eight voters signed a paper binding themselves to abide by the decision of the committee. Sept. 27, 1791, the committee set the stake near the house of Moody Morse. This decision dissatisfied many residents; a call extended to Rev. Israel Chapin to become the settled minister of the town failed of acceptance; the meeting-house was not built. The first church organized

(1784) was Presbyterian, but it languished and was dissolved. In 1794 a new church was organized on the Congregational model. The town proceeded again to choose a committee to set a stake for the meeting-house; but in 1795 a building was erected for the Caledonia County Grammar School, and this was used for church services until 1806. It would appear that this dispute concerning the location of the meeting-house did not lessen General Chamberlin's popularity in the town. September 1, 1795, in casting its votes for governor and councillors, the Town cast for him as councillor eight votes more than the sum of all the votes it cast for the four candidates for the governorship.

While a member of the Vermont Assembly, General Chamberlain secured the incorporation of the Caledonia County Grammar School and its location at Peacham. Sept. 2, 1795, a warning was issued for a town meeting on Sept. 15th containing the item, "2d to see if the town will Authorize Wm. Chamberlin, Esq., to engage in behalf of the Town to build a Court House or County Grammar School House or any other Publick Building upon the Expense of the Town with what will be subscribed, if any of the above privileges are granted by the Legislature." At the town meeting it was:

"II. Voted That in case a Grant of the County Grammar School can be obtained by Act of Assembly and established in the town of Peacham, that the Town will support a Preceptor for the term of three years from the first day of January, A. D. 1797, Provided the Persons who live in the vicinity of the place where the Buildings will probably be built will subscribe a sum sufficient for erecting the Buildings that shall be required by the Trustees and that the Town Clerk [William Chamberlin] be Directed to receive subscriptions to the amount of three Hundred Pounds. And that each person be holden to pay the sum by him subscribed when the sum of 300 Pounds shall be subscribed in the whole. And also receive subscriptions for a Court House if the Grant shall be obtained.

"3d. Voted That Jonathan Ware, Wm. Chamberlin and Wm. Buckminster be a Committee to draft a Memorial to be presented to the Legislature for the Purpose of obtaining a grant of the County Grammar School."

General Chamberlain did not forget his boyhood's desire for the best education the country could offer, and threw his influence for the school in preference to the court-house and prison, notwithstanding the fact that as a judge of the county he would have a drive of six miles to the court-house in Danville. On the first Friday in October the town accepted the memorial drawn by this committee of three, and authorized William Chamberlin, the Town's Representative, to present it to the Legislature. It agreed to pay the salary of a preceptor for three years, and to relinquish to the County Grammar School, if located in Peacham, the lot reserved by the Charter of the Town for the British missionary society, the Society for the Propagation of the Gospel in Foreign Parts. General Chamberlin carried the memorial to the Legislature, and Oct. 28, 1795, secured the passage of an act locating the Caledonia County Grammar School in Peacham. Eight days before, Oct. 20, an act had been passed appointing a committee, "to Determine the Place for erecting the County Buildings in the County of Caledonia". This committee located them June 16, 1796, in the adjoining town of Danville, nearer the geographical center of the county. (Records of the Governor and Council of Vt., iv. 94, 96; Journal of the General Assembly of Vermont, 1796, p. 30.) Peacham retains to-day its endowed school, but the county seat has been removed eight miles further away to St. Johnsbury.

The act incorporating the school named nine trustees, leading men in their respective towns, William Chamberlain alone living in Peacham; and appointed the first meeting of the Board of Trustees at his house on the third Tuesday of November, 1795. At this first meeting, Alexander Harvey, who represented the adjoining town of Barnet in the Legislature, and had many years before served as colonel of the regiment of militia of this region, was chosen President of the Board of Trustees and General Chamberlin, Secretary. Dec. 2, the town voted that, "a Committee consisting of John W. Chandler, Wm. Chamberlin, R'n Blanchard, Jonathan Ware, Abiel Blanchard, Jonathan Elkins, Jr., Jacob Guy & Abel Blanchard, be appointed to wait on the Trustees and express their wishes with respect to the place for erecting the County Grammar School House." The question seems to have been promptly settled by the choice of a site half a mile further from General Chamberlin's house to the east than the stake struck for the meeting-house in 1791, a somewhat bleak location on what has since been known as Academy Hill. December 23, a building of two stories, forty feet long by thirty feet wide, was decided upon, and the Board of Trustees and the Town agreed upon General Chamberlin and Captain Jonathan Elkins as a committee to superintend the building operations. General Chamberlin was also appointed, with three trustees from three adjoining towns, to devise, adopt and execute the best method of securing to the institution the profits of the lands and other property of the school. Caledonia County was then more extensive than now, and the school received as its endowment lands in Montpelier, St. Andrews (now Plainfield), Calais, Cabot, Marshfield, and Woodbury, as well as in the several towns now included in the county. It was decided to lease the lands on long or perpetual leases. Possibly the leasing of the lands in Hopkinton, Mass. (where General Chamberlin spent his boyhood) for the benefit of Harvard College by the Trustees of Edward Hopkins' estate suggested this. In November, 1796, he and one other trustee were appointed to secure a preceptor and regulate the school. He journeyed in person to Concord, N. H., to hire the first principal, Ezra Carter, a great-grandson of Captain Ebenezer Eastman, a graduate of Dartmouth College, and so well beloved that both General Chamberlin and Rev. Leonard Worcester, the first pastor of Peacham, named a son Ezra Carter. The Board of Trustees met annually at William Chamberlin's house as long as he lived. He was Secretary of the Board from 1795 to 1812, and President from 1813 until his death in 1828. ("100th Anniversary of Caledonia Co. Grammar School", pp. VII, 41; MSS. records of the Trustees. See also "Rec. of Gov. and Council of Vt.", VI. 53. 54. 58.)

Oliver Johnson, the well-known anti-slavery leader, said in 1871:—"Two things early gave Peacham an honorable pre-eminence among the towns in this part of the State. The first was the settlement of a minister of rare ability, catholicity, and worth; a man, taking him for all in all, such as is not often found in the pulpit of a small frontier town. The second was the establishment here of the Caledonia County Grammar School; an institution which has been of unspeakable value to each successive generation of the boys and girls of the town, to say nothing of the hundreds who came from other places to avail themselves of its advantages. * * * The effect of such a ministry and such a school was seen in the high standard of morals that prevailed here, in a thirst for knowledge on the part of the young, and in the fixed habit on the part of the people of attending public worship. I doubt if there is another town in the whole State, in which, fifty or sixty years ago, there was so small a fraction of the inhabitants who did not go to meeting on Sunday as there was in Peacham." (Addresses delivered at the Re-Opening of the Congregational Church in Peacham, Vt., Sept. 28, 1871. Publ. Montpelier 1872, p. 34.) Rev. Leonard Worcester, the first minister of the Church in Peacham, said: "The establishment of a County Grammar School here was pretty early sought for and obtained, on terms which were honorable to the inhabitants generally; as, while several individuals made very considerable donations, the town at large subjected itself to no little expense to secure the grant. That this institution has been of inestimable value to this people, and to all the region round about * * * is beyond all question. No less than twenty-six young men, from among the inhabitants of this town, have obtained a college education, having been prepared to enter college in this institution. Six of these are, or have been, favorably known as preachers of the gospel; one of whom is now a missionary among the Cherokee Indians, and another in the Sandwich Islands." Twelve, he adds, after completing the course of instruction in this school, studied medicine without pursuing a college course. This was written in 1839. (Ibid, p. 51.) Until the building of the railways, Peacham, a hilltown, was one of the most prosperous in the county. The market road from Boston to Montreal passed through Newbury and Peacham. To-day the population is less than it was in 1800, when Peacham was next to Danville the most populous town in the county. According to the General List of the State of Vermont in 1813, the town ranked third in Caledonia County in the number of polls (Danville, Barnet, Peacham, Wheelock); fourth in the number of acres of improved land (Danville, Barnet, Ryegate, Peacham, Lyndon); second in the number of its houses (Danville, Peacham, Barnet);

second in the value of its mills (Barnet, Peacham, Burke, Wheelock); second in its tax on mechanics (Danville, Peacham); third in the number and value of its oxen and other cattle, and of its horses; fourth in luxuries (pleasure-carriages, clocks, watches); third in its total assessment (Danville, Barnet, Peacham, Ryegate). In 1832 the number of names on the church roll was 370, "which, I think", Rev. Leonard Worcester added, "was the largest number then belonging to any one church in this state, excepting that of Middlebury." (Ibid, pp. 59, 60.)

William Chamberlain, Captain Elkins and John W. Chandler were chosen a committee to "obtain subscriptions for the printing a Paper at Peacham". As a result the *Green Mountain Patriot* was published in Peacham by Samuel Goss and Amos Farley from 1798 to 1807, when it was removed to Montpelier, Vt. Several times William Chamberlin served on a committee to secure as preachers candidates for the pastorate of the church, and he was appointed on many other committees of the Town. Rev. Asaph Boutelle wrote to the "Gazetteer of Vermont" that General Chamberlin "ran lines both for land and conduct".

October 24, 1786, William Chamberlain was commissioned a Justice of the Peace for Orange County by Governor Thomas Chittenden. In 1795 he was chosen an Assistant Judge for Orange County. November 5, 1792, an act had been passed for the division of Orange County, appointing the years 1795 and 1796 for the reorganization. October 19, 1796, William Chamberlin was chosen the first Chief Judge of Caledonia County, with Benjamin Sias and David Wing as Assistant Judges. A little later, November 8, 1796, an act was passed fixing the times for holding the Supreme and County courts in Caledonia County. (Records of Gov. & Council of Vt., iv. 15, 33, 36, 94, 101, 123; Journal of the General Assembly of 1796, pp. 30, 45, 136, 167, 184.) He held this office from 1796 until elected to Congress in 1803.

He represented Peacham in the Constitutional Convention held at Bennington in 1791, and signed the ratification of the Constitution of the United States on January 10, 1791. (Records of Governor and Council of Vermont, iii, 467, 481.)

His interest in military affairs during this period of his life is evinced by the following commissions in the possession of his descendants: Major, October 7, 1787, in the 2d Regiment, 5th Brigade (Alexander Harvey, Colonel); Lieutenant Colonel in the same regiment April 29, 1791; Lieutenant Colonel Commandant of the same regiment January 1, 1794 (a reorganization makes this regiment in the 2d Brigade instead of in the 5th Brigade); Brigadier General of the 2d Brigade in the 4th Division of the Militia October 20, 1794; Brigadier General of the 3d Brigade in the 4th Division of the Militia October 29, 1798; (he took the oath of office November 8th); Major General of the 4th Division October, 1799. He resigned from the militia

October 27, 1799, in favor of Brigadier General Zebina Curtiss, as he found that some officers felt that General Curtiss was the senior Brigadier General, and should have been promoted. (Records of Governor and Council of Vermont, IV, 239.) The militia at this time consisted of all able bodied men from sixteen to forty-five years of age. It was customary for companies to elect their captains and lower officers; for the captains and subalterns to choose the field officers; and for the Governor and Assembly to elect the eight Brigadier Generals and the four Major Generals. It is interesting to note that his promotion in 1794 came at a time when there was danger of war with England, because of her interference with American commerce during the war then raging between France and England. The news of this war arrived in America in April, 1793. In May, 1794, Congress ordered Vermont to have 2,139 militia ready to march at a moment's warning, and the danger did not pass until the ratification of Jay's Treaty with England in 1795. There was danger of war when his next commission was signed in 1798. In October of that year, a few days before this commission, he had voted as a member of the Council for the address to President Adams, approving his administration in general and especially his course toward France. This was a few months subsequent to the famous X. Y. Z. disclosures and the suspension of intercourse with France. (Records of the Governor and Council of Vermont, IV, 187, 201, 237, 239, 438, 471–484, 492; J. B. McMaster, Hist. of People of U. S., ii, 168–170, 212–282, 374–384, 432, etc.)

A member of the General Assembly of Vermont in 1785 and from 1787 to 1796, William Chamberlin was a member of the Governor's Council from 1796 until his election to Congress in 1803. Before his election to the Council, he had frequently served on joint committees of the Assembly and Council, serving on four for instance in 1794. (Records of Governor and Council of Vermont, IV, 69, 74, 76.) The Governor's Council consisted of the Governor, the Lieutenant Governor and twelve Councillors, all elected on the same day, and by the State at large. He was active in the Council, serving frequently on joint committees of the Assembly and Council. (See Records of Governor and Council of Vermont, iv, 110, 115, 125, 129, 138, 141, 143, 148, 149, 152, 153, 181, 184, 196, 198, 220, 221, 224, 230, 232, etc.) He served on many important joint committees, as those to consider amending the laws, to consider amending the judiciary system, on the militia, and on the University of Vermont. (Ibid, 308, 335, 339, 340, 341, 349, 351, etc.) In 1800 he was a Presidential elector. (Ibid, iv, 278.)

General Chamberlin was a Member of Congress from October 17, 1803, to March 3, 1805. It was a long journey to Washington over rough roads, yet he and the three other Representatives from Vermont were present on the opening day of each session. He served for both sessions on the Committee of Claims, one of the five Standing Committees of the House. He was a Federalist, and seems to have voted with his party on the important questions of the day. He was defeated for reëlection by James Fiske, Republican. The election was a very close one. January 9, 1805, W. B. Banister wrote from Caledonia County to General Chamberlin in Washington that neither candidate had received a majority of all the votes cast, and that a second election would be necessary. (MSS. letter.)

Returning from Washington he represented Peacham in the General Assembly of Vermont in 1805 and 1808. He represented Caledonia County on the joint committee of ten from the Assembly and two from the Council that located the seat of government at Montpelier in the autumn of 1805. (Records of Governor and Council of Vermont, v, 66, 426, 427.) Previously to this time the Legislature of Vermont had been migratory. Montpelier was in the southwest corner of Caledonia County (until 1810), about twenty-five miles from Peacham. It was within ten miles of the geographical center of the state, and the lines of travel passed through it in all directions.

General Chamberlin was elected to the Eleventh Congress, receiving a majority of 169 votes over James Fiske. The four Representatives from Vermont were present, May 22, 1809, on the opening day of the first session, which lasted until June 28. The appointments assigned to Vermont on the Standing Committees were given to the two Representatives who had served in the preceding Congress,—Martin Chittenden, Federalist (M. C. 1803–1813), and Samuel Shaw, Republican (M. C. 1808–1813). General Chamberlin was appointed on the Select Committee of seven to whom that part of the President's message relating to "the fortification of our seaport towns", was referred on May 26. This was an important committee appointment, as war was then in progress between England and France, and it was feared that America would become involved through the ill feeling aroused by the search of American ships on the high seas and the impressment of American seamen. On May 27, the House of Representatives, at the request of the Committee, called on the President for information from the Secretary of War, which was received June 6. On June 7, a bill was reported from this committee making an appropriation to complete fortifications already commenced at the seaports, etc., and also for fortifications on the northern and western frontiers. On the following day a bill was received from the Senate appropriating $750,000 for these same purposes, and this bill was passed the following day, William Chamberlin voting against reducing the appropriation and for the bill. Measures were moving rapidly at this extra session of Congress, but he wished the pace accelerated as he voted June 7 with the minority (17 to 104) who wished all petitions of a private nature excluded for the remainder of that session. On June 6 also he voted with a minority (59 to 60), who wished instructions given to the committee on that part of the President's Message referring to foreign affairs directing them to reduce to one act all provisions relating to embargo, non-intercourse, etc. On June 7 he voted for a resolution directing the Secretary of the Treasury to report to the House at the next session a plan for protecting and fostering manufactures, with a statement of the manufacturing establishments begun, and such other statistics and facts as would give a general view of manufactures throughout the United States. But it will not be possible to follow his Congressional career in this detail. The second session lasted from Nov. 27, 1809, to May 1, 1810. He was appointed December 1 on the Select Committee of nine to whom was referred that part of the President's message concerning the relations of the United States with foreign nations, and he served on sundry other select committees during the session. On December 7, he wrote his wife that he arrived in Washington November 25, and was amidst congenial surroundings in a boarding house with Messrs. Pickering, Hillhouse and Hubbard. Surely at this point a reminder that he was a Federalist, and supported Federalist measures is not necessary. In October, 1810, he was defeated for reëlection by James Fiske, Republican. The Governor and both branches of the Legislature were Republican that year, and only one Federalist was reëlected to Congress, Martin Chittenden, Member of Congress from 1803 to 1813, who won his seat by a majority of twelve votes, it was said. (*Vermont Republican*, October 22, 1810.) Peacham and Barnet were strongly Federalist, but Danville was Republican and supported a Republican newspaper, *The North Star*. General Chamberlin and the other Federalist members from Vermont arrived two days late for the third session of this Congress, taking their seats December 5, just in time to hear the President's message read. He represented Vermont on the Select Committee of seventeen appointed to consider "that part of the President's message in regard to the militia". He represented Vermont, also, on the Select Committee appointed December 18, 1810, to consider the petition of the stockholders of the Bank of the United States praying the renewal of their charter. This committee introduced a bill "continuing for a further time the Charter of the Bank of the United States". After several days of debate this bill was postponed indefinitely on January 24, 1911, by a vote of 65 to 64, General Chamberlin voting against this postponement.

The War of 1812 was unpopular throughout New England, and the Federalist Party regained control of the Legislature of Vermont and elected Federalists as Governor and Lieutenant Governor. From 1813 to 1815, William Chamberlain was Lieutenant Governor of Vermont. The elections of 1813 and 1814 were very close. Neither the Federalist nor the Republican candidates for Governor and Lieutenant-Governor received a majority of the votes cast, so that Governor Martin Chittenden and Lieutenant Governor William Chamberlin were elected in both years by the two houses of the Legislature in joint session. While Lieutenant Governor he was an active member of the Council, serving frequently on committees. (Records of Gov. and Council, VI. 17, 20, 28, 52, 53, 58, etc.) In November, 1813, he voted with the Republicans to postpone till the next session the repeal of the act "to prevent intercourse with the enemies of the United States," which the Federalists, forgetting the Alien and Sedition acts of 1798, regarded too great an infringement of personal liberty. A year later he voted against sending delegates to the Hartford Convention. Obviously he was an independent Federalist. (Ibid, VI. 36, 94.) For two-thirds of his term as Lieutenant Governor the War of 1812 was in progress, and hence his post on the joint military committee was an important one. (Ibid, VI. 66, 73, 74, 75, 77, 86, 89, 94, etc.) He was the sole representative of the Council on the joint committee to consider a revision of the militia laws. (Ibid, 67.) Apparently he was placed on all the special, as well as the permanent committees on military matters. (Ibid, 72, 80, 85, 89, 92, 93, etc.)

In 1814, on the receipt of a letter from the Secretary of War of the United States ordering 2,000 militia to be drafted for immediate service, the Legislature appointed a committee of three to consider whether the militia called into the Federal service could remain under State officers. General Chamberlin as chairman presented, October 28, a report to the effect that the President of the United States must command the militia "in person or exercise his command over them by officers appointed by the States." This report was accepted November 1, and it was resolved unanimously November 31,—"That it is the opinion of the Council, that it is not made the duty of his Excellency, by the Constitution of the United States, to put the detached militia of this State, when in actual service of the United States, under the command of any officer commissioned by the President; but such militia are to be commanded by officers appointed by the State or by the President in person." (Records of Gov. & Council of Vt., vi 80, 85, 89, 92; Niles Register, vii. 105.) It will be remembered that General Stark, with the militia of New Hampshire and Vermont, won the Battle of Bennington and protected the Vermont frontier in 1777 by ignoring the orders of the commander of the Continental Army in that region. Vermont, a sparsely settled country facing the Canadian frontier, was fearful of being denuded of its military strength. Under changed conditions, this became a vexed question during the Civil War. Peace with England was proclaimed in February, 1815, and the Federalists in Vermont, as in other parts of the country, lost their hold upon the people. The Federalist candidates for Governor and Lieutenant Governor were defeated in 1815, 1816 and 1817. In 1818 the Federalists placed no ticket in the field. (Ibid, 108, 176, 213.) Thus ended the political life of William Chamberlin.

During his term as Lieutenant Governor, he served in 1814 as Chief Justice of Caledonia County, and also as a delegate to the Constitutional

Convention which met at Montpelier July 7 to 9, 1814, to consider amending the State Constitution. Lieutenant Governor Chamberlin voted with the minority (20 yeas to 188 nays) for abolishing the Governor's Council and establishing a Senate as a co-ordinate branch of the Legislature of Vermont. All the amendments proposed were rejected by the Convention. (Journal of the Convention, publ. 1814.)

Later in life General Chamberlin wrote:—"In the variety of Business that I have engaged in the course of my life I have always found that where my personal attention was not bestowed my profits all went to the Leeward." (Letter from Wm. Chamberlin to his son Mellen, April 30, 1827.) Yet notwithstanding his devotion to public affairs his private business seems to have prospered. His wife was an excellent manager and remained with the

Jane Chamberlin

children at the home in Peacham. An agreement signed by William Chamberlin and Israel Page Oct. 2, 1795, shows something of his careful attention to details. Page was to take the whole care of the cattle, sheep and horses through the whole of the winter, care for the barn in the neatest and best manner, do all the thrashing, cut and haul the wood, cutting the wood both in the woods and at the house, and tend all the fires. Dec. 17, 1798, General Chamberlin drew up a list of his property on which the direct tax authorized by Congress in that year was assessable. This list included nearly 1,000 acres in Peacham, 100 acres in Danville, 100 acres in Walden, 100 acres in Cabot, and over 2,000 acres in Barton, Vt. His list of assessable property April 1, 1815, describes the home-farm more fully. It contained 275 acres, 50 acres of improved land; two dwelling houses, the one 29 x 38 ft., of two stories, with a back kitchen; the other about 24 ft. square, two story on one side and one story on the other. There were two barns, one 32 x 100, the other 24 x 36 feet, and sundry outhouses. During the years 1807 to 1813 he purchased several parcels of land, which formed a farm of 156 acres in the east part of the town, called his "Hollow farm", with a grist mill, a barn 36 x 80 ft., and a corn barn. The land lay on both sides of the road from Peacham to Danville, the mill brook being east of this road. Dec. 17, 1811, he and his son-in-law, Dr. Josiah Shedd, purchased for $1,000, three-fourths of an acre of land with a house thereon at "Peacham Corner", the southeast corner, on "the Highway leading from the Academy to Danville where Hazen's road intersects the same". It was a house of two stories, 30 x 40 ft., with a barn 30 ft. square, a woodshed, etc. Several years later he bought about nine acres adjoining this lot, removed an old store (McLean's store) and built a new barn and outhouses.

April 1, 1812, William Chamberlin leased to Thomas Russell of Cabot for three years "that farm in Peacham on which the said William Chamberlin now lives, the House in which he now lives and Garden adjoining excepted, as also excepting the mill house and one acre of land for tillage occupied by the miller for a number of years past". How long he continued to live on this farm west of the village is not known. April 15, 1817, he was living in the house at Peacham Corner, but was planning to move to his farm at Peacham Hollow, as soon as a house on that farm could be prepared for him. The total disintegration of the Federalist Party in Vermont meant that his political life had ended, and he was, presumably, too active a man to cease work. In 1821 he was living on one of his farms, but was thinking of returning to the house at Peacham Corner. (MSS. Letters from William Chamberlin to his son Mellen, April 15, 1817, and Feb. 25, 1821.) February 18, 1823, he conveyed to his son, Ezra Carter Chamberlin, one-half of the old home-farm west of the village with adjoining lots of land, in all one-half of 520 acres. This was General Chamberlin's youngest son, born Oct. 17, 1799. As a boy he strained his eyes by close reading on the long winter evenings, often by the light of a pine knot in the fireplace when he was supposed to be asleep, and hence was unable to follow his two elder brothers to Dartmouth College. As early as 1820 he was living on this farm with his sister Abigail, as several letters to and from their brother Mellen show. "Dear folks at the Yellow House", was a favorite phrase of this brother. He married March 22, 1827, at Peacham, Deborah Shedd, only child of Henry and Sarah (Bickford) Shedd, and a niece of his brother-in-law, Dr. Josiah Shedd. His love for books and for public affairs never wavered, and during his long life no one in his household escaped being impressed into the service of reading aloud to him during the winter evenings. So, though not educated at college, he was a highly intelligent and well informed man, and a delightful conversationalist. His father felt it absolutely essential to his comfort to have the assistance of this one son in his wide business interests. He had the pleasure, also, of seeing him a Justice of the Peace, holding his first court in December, 1826. After the father's death this son took his place in the community. He was a Trustee of the Caledonia County Grammar School (Peacham Academy) thirty-eight years (1839–1877), and its Treasurer for fourteen years (1856–1870); he was Treasurer of the Town and also of the Church for many years, and represented the Town in the State Legislature in 1842 and 1843; he was a deacon in the Congregational Church for thirty-five years and one of the most liberal supporters of the Church, the Sunday School (an innovation in his day), and the cause of Christian missions at home and abroad. He had his father's love for the Union, and during the Civil War gave $700. to send a man to the front because he was too old to go in person. In 1823 and 1826 General Chamberlin sold his "Hollow farm" and other lands, and made

HOME OF E. C. CHAMBERLIN, PEACHAM

Ezra C Chamberlin

improvements in the house at Peacham Corner. His will, signed May 4, 1827, and probated Nov. 20, 1828, covers three closely written folios. He bequeathed land and securities to his three sons,—Mellen, William, and Ezra Carter,—and to his four daughters,—Betey Bradley, Lydia Shedd, Jane Strong and Abigail Chamberlin. The house at Peacham Corner was included in the portion of his unmarried daughter Abigail, who cared for her parents during the last years of their life. The other half of the old home-farm was included in the portion of his son, Ezra Carter Chamberlin. His wife's will was probated Dec. 9, 1830.

General Chamberlin was buried in the cemetery on Academy Hill in Peacham. The stone table which stands above his grave reads: "In memory of Gen. Wm. Chamberlain, this tablet is inscribed by the affection of his wife and the gratitude of his children. Trained in the active service of his Country, & long employed in its civil Councils; abroad respected, & at home beloved. He closed an honorable and useful life on earth in humble hope. Through the Mercy of God his Redeemer of a better life in Heaven. Born 1753 [1755]—died Sept. (27) 1828, aged 75 years." The stone table over his wife's grave reads: "In memory of Mrs. Jane, Relict of Gen. Wm. Chamberlain, obt. Oct. 23, 1830, aged 68 years. In early life she devoted herself to her Redeemer and manifested an attachment to His cause by a faithful discharge of her duties as a wife, a mother, and a Christian."

A brief biographical sketch written at the time of his death, contains these words: "In private life General Chamberlin was an upright and honorable man, a friend of order, a steady supporter of all religious institutions, and a patron of learning within his sphere of influence, and was one of the founders of the comparatively old and valuable Academy at Peacham, and was perhaps more influential than any other in laying its foundation, and till his death most of the time president of the Board of Trustees, and also of the Bible Society in that county. In his old age he could look around on every side on a cultivated region which had become so under his observation and in some good measure perhaps by his exertions". As a résumé of his public record, the following sketch by Walton in the "Records of the Governor and Council of Vermont", may fittingly close this paper:

"Gen. William Chamberlain, born at Hopkinton, Mass., April 27, 1753 [1755], removed with his father to Loudon, N. H., in 1773; volunteered in the army in 1775, and served as orderly sergeant in the invasion of Canada, suffering all sorts of privations, and being one of the nine officers and privates, out of a company of seventy, who survived to take part in the battle of Trenton, N. J. At the expiration of his enlistment he returned to New Hampshire, but on Burgoyne's invasion he again volunteered, and was in the battle of Bennington, from which he is said to have brought away some trophies of personal combat with his enemies. About 1780 he removed to

Peacham, being then clerk of the proprietors of the town. He was town clerk twelve years; justice of the peace twenty-four years; town representative in 1785, 1787 until 1796, in 1805, and 1808—twelve years; Chief Judge of Caldonia County Court 1787 until 1803, and again in 1814—seventeen years; Councillor from 1796 until 1803—seven years; Lieutenant Governor 1813 to 1815; a delegate to the Constitutional Conventions of 1791 and 1814; a Presidential Elector in 1800; and a Member of Congress two terms, 1803-5, and 1809-11."

Mellen Chamberlain

MELLEN CHAMBERLAIN, ESQ.

By Abbie Mellen Chamberlain

Mellen Chamberlain, the subject of this sketch, was the sixth child of General William and Jane (Eastman) Chamberlain, born in Peacham, Vt., June 17, 1795. His short and eventful life might be divided into three parts; the first was his preparation for college in the then well-known Caledonia County Grammar School in his native town. This academy was the sixth institution of the kind founded in the state of Vermont; and his father was one of the founders, and also one of the leading officers in the school for years. He graduated from Dartmouth College in Hanover, N. H., in 1816. His first engagement to teach was in the academy at Bellefonte, Pa. Afterwards he became an instructor in the academy at Peacham. Later he read law with Judge Samuel Prentice at Montpelier, Vt., and finished his course at the famous Law School at Litchfield, Conn. By 1820 he was ready to practice law at Castine, Me., as junior partner of Mr. Hale, formerly of Rutland, Vt., but for many years a resident of Castine.

Personally Mr. Chamberlain was a responsive, generous-hearted man, delicate in sensibilities, fastidious and highly cultured in tastes, with a courtly bearing and possessing a deep interest in the sciences and inventions of the day. He was five feet eleven and one-half inches high, with light brown hair, blue eyes and a fair complexion. The portrait which accompanies this sketch is copied from an oil painting darkened by age.

His legal practice furnished him a comfortable living, but did not satisfy his energetic temperament. May 29, 1826, he wrote to his father: "Besides my law business which is about as usual I have undertaken or entered into a partnership for making cordage which promises well. My partner has lived in this town four years & in that time has made by his business $1500 pr ann. There is every prospect of his doing twice the business in Thomaston (where we have erected a rope walk) that he does here. He is considered an honest & religious man. I have been able to advance my proportion of the contingent & we commence soon. The firm of Chamberlain & Williams is building a quarter of a vessel of 120-30 tons. The cost will be about $1000. which the company will pay without encroaching upon private property. I have some other matters on hand which bid fair to be productive & will I hope rather augment my income." April 23, 1827, he was visiting New York City, and engaging in what his father feared would prove "wild Speculations and Partnerships", although the "new-fashioned steamship may be an Exception" to the old maxim that "Partnerships are Bad Ships to sail in". In 1828 Mellen Chamberlain was an officer in the Custom House in Castine. February 26, 1831, he wrote his sister about "my coal mine & my ship".

October 20, 1832, he wrote his sister Abigail: "My ship has arrived from Liverpool with plenty of salt & coal & we are now engaged in discharging it. As soon as that is done & we have loaded her for the West Indies I shall start for Florida where I expect to meet her in January & should I not succeed in my projects at Apalachicola I shall go out to Europe with her. She has been a good servant this year having earned for me clear of all expenses $1800.00". Six weeks later, Dec. 2, 1832, he wrote to his brother Ezra Carter Chamberlain from New York City: "I have concluded to sail to-morrow in the Ship *Mason Barney* for St. Thomas. I decline going to Apalachicola on account of the cholera. You of course have no idea of pursuing your proposed enterprise on the same account. I think it likely that I shall go to N. Orleans some two months hence if the pestilence entirely disappears. I go to St. T. to meet my vessel which is about sailing from Castine for that place. * * * I expect to go with the ship whether she comes back, goes South or to Europe.

"The tariff will I believe be repealed either this or the next session. The president will indicate to day his views. Let the people of N. England look for a tremendous reaction in their prosperity. It is impossible to put down the Yankee nation. If they cannot be profitably employed at home, they will go forth & by their superior powers possess the inheritance of their oppressors. As sure as knowledge is power so certainly must the estates of the Southern planters pass into the hands of the people of New England.

"Much anxiety is felt on the subject of our union. * * * I imagine that the tariff being taken off the causes of dissatisfaction will be removed but such is the violence of the South that there may be much embarrassment."

March 15, 1833, he wrote from New Orleans: "It is exceedingly pleasant again to set foot in one's own country especially when we compare it with the Spanish West Indies misgoverned as they are. I am also a little more reconciled to Jackson since he has changed his politics. You can conceive nothing more stunning than the conversation of political gentlemen when I first arrived here. The executive depending upon the opposition with Mr. Webster at their head for support, Mr. Clay the first to give a death blow to the tarriff. The whole seemed a sort of Phantasmagoria. I have been long in ascending this wonderful river. Turbid though it be & its banks thus far all unlovely, yet there is such a magnificent rush of waters such evidence of mighty enterprise on its current that you cannot with hold your astonishment.

"I have enjoyed myself very well on my tour, had many opportunities of seeing the manners & customs of the Islands of which I have advised you from time to time & have other notes on hand which I hope may amuse you at some future time. * * * The city [of New Orleans] is increasing rapidly but cannot be a pleasant residence. God be thanked for hills, said someone. I echo the thanksgiving from my heart. Nothing has so much of nothingness in it as this dead level. It is more monotonous than the sea for there you can get above surrounding objects by climbing the mast. * * *

"How I should relish your firesides—for a time. For the spirit of adventure is not yet gone. I must wander still farther. I find within me still the power of enjoyment. Novelty and contrast together with employment are the ingredients of the highest flavored dish. * * * But you will show such interest in the Quixotic Knight Errant as to ask, where are you bound next? To Florida forsooth. The ship let me tell you made a loosing voyage to the W. Indies. She has now taken freight for Providence & will return here or to some Southern port & probably I shall join her for Europe in about two months."

The journey to Europe was not made that year. Early in June he appears to have been in New York City, where a letter was addressed offering him certain rights in the sale of the Fairbanks scales. E. & T. Fairbanks & Co. offered him the sole right to sell the scales, both hay-scales and the smaller ones used in stores, in the state of Pennsylvania for $5,000., in the state of Ohio for $4,000., or in Ohio and all the Valley of the Mississippi to the Gulf of Mexico for $10,000. He had become interested in the scales during a visit to his friends in Vermont the previous summer, Erasmus and Thaddeus Fairbanks living in the neighboring town of St. Johnsbury and being old friends and connections of his father's family. He decided to purchase the rights in the Ohio and Mississippi valleys, visited Vermont in the summer, and in the autumn located in Pittsburg, Pa., a central location for his new business. He was now, as he phrased it in a letter written Oct. 5, 1835, engaged in "land, sea & scale speculations", and was exceedingly successful, expecting to net from these various ventures between $8,000 and $10,000. that year, a sum which represented far greater wealth then than it would now. In the autumn of 1834, he married, in New York City, Mrs. Catharine (Hill) Crosby, widow of Rev. John Crosby of Maine. This proved a happy union. Later, her health being delicate, a milder climate was imperative and they spent a winter in the West Indies. She rallied for a time, and returned to the United States, but finally passed away in 1837, leaving a young daughter, Catharine. During his sojourn in the islands he did not forget his friends at home, sending a box of shells for his nieces to the care of Daniel Chamberlain in Boston. And after his return to the United States he sent to Hicks & Swift at Saint Thomas the first Fairbanks scales seen in the islands. "We think they only require to be seen to be in great demand", was the cordial greeting given by the firm to these "six platform Balances" in their letter of June 22, 1837. Two of them had been sold, they reported, to go to Porto Rico, and "we have no doubt when they are seen there we shall have orders for others".

Dec. 20, 1837, he wrote from Pittsburg, Pa., to his brother Ezra Carter Chamberlain: "* * * I would be very far from wishing you to put your substance at the mercy of the seas or political quacks especially if it would disturb your peace. But after all there is something even in this very jeopardy that is not unpleasant. * * * There is the Ship *St. James* loading at London for N. Orleans. Shall I insure? I have a policy for $1500 but that is not a third in case of loss. Let her go. She made me that last year & if the Insurance Offices can make money by insuring so can I by not doing it. The *Valhalla* has not arrived at N. Orleans yet. Is she lost? Freights I see are good for nothing. If they don't run me in debt I shall be glad. Then there is the scale business—$600. burnt at Natchez. Loss by Young $2,000. or rather by the harpies at N. O. probably. Suspension cuts down sales one half. Shall not make more than $3 or 4,000. this year by that. However hope the year's business will wind up with $6 or 8,000 advance. Stay here & make a purchase of Scott's patent for Asbestos chests? Think it equal to scales. There is some excitement in such various interests which helps along the time & leaves the contrast you have drawn between your occupations & mine not so much in your favor as you have drawn it. Though I admit that it is much in your favor.

"But my dear brother I have thoughts more worthy of me than such as these. My most serious troubles arise from my own shortcomings of duty. With perhaps the faculties of doing good & abundant means, how little do I in fact accomplish! I am not likely to be led away by any scheme of splendid benevolence yet some thing every one should do for the benefit of his kind. Nothing will be looked back to in our declining years (& mine are so) with half the satisfaction, as active untiring effort to do good to others.

"I love my relatives but they do not need my charities. Apropos—I have written but not sent a letter to ——— offering to give or loan to Wm. as may be thought best the means of getting an education. I have not sent it not knowing the real situation of their affairs or how she would take such or whether he desires or would be benefitted by that kind of education. For I hold it quite doubtful whether it is of much use. Still if he earnestly desires it I will not suffer him to lack the means. Without saying anything of this you might obtain the information I wish & let me know.

"I am very glad the shells please you & wish the collection was more choice. I supposed they would be a rarity among you & would be in most parts of the country.

"I still think it would be a grand plan to buy a township to be called Ezraville &c. & plant it with the mulberry & wear silk & eat but sugar. Were it not for going to Europe, the spring would find me in some such matter.

"I shall go to Washington in a few days where write me. Mr. Adams thinks he is playing the old Roman in fine style but it appears to me that he has forgotten one of their deities the Goddess of Prudence. I fear the Abolitionists will bring about disunion not by their objects but by the means they take to accomplish them. * * * "

This letter lacks something of the buoyancy of spirit which made him so refreshing a companion or correspondent. His wife's companionship was sorely missed. His business agents addressed him Feb. 10, 1838, at Washington, D. C.; March 6, at Philadelphia, Pa.; March 13 at Andover, Mass., where his little daughter Catharine was staying with the widow of his brother William; March 16 at Washington, D. C.; and April 16 at New York City. March 15, 1838, he was given a letter of introduction by Saml. Upton in Washington, D. C., to Robert Grant Esq., of Baltimore. Mr. Upton wrote: " * * * Mr. Chamberlain proposes, in a few weeks, to visit Europe, and may, perhaps, be servicable to you in reference to your important invention; or there may be a reciprocity of benefits conferred. Mr. Chamberlain is worthy of unlimited confidence, both as to property and probity. His judgment and skill, in matters of science, as connected with the useful arts, are such as to commend him to your acquaintance." Apparently Mr. Chamberlain did not deliver this letter.

July 9, 1838, he wrote from Havre, France, to his sister Abigail in Vermont: "My purpose is now to inform you that I have just arrived after a passage of 20 days in this frog eating land. I've not eaten any as yet that I know of though it may well be without my knowledge. What it is that appears at table it would [puzzle] any Yankee to tell. The bread is the best I have seen in any country & I shall devote the next six months to learning how it is made. There is nothing very new to see here. I have seen the same manners & customs elsewhere. Havre is a place of 30,000. It has a fine dock for ships. But we build up a town of equal pretensions in a few years & superior in architecture. * * * There is a steamer just starting from under the windows. I'll give you the remarks of the rest of the party as the best account of the novelties.

"Oh says a Danish lady fellow passenger—see those two old men kissing each other & those nuns with black head dresses & white bibs under their chins—those monstrous caps a foot above their heads & wings a foot long each as if they were about to fly away. What lots of soldiers!

"We go for Paris to-morrow. Our party is Major & Mrs. Reilhrup (?) of St. Thomas W. I., Mr. Brown of Andover & Mr. McLellan of Boston. We are chattering French as fast as we can. The children even here are so learned that they talk French—but [it] is with the greatest difficulty that we grown people can be understood.

"I think it most likely that I shall return in about a year & may much sooner. You have learned that I gave up my visit with great regret to Peacham. I rec'd your letter & am glad that you considered Kate a good apology for my deficiency. How did you like her? was not she a fine little fellow? I see none I like as well.

"It is long before I can get an answer to this but write as soon as you can to the care of Edwards & Co.—Paris. I shall be there three months. The winter we expect to spend in Italy & perhaps [go] to Palestine. I will give you from time to time account of my doings—but you will not expect much from so lazy a fellow. * * *

"I think I am not good at description. Others see everything wonderful & nothing is wonderful to me. However we will see what Paris will do for me."

A journey to Europe in 1838 was a great undertaking compared with a trip to-day; for there were no telegraphs, cables nor wireless signals; little communication could be had with friends abroad. It became a part of his mission to aid Professor S. F. B. Morse in his great undertaking of trying to introduce the magnetic telegraph into European countries. One of our historians has said that never before had our country experienced such a transition from apparent prosperity to a fatal prostration of business as during Martin Van Buren's administration in 1837, after the failure to re-charter the United States Bank during Andrew Jackson's time, and the establishing of many State banks. Legislators became opposed to costly internal improvements at public expense, hence Prof. Morse could not obtain the pecuniary aid and assistance from Congress which he so much needed, and he resolved to seek recognition in Europe. When Mr. Morse exhibited his invention February 21, 1838, to President Van Buren and his Cabinet, Hon. F. O. J. Smith, a congressman and chairman of the Committee on Commerce in the House of Representatives, resigned his office to become a partner, with several other distinguished gentlemen, in the new invention. Mr. Morse sailed for England May 16, 1838, to secure foreign patents. In a hearing before Sir John Campbell, the British attorney-general, July 18, 1838, he was not given an encouraging reception. The hostile feelings aroused in 1776 and 1812 had not abated. Campbell preferred, evidently, Wheatstone's invention with its six wires to Morse's with a single wire and a much simpler construction. He claimed that Morse had published a description of his invention before this, but there had been printed only a statement of results.

This unjust decision led Mr. Morse to go to Paris to memorialize the French Government, which was more friendly and hospitable to new inventions. He established himself in Paris with his old friend, Dr. Kirk, later of Boston. They made Tuesday their levee-day for several weeks to exhibit the telegraph. Prof. Morse was delighted with the great enthusiasm manifested by all classes, especially by the best known savants, such men as Arago, the noted physicist and statesman, secretary of the Academy of Sciences, who urged him to appear before that body of noted men with his invention. At this exhibition, September 10, 1838, Arago explained the telegraph and its workings to the great surprise and delight of his audience. Humboldt declared it to be the best instrument he had ever seen, as did also Gay-Lussac and other scientists. Yet it seemed difficult for all to realize that it was destined to revolutionize the conduct of nations in war and in peace, as well as to flash news all over the globe; for instance, that it could have telegraphed the victory of the English over the French at the battle of Waterloo, June 18, 1815, in a few seconds or moments, instead of the news taking two days to reach London. Mr. Morse was gratified by the universal sentiment in his favor, but he alternated between hope and fear as to practical results, which were of great importance to him. He secured a patent. By French law, an invention must be put into practical operation within two years from the issuing of the patent. He tried in vain to introduce it on the line of the Saint Germain Railroad near Paris. He found that the telegraph was considered a government monopoly and that he could not enter into relations with private parties. He resolved to return to the United States and try Congress again. The attention of French scientists had been divided between the pictures of Daguerre and Morse's telegraph, but the French Government purchased Daguerre's invention of the daguerreotype. Prof. Morse, himself a portrait painter, declared that it was beautiful to see an artist paint with sunbeams. Napoleon had been more interested in new inventions than the present sovereign, King Louis Philippe. Hon. H. L. Ellsworth, an American gentleman in Paris, wrote home that although Prof. Wheatstone of London and Dr. Steinheil of Munich had shown their telegraphs in Paris, that of the Yankee professor had carried the palm by its simplicity of design, cheapness of construction and efficiency, as well as by its priority of discovery. Baron Meyendorff, the agent of the emperor of Russia to report new discoveries to the home government, became much interested.

Mellen Chamberlain was introduced to Professor Morse by a mutual friend in Washington, D. C., as a man worthy of unlimited confidence both as to property and probity. This friend commended also his judgment and skill in matters of science with regard to the useful arts, and he felt sure that the acquaintance would prove mutually agreeable. It resulted in a partnership in the new invention. Mr. Chamberlain's familiarity with different kinds of machinery from his connection with the Fairbanks' scales, his knowledge of the technical points of law and of the French language, his being independent financially, and somewhat of a diplomat, together with his enthusiastic belief in the value of the new invention to the world, made him a valuable partner and associate for Prof. Morse.

A letter written by Mellen Chamberlain from Paris September 19, 1838, to his sister, Miss Abigail Chamberlain in Vermont, refers to his partnership with Prof. Morse, stating that the latter had chosen the countries of Great

Britain, France and America in which to introduce the telegraph, and had left to him the rest of the world, which fell in with his humor for travel, and would be a good introduction to the best society of the countries he was to visit, even if nothing more was realized. He wrote that all Paris and the Institute were agog with the marvelous American experiments; and he was proud of the telegraph as an American citizen; and also of the acquaintance of Mr. Morse, a gentleman and a fine painter. He could not doubt that a system so much cheaper and surer than the one then in use, would be adopted by all governments. He had seen the king, attended the Institute, dined with General Cass, our American minister there, and eaten frogs and a thousand nameless things. He was not very much in love with the French people that he had seen, but thought one Yankee was worth a dozen of them, for he had been all over Paris for a week to get a machine made which one of our turners would make in three days, and they would not promise it in less than three weeks; but he would procure it when he went to London to meet a ship which he expected would bring him the sinews of war. Prof. Morse had decided that he would have a better instrument made than the clumsy one brought from Speedwell, N. J., to give Mr. Chamberlain to exhibit in the East. In order to avoid delay, the latter procured a common brass clock-movement in London, took out all but the wheels of the train and put in four box-wood rollers he got turned for one shilling sixpence; the whole expense about twelve francs. At Boulogne the officers of the custom house, finding it in his trunk, declared it must be sent to the administrator at Paris. He called daily for a week before the box arrived. A letter from Prof. Morse to Hon. F. O. J. Smith Nov. 22, 1838, gives one some idea of the great annoyance the long system of red-tape caused them before they were able to obtain the box; how they were sent from one office to another until they offered to give up the box; but no, they must make a sketch and explain what such an ominous looking thing was intended for. After the box had been shown to four or five officers, it was still kept until they had sketched and painted the design of the instrument, signed various papers and obligations and receipts, obtained French security and paid twenty-one francs in customs duties and transportation charges for a box which cost originally twelve francs. Prof. Morse said that he took the box and ran round several streets and corners as if he had stolen it, expecting the whole *Douane* would be after him to call him back to do everything according to rule.

Mr. Chamberlain parted with Prof. Morse in November 1838 in Paris with high expectations of pleasure and profit in the East, while the latter left for the United States in March. Hon. F. O. J. Smith wrote: "Before I left Paris we had closed a contract with Mr. Chamberlain to carry the telegraph to Austria, Prussia, the principal cities of Greece and of Egypt, and put it upon exhibition with a view to its utilization there. He was an American gentleman (from Vermont, I think), of large wealth, of eminent business capacities, of pleasing personal address, and sustaining a character for strict integrity." (S. I. Prime, "Life of Samuel F. B. Morse, LL.D.", p. 411.) November 20, General Lewis Cass, the American minister in Paris, who had recently returned from a trip through Italy, Greece, Egypt and Palestine to Constantinople, gave Mr. Chamberlain a complimentary letter of introduction. His passport was viseed at Marseilles Nov. 24, Genoa Nov. 27, Leghorn Dec. 13. He wrote from Athens Jan. 5, 1839, that they had exhibited the invention to the learned of Florence and to the King and Queen of Greece, who were "highly delighted", as were also the principal inhabitants of Athens. But he added: "Fame is all you will get for it in these poor countries. We think of starting in a few days for Alexandria, and hope to get something worth having from Mehemet Ali. It is, however, doubtful. Nations appear as poor as individuals, and as unwilling to risk their money upon such matters. I hope the French will avail themselves of the benefits you offer them. It is truly strange that it is not grasped at with more avidity. If I can do anything in Egypt, I will try Turkey and St. Petersburg". January 9, he wrote from Syra, Greece, in good spirits. "The pretty little Queen of Greece", he said, "was delighted with Morse's telegraph. The string which carried the cannon-ball used for a weight broke, and came near falling on her Majesty's toes, but happily missed, and we, perhaps, escaped a prison." His passport was viseed in Alexandria Jan. 16, 1839, and later in Cairo. From Egypt he journeyed through Palestine, being at Jaffa Feb. 2, 1839.

He wrote from "Ramle Rama or Arimathea Palestine", February 22, 1839: "We are just celebrating the birth of Pater Patriæ. At the house of our polite consul Ahbout Montas, where we slept, we hoisted the broad flag of our country this morning at sunrise & fired the salute. We are to have a great dinner at 12. Think of celebrating such an event in Palestine. We are much gratified to see the numerous places so of[t] mentioned in the scriptures. The particular localities which are shown us such as the scenes of Christ's birth & suffering, the place whence the wood of the cross was taken, the fountain whence he brought water & a thousand other things are probably fabulous. Nevertheless we do know that in these cities He was born & suffered. You know that I am not apt to fall into fits of enthusiasm yet when I think of the consequences of His appearance I perceive a gush of gratitude & affection thrilling through me. Few can visit the small village of Nazareth & not feel that it has had more influence on the world than any other city.

"Now as you are aware these countries are possessed by people foreign to the laws & the religion of the Jews. Scarcely ten thousand of the people of God as they thought themselves remain. All the glory of the land has departed. The country is depopulated & barren. An iron rule grinds the poor remainder of the inhabitants to the dust. We believe that it will be restored because it is so written, but I have less confidence in my theories the more I see. It must be that Mehemet Ali the present tyrant of Egypt & Syria is killing the hen that lays the golden egg. They cannot sustain the exactions of men & money. It would sicken you to hear the particulars of his oppressions. It suffices to know that probably half the able bodied men have put out their eyes or cut off their hands to escape being pressed into his enormous armies."

April 22, 1839, he wrote from Constantinople to his brother in Vermont, in a letter defaced by time: —

"After suffering twenty days from cold such as I have not felt during the colder months in Egypt or Syria, we start on our voyage up the Danube to Vienna. I enjoyed the journey through the Holy land notwithstanding much fatigue. It is by no means pleasant to ride on camels, mules & jackasses, especially when you cannot make more than twenty miles by ten hours hard beating of your lubberly beasts. But the compensation is in treading the same ground which has been trodden by our Saviour. Of this you are *sure* but by no means sure of the truth of the thousand stories they tell * * * but you are confident that you see the Nazareth in which He dwelt, Jerusalem where He suffered & Mt. Zion & Mt. Olivet. For this cause it is the most interesting country on Earth. Otherwise it is barren desolated & accursed. We sailed from Beyroot to Alexandria in a steamer. As we left the harbour she was struck with such a shock of lightning as I never heard filling the cabin with a sulphurous smell, blinding the crew for a time, tearing off the plank above the water's edge, killing a goat &c. This is the [only] striking of a steamer within my knowledge. We saw Messrs. Goodale & Temple (whom you know) at Smyrna & here. Indeed we have become acquainted with all the missionaries in the Mediterranean—at Athens, at Beirout, &c. They [are in] comfortable situations & appear to be sincerely occupied in effecting the purpose of their missions.

"It is a splendid city this of the East. Resting as it does upon Europe & Asia it commands the products of both & might be the mistress of this Eastern world in other hands. But the genius of Mahommetainism is adverse to the de[ve]lopment of the powers of men. There is hope that that religion will perish in the presence of a purer. They are certainly admitting modern improvements with unwonted rapidity. The Sultan himself no longer wears the turban but has substituted the red cap so universally worn in the Levant. In company with Mr. Rhodes his principal naval architect (an American) I visited some of his palaces and mosques & saw him in grand procession—with his gorgeous [escort] as they swept along in state to the mosque at mid day. It is said that he cares little for the faith he holds except for political reasons. Some of the mosques are prohibited to infidel feet. Yet [I deter] mined to see that of St. Sophia if possible. We put off our shoes at [the] door & lifting the curtain entered but were soon ordered out in no civil tone but without other violence. It is said to be second to no other structure except St. Peters at Rome. The bazars of which you have heard much are splendid in gold lace & embroidery, but for nothing else. The Turks squatting on their hams & lazily smoking are picturesque enough in the distance but very indifferent shopmen. It [is] supposed that the city itself & the adjacent villages on the Bosphorus & in Asia have a million of inhabitants. I think a more indolent million could scarcely be found except in the adjoining grave yards. These extend for miles in every direction covered with the tall cypress which sighs solemnly in every breeze. They have held these places most sacred until [recently]. They have now built some large & handsome buildings [of] funereal marbles & there seem to be enough for such another city. Indeed they would be much better applied, for their houses being of wood are often burned. I never saw such terror as the other night at an alarm. Mr. Goodale, though at a distance, seized his translation & was prepared to flee with his family.

"I have not heard from home these six months & am almost afraid to receive my letters at Vienna. We must pass through a quarantine to get into Europe which will delay us some. I am getting very impatient. My design was to go to St. Petersburg across the continent & it still depends upon the tenor of my letters. If they are such as I expect perhaps I may as well spend the summer in Europe & return in the fall. I long to see you all & to tell you of what I have seen."

At the home of Dr. William Goodell, his college friend, he met Rev. Cyrus Hamlin, who had recently arrived in Turkey, and who rendered later such valuable service during the Crimean War by his inventions. The telegraph was set up in his library. Cyrus Hamlin wrote: "I have been at work nearly all day helping Mr. Chamberlain, an American traveller, prepare Morse's Electro-Magnetic telegraph for an exhibition to a party of gentlemen to-morrow evening. He thinks of inviting the Sultan's prime minister." (M. W. Lawrence, Light on the Dark River, p. 140) Dr. Hamlin told Mr. Chamberlain's niece that he advised Mr. Chamberlain to go to Vienna to have a better instrument made, as there were more skillful artisans living there.

In July, intelligence was received by Professor Morse of a fatal calamity on the Danube River by the upsetting of a boat, and that Mr. Chamberlain was amongst those who were drowned. July 29 he wrote, "Our hopes from that quarter are thus darkened by this melancholy event, and in all probability (unless Mr. Brown, when he returns, can give us information), we shall not know what has been done with the Telegraph in Constantinople or Egypt." This was Mr. S. G. Brown of Andover, later a professor at Dartmouth College, and still later President of Hamilton College, N. Y. Mr. B. B. Edwards of Andover, Mass., wrote to Mr. Chamberlain's friends in Vermont, July 26, 1839, some account of the disaster. Mellen Chamberlain was travelling from Constantinople to Vienna up the Danube on a steamboat with fifteen passengers, two of whom were his fellow travellers in Syria, Mr. Bennett of South Carolina and Mr. Swords of New York City. In consequence of the rapid course of the Danube between Drinkova and Orsova, steamers were not able to ply, and the link was supplied by boats that were towed as on a canal. Within an hour of its destination, on May 14, 1839, the tow-boat was overturned by the action of the water with that of the tow-line secured to the mast. Eleven of the fifteen passengers were lost. Mr. Chamberlain was walking the deck a few moments before in excellent spirits, and but a second before entered the cabin. It was not until the next day that the boat was righted. There, amidst the luggage, he lay pleasant in death. A heavy blow on the temple was all that disfigured him. The authorities interested themselves to obtain a grant in the Catholic Cemetery at Sevenetzi, a favor never granted before to Protestants. Mr. Bennett took effectual measures to have a stone erected to his memory. A nephew, Dr. William M. Chamberlain of New York City, afterwards visited his grave there. President Francis Brown of Union Theological Seminary has favored us with some further details from his father's diary. Prof. S. G. Brown of Dartmouth College travelled with Mr. Chamberlain through Italy, Syria and Egypt in the winter of 1838. In a letter to his mother from Milan, Italy, dated July 19, 1839, he said that he had just met Mr. Swords of New York, who was with Mr. Chamberlain on the boat, and learned the particulars of the sad disaster. The boat had passed through the dangerous cataracts of the Danube, but in going past a jutting point they were compelled to steer into the stream, and, for some reason, the helmsman failed to turn the rudder to bring the boat towards the shore; strong currents forced it farther into the stream, the tow-rope attached to the top drew it over and the boat turned bottom-side up, launching those on deck into the water. The boat drifted down the stream (nearly a mile wide) three or four miles into the smaller cataracts, falling into a whirlpool, where a boat from the Servian shore picked off the passengers. They were met on the northern or Austrian shore by soldiers with fixed bayonets, and marched to the guard-house, and, owing to their contact with the Servian boat, they were compelled to be in quarantine ten or twelve days in the very same room in Orsova which they had so joyfully left a day or two before. The English Consul at Bucharest, owing to the barbaric cupidity of the people, advised them to adopt a pyramidal form for a tombstone with a simple inscription. Mr. Chamberlain's effects were forwarded to the American consul at Vienna to await orders from his friends. "How mysterious are the ways of Providence!" Prof. Brown kept exclaiming. A notice of Mr. Chamberlain's death in a copy of the N. Y. *Journal of Commerce*, closes with these lines: "He has left an only child and a very extensive circle of friends to mourn his melancholy loss; he was a gentleman of highly cultivated mind and manner, of rich and varied acquisition, and of amiable and exemplary character." If Mellen Chamberlain was not permitted to live to see the introduction of the magnetic telegraph into Europe and Asia, he had the honor of aiding Professor Morse in his initial efforts and struggles to interest those nations in one of the most useful inventions of his day, and eventually lost his life in the effort. But Professor Morse struggled bravely on more than four years longer before Congress "in the midnight hour of the expiring session" (March 3, 1843) voted him the money to make the experiment between Washington and Baltimore. Then that well-known Biblical verse, "What hath God Wrought?" was sent. Mellen Chamberlain's prediction that eventually all countries would adopt this invention was verified years afterwards, as Mr. Morse lived to be highly honored and rewarded by nations and individuals for his services and inventions. Much time and money have since been expended to make the navigation of the Danube safe for future travellers.

Agreement with S. F. B. Morse

"This Memorandum of an agreement made by and between Samuel F. B. Morse of the City of New York in the United States of America, of the one part, and Mellen Chamberlain also of the United States, of the other part, witnesseth as follows:

"First, that the said Morse is the inventor of a new system of Telegraph, called the Electro Magnetic Telegraph, and the same which he has patented in the United States of America, and in France.

"Secondly, That the said Morse hath released and quit-claimed unto the said Chamberlain, all of said Morse's right, title, privilege and opportunity of obtaining patents in his own name or otherwise, for said invention, and of establishing agents for selling said invention and bringing the same into use, in all of the kingdoms, governments and countries in Europe, Asia and Africa, excepting only the kingdom of France and its dependencies, and the kingdom of Great Britain and its dependencies.

"Thirdly, That said Morse hath released and quit-claimed and hereby doth release and quit-claim in manner as before named, to the said Chamberlain, as well for and in behalf of all said Morse's co-proprietors in said invention now existing, and for them in like manner, as for himself.

"Fourthly, That in consideration of the aforesaid release and quit-claim, the said Chamberlain hath agreed and obligated himself, and hereby doth agree and obligate himself, to use his best endeavors and good diligence, in causing said invention by himself, or through agents, to be introduced by patents from governments or otherwise, as he may deem most advantageous for those interested therein, in as many of the kingdoms, governments and countries aforesaid, by these presents intended to be embraced, as he shall find to be practicable, and upon such terms, the most advantageous to the said Morse and his co-proprietors and to the said Chamberlain, as the said Chamberlain shall be able to effect in any of the modes hereinbefore contemplated.

"Fifthly, That the proceeds of every disposition, sale, transfer or introduction of said invention, made by the said Chamberlain as aforesaid, into any of said kingdoms, governments or countries, at any time hereafter, and whether said proceeds shall consist in money, or presents of other articles or property, shall be apportioned and divided between the said Morse, of the one part, and the said Chamberlain of the other part, in manner following—that is to say—1st. The said Chamberlain shall deduct therefrom the full amount of all moneys that may have been advanced by him for counsel fees and for patent fees, paid for any patent that he shall obtain in any of said governments.

"2dly. He shall deduct therefrom all monies that he shall have advanced in any country or kingdom where he shall obtain a patent for said invention, for his own personal expenses of travel and support in such country or kingdom during his residence there on the business of said invention—and—

"3dly. He shall deduct therefrom all monies that he shall necessarily advance in providing apparatus for exhibition of said invention in any of said governments or countries.

"4th. All the excess of such proceeds, beyond the aforesaid three classes of expenses enumerated for deduction shall be divided equally between said Morse for himself and his co-proprietors, of the one part, and the said Chamberlain, of the other part, share and share alike.

"It is further agreed, *Sixthly*, The said Chamberlain shall have the right to retain any presents which may be made to him by any prince, potentate or government, for or on account of said invention, if he shall elect so to do, by substituting therefor in money the fair value thereof, to be ascertained by disinterested judges, so that said substitute shall enter into the division aforesaid.

"Seventhly. All improvements that shall be made in or to said invention by the said Morse or any of his associates, shall enure to the use and disposal of the said Chamberlain to the same extent, and upon the same terms and for the same purposes as said invention in its present form is by this instrument transfered to him.

"Eighthly. All requisite advances of money in fulfilling the purposes contemplated by these presents are to be made by the said Chamberlain, to be refunded in such extent and upon such conditions only as are herein specifically set forth, and without recourse otherwise to the said Morse or his co-proprietors in any event therefor.

"Ninthly. The said Chamberlain shall account to the said Morse as often as once in each year, if requested so to do, for the proceeds of said invention, that may have been realized by said Chamberlain, and complete the division thereof according to the terms of this instrument.

"Tenthly. After the term of four years from the date hereof, any and all of said kingdoms, countries or governments wherein said Chamberlain shall have omitted to introduce said Telegraph by obtaining patents therefor, shall be considered as from that time excluded and excepted from the purview and meaning of the provisions of this instrument, and open to the use and improvement of the said Morse in the same manner as if these presents had not existed. But until the expiration of said term the said Morse and his co-proprietors hereby are excluded and disqualified from introducing said invention in any way to prejudice the rights or arrangements of the said Chamberlain, unless the same be done by his concurrence and assent.

"In testimony whereof said Parties have hereunto interchangeably set their hands this twentieth day of September, A. D. 1838.

WITNESS SAM: F: B: MORSE:
SAM[l]. G. BROWN. MELLEN CHAMBERLAIN."

THE DESCENDANTS OF JACOB CHAMBERLAIN

By General William Chamberlin

The following sketch was written ninety-one years ago. The words included in parentheses were interlined in the author's handwriting in a different ink from that used in the body of the manuscript, but in the same ink that was used for the last two paragraphs describing Edmund and Abial Chamberlain and their children, two of Abial's children being omitted. The editor has added in brackets the names of such descendants as are members of this Association. As the offspring of Jacob Chamberlain wandered into many towns and even into many states, and settled not infrequently where other families bearing the name Chamberlain resided, this record by General Chamberlin of where his uncles, cousins, nephews, and nieces had lived and died, or were living in 1820, has proved very helpful to many descendants of his grandfather. Through the printing of the record, some with whom the heirs of General Chamberlin have no personal acquaintance will be able, it is hoped, to trace their ancestry to Jacob Chamberlain. Will all descendants of this progenitor kindly send information concerning themselves and their ancestors to Miss Jenny Chamberlain Watts, 6 Exeter Park, Cambridge, Mass., in order that records of all the members of this branch of the family may be compiled. The autograph of Jacob Chamberlain is a facsimile of his signature as collector on a tax receipt Jan. 16, 1733-4, from the collection of autographs presented by Judge Mellen Chamberlain to the Boston Public Library. The autograph of Abihail Chamberlain is from her signature as administratrix in the Suffolk County Probate Records.

Peacham, Vermont, Jan'y 6th 1820.

The following Historical account of the Chamberlain Family in America May not at some future time be uninteresting to my Posterity and others of the name. Taken from the most authentic account I have been able to collect being derived principally from the information received from my Grandmother, Relict of Jacob Chamberlin who died at Chelsea, M's. A. D.

Jacob Chamberlain

1734 in the 44th year of his Age, leaving my Grandmother, Abihail Chamberlin, whose Maiden name was Hasey with the Issue which Will be Hereafter men-

Abihail Chamberlain

tioned. [His gravestone is still legible in the old graveyard at Revere, a part of Chelsea in 1820, a part of Boston in 1734.] She informed [me] that the first Emigrants of the name were four Brothers, one of whom settled at Newport Rhode Island, one in Rochester N. Hampshire, one in Newtown, and one in Chelsea near Boston, M's. That on the Death of my Grandfather, she had the following Issue, Vizt,

1 John Chamberlin born about the year 1714. [John was the eldest son, but not the eldest child. He was born about 1720, as he died in 1792 aged 72.]

2, 3, 4 the Next were three Daugters born between the years 1714 & 1722, all of whom died without Male issue. [There were four daughters: Sarah, b. in December 1714; Martha, b. Jan. 19, 1717-8; Elizabeth, bapt. Sept. 18, 1726; and Phebe, b. Sept. 4, 1728. Nothing is known of Phebe after 1735.]

John lived at Hopkinton M's until about the year 1780, and removed to Jaffrey, New Hampshire, [died] about 75 years of age and left four Sons, John, Joseph, Nathan, and Phinehas. John and Phinehas settled at or near Whitestown, N. York. Joseph and Nathan still living reside at Jeffrey, N. H.

5th Jacob Chamberlin who died at Danville, Vt. about the year 1798, leaving 3 Sons, Jacob, Nathaniel & James. He married Lydia Mellen a sister of my mother, a very pious woman. Jacob died at St. Johnsbury, Vermont, 1818 without Male issue. Nathaniel is now living at Wardsborough, Vt. James died at Danville Vermont leaving one son Henry Chamberlin and two Daugters. [Mrs. Helen M. Guilford is a daughter of Pamela and a granddaughter of James.] Abigail Chamberlin daughter to the Jacob Sen'r Married in Hopkinton M's a Mr. Cody where she still resides.

[6th] My Honoured Father Samuel Chamberlin was the 6th Child and 3'd Son of my Grandmother—he was born at Chelsea M's A. D. 1724, lived at Hopkinton M's until the year 1774, when he removed to Loudon in the State of N. Hampshire until 1797, he then removed to Peacham and lived with me untill his Death A. D. 1802 in the 79th year of his age, leaving my mother, Martha Chamberlin now in the 90th year of her age with the following Issue—(She Deceased No. 14th 1820.)

[1st] Hon'ble Samuel Chamberlin of Danville Vt. Born May 2d 1750 who died at Danville A. D. 1812 leaving his wife Abigail and the following issue Vizt.

1st Timothy Chamberlin who lived and died at Danville before his father leaving a widow and one Daughter Harriet Chamberlin still a Minor.

2d Nancy Chamberlin Married to the Rev'd Luther Jewett of St. Johnsbury, Vt.

3d Abigail Chamberlin. Married to Colo. Ellis Cobb Merchant at Barton, Vt.

4th Sophia Chamberlin, Feme Sole

5th Sally Chamberlin. Married to Samuel Sias Esqr. of Danville.

6th Samll Chamberlin Jun'r Merchant at Barton Vt. [William S. Boynton is his grandson.]

7th William Chamberlin now residing on the Paternal Estate at Danville, Vt.

2 The 2d Child of my Parents was Patty Chamberlin who died in the 15th year of her age A. D. 1768.

3d William Chamberlin Born April 27th 1755 Married to Jane Eastman

1780. Settled at Peacham Vermont now living at Peacham and has the following Issue.

1st Joseph Chamberlin who Died in the 4th year of his age.

2nd Elizabeth Chamberlin Born September 2d. [Illegible. Sept. 25, 1784, Town Record of Concord N. H.; Sept. 28, 1784, Records of Peacham, Vt.] Married to Nehemiah Bradley Esq. of Peacham. [Dr. Edward Cowles is her grandson.]

3 Abigail Chamberlin. Born Nov'r 14th, 1786. Feme Sole.

4 Lydia Chamberlin. Born April 18th, 1790. Married to Dr. Josiah Shedd of Peacham.

5th Jane Chamberlin Born June 7th 1792 Feme Sole (Maried 1820 to Elnathan Strong Merchant, Hardwick.) [Rev. E. E. Strong, D. D., a Vice President of this association, is her son.]

6 Mellen Chamberlin A. B. born June 17th 1795 Graduate at Dar[t]mouth College August 1816—in Practice of Law at Castine Maine. [His biography by his niece, Miss Abbie Mellen Chamberlain, is printed in this Report.]

[7th] 6th William Chamberlin Jun'r A. B. Born May 24th 1797. Graduate at Dartmouth College 1718. Professor of languages and literature Dartmouth College. [William C. Chamberlain of Charlottesville, Va., is his grandson.]

[8th] 7 Ezra Carter Chamberlin Born Oct'r 17th 1799. Farmer. (Residing on the Paternal Estate in Peacham.) [Miss Abbie M. Chamberlain, Corresponding Secretary of the Association, and Miss Laura B. Chamberlain are his daughters, and Miss Jenny C. Watts his granddaughter. The house pictured here was his home at Peacham Corner. Its windows command a beautiful and extensive view across the Connecticut Valley to the White and Franconia mountains.]

[9th] 8 Joseph Chamberlin 2d born Dec'r 21st 1781. [1801] Drowned Nov'r 2d 1803.

4 3d Son [4th child] of Sam'l and Martha Chamberlin was Major Moses Chamberlin who was born Oct'r 1757. Married Rebeckah Abbot 1780 [1781]—lived on his paternal Estate at Loudon and died Oct'r 1811 leaving his wife and the following Issue.

1st Rebeckah Chamberlin Married to Capt. Cate of Loudon.

2d Judith Married to Mr. Sam'l Elliot Merchant at Boscawen, N. H.

3d Patty Deceased Oct'r 1817 [1816]

4th Amos Chamberlin who lived and died on the Paternal Estate at Loudon A. D. 1818 leaving a widow and four Children.

5th William Chamberlin Merchant at Loudon unmarried.

6th Moses Chamberlin Merchant at Pembrook N. H. [Hon. Mellen Chamberlain of Chelsea, Mass., and Hon. Henry Chamberlain of Michigan, lately deceased, were his sons; Paul Mellen Chamberlain, Mrs. Edward K. Warren and Mrs. Lee Chamberlain are his grandchildren.]

7th John Chamberlin Settled on the Paternal Estate.

8 Betey Chamberlin Married to Mr. Emery Loudon (died October 1825)

[9] Samuel Chamberlin—Minor living with William. [Lee Chamberlain and Mrs. William T. Dale are his grandchildren.]

[5] The 4th [5th] Child of my Parents, Sibel Chamberlin Married to Capt. John Eastman of Concord, N. H., by whom she has Issue— 1 Patty Feme Sole [The second child; Samuel was her elder.] 2 Samuel Settled in Exeter State of Maine (re'ved to Charleston) 3 Cyrus

HOME OF EZRA CARTER CHAMBERLIN

Now at Natchez (returned and resides at Amherst, N. H.) 4th Thomas Settled at Montreal. 5th John living at Concord. 6th Moses at Savanah, Georgia. 7th Betsey Feme Sole. 8th Mellen a Minor (died at Troy N. York 1821 [Sept. 1, 1822]). 9th Joseph—(not settled)

6 The 5th [6th] Child of Sam'l & Martha is Elizabeth Born A. D. 1762. Married to N. C. Buswell Esqr of Peacham Vt. about A. D. 1786. Issue by Buswell still living—Betey, Polly, James, Silas, Rebeckah, Lucinda & Colby. Betey Married Mr. Winslow at Mon[t]pelier. Polly Married a Capt. Daniel Tower of Peacham, Vt. The others are now unmarried. (James Buswell since married to a Cloe Pratt, settled at Peach. Silas married a Lee. Settled at Atkinson Maine.)

7th Child Lydia Chamberlin. Married to Capt Ashbel Martin of Peacham Vt. She died Oct'r 1811 leaving Issue by Martin—Patty Married to a Mr. Goodhue Merchant Merredith, N. H. Lyman Martin Physician Settled at New Liberty, Kentucky. Joseph Deceased while young. Moses Martin Settled in Peacham. [The late Rev. Moses Mellen Martin was his son; Mrs. George B. Harvey and Mrs. Julia Woodhull Hayes are his grandchildren.] Leonard Martin a Minor (living with his father in Peacham) Lydia Martin (Unmarried at this Time)

8th Patty Chamberlin Married to Walter Brock Esqr, of Barnett, Vt. Issue Samuel Brock a Minor.

9 Joseph Chamberlin Born 1771 Married to Ruth Blanchard about 1805. Deceased Dec'r 1808. Killed by the fall of a Tree leaving one son Ryley Chamberlin & a Posthumous Child named Joseph now living with his mother in Barnett who Married to a Mr. William Gillfillan.

The 7th [8th] Child of my Grandfather Jacob Chamberlin was Edmund Born about the year 1726. Maried Mary Caryl and lived at Hopkinton and afterwards at Rockingham Vermont and last at Lunenburgh, Vermont and died there about 1810 leaving Issue Male, Viz. Eli and Aaron Settled at Albany, Vermont. Moses & Joel—Joel a Physician—settled at Townshend, Vermont. Edmund Settled at Colbrook N. Hampshire & David at Lunenburgh.

8th [10th] Child of my Grandfather Jacob Chamberlin a Posthumous Son was Deacon Abial Chamberlin Born at Chelsea in 1734 he lived the last twenty five or thirty years in Peacham Vermont Deceased in 1823. Leaving the following Issue Vizt.

[1] Lois Married to Saml. Crosman living at St. Johnsbury Vermont. [Mrs. George N. Conklin is her greatgranddaughter.]

[2] Lucy Married to a Mr. Ordway, Deceased, Loudon N. Hampshire. Now a Widow. [The late John Chamberlain Ordway was her grandson.]

[3] Ebenezer living at Hebron, N. H.

[4] Ephraim Chamberlin Esqr living at Lyndon Vermont. [Mrs. Emily S. Bartlett and Mrs. Sarah M. C. Bodwell are his granddaughters.]

[5] Abial at Brookfield, Vt.

[6] Susanah Married to a Mr. Hopkins Peacham and

[7] Persies Married to Capt. Charles Eastman, Concord, N. H.

[8] [Abial Chamberlain had two sons not recorded here,—John, from whom Hon. Daniel U. Chamberlin of this Association was descended,

[9] and Daniel.]

[Jacob Chamberlain had ten children, all of whom were living in November, 1735,—six sons and four daughters. The son not recorded here was Nathaniel, born Oct. 27, 1732. Presumably he died young, as no record of him has been found after 1735.]

WILLIAM CHAMBERLAIN OF BILLERICA, MASS. AND HIS DESCENDANTS

By George Walter Chamberlain, M. S.,

Member of New England Historic Genealogical Society

What our ancestors were deserves preservation in the annals of time—
(Original)

FIRST GENERATION

1 WILLIAM[1] CHAMBERLAIN, the immigrant, was born undoubtedly in England about 1620, and died at Billerica, Massachusetts, May 31, 1706, "aged about 86 years." (*Billerica Town Records.*) After considerable effort to ascertain his parentage, his ancestry and his English home, they have not been discovered. The publication of the marriages in the English parish registers, now in process, is likely to enable us to identify him, provided he were married in England and the parish register where he was married is still preserved. Of the forty proprietors of Billerica and Chelmsford with whom he was closely associated from 1648 to 1665, at least six are known to have come to New England from East Anglia, one from the County of Surrey and one from Kent. An abstract of every Chamberlain will which was probated in East Anglia between 1620 and 1700, Cambridgeshire excepted, has been obtained, and from that number one abstract is given as follows:

"Francis Chamberlyn, senior, of Narburgh, Co. of Norfolk, made his will June 1, 1676, bequeathing to his sons William Chamberlyn and Clement Chamberlyn £25 each when they arrive at the age of 21; to his grandchildren Mary Woodhouse, the daughter of John Woodhouse, and to Alice Chamberlyn each £5; to his son Francis Chamberlyn ten shillings; to his son Thomas Chamberlyn his mansion house and lands in Pentry, the said Thomas and his wife Mary to be executors and Noah Clarke of Narburgh to be supervisor. Witnesses: John Roberts and Noah Clarke." Will proved, Sept. 16, 1677, in the Consistory Court of Norwich.

The rare Christian name Clement found in this Narburgh family and which occurs in the early generations of our New England family is suggestive of kinship, although it may be a coincidence in names. The names William and Thomas are common in the majority of English families.

The parish registers of St. Mary, Reading, Co. of Berks, show that William son of John Chamberlain was bapt. there Jan. 23, 1619/20, but they also show that one William Chamberline was buried there, Nov. 28, 1665, and another William Chamberlain, July 8, 1686. These data seem to indicate that this first-mentioned William Chamberlain remained and died there. An examination of all Chamberlain probate records for Berkshire from 1620 to 1700, shows no will nor administration of any one of the name living in Reading, although the parish register gives four, viz. Robert Chamberline, William Chamberline, John Chamberline, and William Chamberlain, presumably adults, buried there between 1653 and 1687. No settlement of the estate of any one of these has been found.

"6th June 1635. Theis under-written names are to be transported to Virginea imbarqued in the *Thomas & John*, Richard Lambard Mr being examined by the Minister de Gravesend concerning their conformitie to the orders and discipline of the Church of England: And tooke the oath of Allegeance. * * * * * * * * * Tho: Chamberlin 20 yeres."

Between Aug. 21 and Sept. 2, 1635 [by inference]:

"Theis under-written names are to be transported to Virginea imbarqued in the *Thomas*, Henry Taverner Mr have been examined by the Minister of Gravesend touching their conformitie in or Religion &c. * * * * * * * * * Wm Chamberlin 16 yeres" [and 57 others]. (*Hotten's Original Lists of Emigrants*, 1600–1700, 84, 127)

"A ship coming from Virginia certified us of a great massacre lately committed by the natives upon the English there to the number of 300 at least * * * *. It was very observable that this massacre came upon them soon after they had driven out the godly ministers we had sent to them and had made an order that all such as would not conform to the discipline of the Church of England should depart the country by a certain day which the massacre now prevented: and governour (one Sir Robert Berkeley a courtier and very malignant towards the way of our churches here) and council had appointed a fast to be kept through the country upon Good Friday (as they called it) for the good success of the king, etc. and the day before, this massacre began in the out parts of the country round about and continued two days for they killed all by sudden surprisal living amongst them and as familiar in their houses as those of the family". [The massacre began, April 18, 1644].

"*Upon these troubles divers godly disposed persons* [including Capt. Daniel Gookin and *others*] came from thence to New England and many of the rest were forced to give glory to God in acknowledging that this evil was sent upon them from God for their reviling the gospel and those faithful ministers he had sent among them." (Winthrop in his *History of New England*, 198, 199).

Savage, in a foot note, tells us that the ship which brought the "*godly disposed persons*" from Virginia to Massachusetts arrived, May 20, 1644. Daniel Gookin, Thomas Chamberlin, James Parker, Allen Convers and others were made freemen of the Massachusetts Bay Colony, May 29, 1644. Did Thomas Chamberlain come with Gookin from Virginia and did William Chamberlain follow a few years later?

No Thomas Chamberlain appeared in Virginia before the latter part of the seventeenth century, but one William Chamberlain was living in Charles City County in 1660 and died there the year following. From the absence of authentic records it is impossible to state whether the immigrants to Virginia in 1635 were, or were not, identical with the immigrants of the same name who appeared in New England within ten or twelve years of that date. Felt stated that there were 70 persons living in Virginia who petitioned for the Puritan clergymen to go there in 1643, but I have failed to find in New England the list of names of the petitioners.

Like every surname the name Chamberlain has many variations. In the first fifty volumes of the New England Historical Genealogical Register, it is found in twenty-two variations. These forms do not represent the variations used by the Chamberlains themselves, but rather the forms found on the colonial records of New England. When we realize that no standard of spelling was in general use among English people until about the period of the American Revolution, it becomes apparent how surnames were corrupted and varied in past centuries.

William Chamberlain, the immigrant, probably first appeared in New England in Boston, Massachusetts, as early as October 30, 1647, when he took a deed of a house and lot of Francis Smith, as follows:

"WILLIAM CHAMBERLAINE HIS POSSESSION IN BOSTON:

9 (9) 1647: Francis Smith granted unto William Chamberlaine his house & garden together wth the shopp & out houseinge unto the same belonging being bounded on the north wth the lane [West Street], on the west wth the Comon [Mason Street], the high streete [Washington Street] east, & Richard Carter South & this was by an absolute deed dated: 30th October 1647: acknowledged the 9 (9) 1647, before M[r] Hibbins. This was againe assigned to ffrancis Smith, see p. 126."

"FRANCIS SMITH HIS POSSESSIONS IN BOSTON.

* * * * * * * *

5 (11) 1648: W[m] Chamberlaine assigned unto Francis Smith & his heires forever his house & ground thereto belonging formerly bought of the s[d] ffrancis being bounded on the north wth the lane [West Street], on the east wth the high street [Washington Street] Richard Carter on the south & the Comon on the west [Mason Street]. This assignment was dated 4 (11) 1648. W[m] Chamberlaine. This house was againe sould to Ri: Wilson p:" (Boston Book of Original Possessions, pp. 132, 126.)

Here on the southwest corner of West and Washington Streets William Chamberlain owned property from Oct. 30, 1647, to Jan. 4, 1648/9,—a period of about fourteen months. All of the early antiquaries identified this man as William Chamberlain who settled in Hull, but as that man was not married until about four years after this William Chamberlain purchased this home, while William Chamberlain, of Woburn had married before he became an inhabitant of Woburn, I have no doubt that the Boston man and the Woburn man of this name were identical. Francis Smith purchased this Boston property only a few months before he sold it to William Chamberlain, and appears to have resided there for many years after it was assigned back to him.

Two days after William Chamberlain disposed of his property in Boston, he was admitted an inhabitant of the town of Woburn—ten miles northwest of Boston—as the following Woburn town record shows:

"the 6 of 11 m° 1648: [Jan 6, 1648/9] William Chamberlin admited an Inhabitant of this Towne and permited to by land for his conuencey in any place thereof prouided hee unsetl not any Inhabitant and bring testimony of his peacebl behaueor which is not in the least mesur questioned." (Woburn Town Records, Vol. I, p. 13.)

In less than one month he received a grant of land there as the following town record shows:

"the 3 of 12 m° 1648: [Feb. 3, 1648/9] and Edmond Chamberlin John Parker and William Chamberlin are to have tenn Acres ether of them or twenty acres as the Committee shall see meete they are to lay it out as shall bee Best for the Towne and proprietors begining at that end next parly medow Brooke and a joyning to Reding line at the out side all the way to bee layd out to the persons as they are in order above Expressed." (*Ibid.* p. 14.)

"the 26th 7 m° 1650: [Aug. 26, 1650.] It is further ordered that Samuel Tidd shall have four acres of meadow laid out in a meadow called Drum Meadow to begin at which end he pleaseth and William Chamberlain to have the residue prouided they continue to improve it to their houses they build." (*Ibid.* p. 16.)

"Parly" Meadow and "Drum" Meadow are in the eastern part of the present city of Woburn but it is doubtful if the exact spot where William Chamberlain built his house in Woburn can be identified.

"the 10 of 11 m° 1651: [Jan. 10, 1651/2] Thomas perce Edward Winn & William Chamberlin are ppointed a committee to looke on the inlargment Allen Convars desirs neer his hous and looke on an inlargment John Parker desirs and make a Return whether it will not bee prejuditiall to the Towne." (*Ibid.* p. 17.)

The town records further show that he and his wife Rebecca had two sons born there (not in Concord as Savage stated), viz. Timothy, b. Aug. 13, 1649, and Isaac, b. Oct. 1, 1650.

On June 9, 1652, the First Church of Cambridge made an agreement for the division of Shawshine. All of the communicants received allotments but comparatively few of the Cambridge settlers removed to Billerica to establish homes there. On March 25, 1654, the proprietors of Cambridge executed "the Great Deed" to the proprietors of Billerica granting the latter "all our respective rights & interest therein unto any part or parcall of the said land now called by the said name of Billerica als Shawshine * * * * excepting & reserving our Joynt & respective interest that any of us have in the farme wherein John Parker now dwelleth comonly called by the name of the Churches farme (ie) the church at Cambridge". To this document the pro-

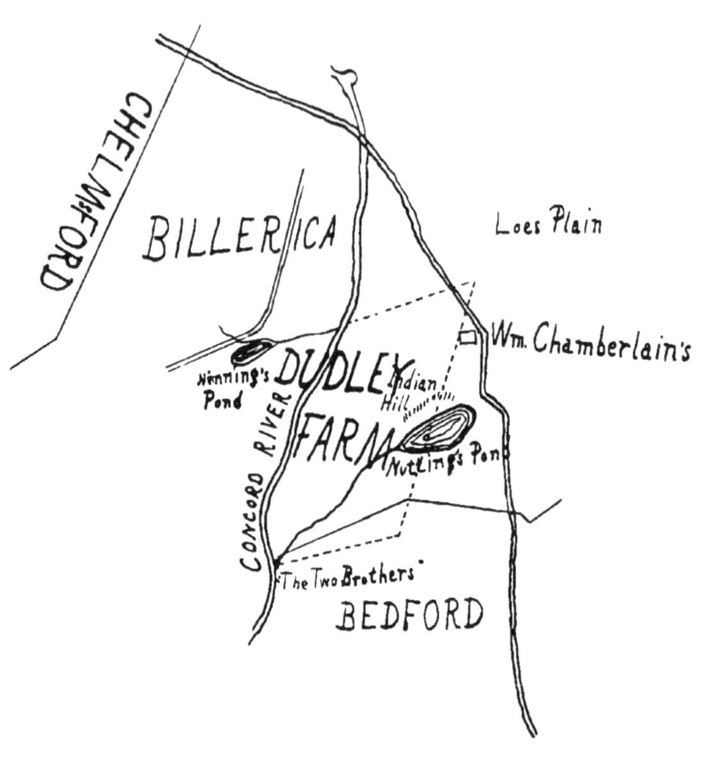
CHELMSFORD
BILLERICA
Loes Plain
Wm. Chamberlain's
DUDLEY
FARM
Indian
Hill
Pond
CONCORD RIVER
Nutting's Pon
"The Two Brothers"
BEDFORD

prietors of Cambridge and the proprietors of Billerica signed their names. "William Chamberline" signed "for Thomas Hamons Lott." (See photograph of the autographs in the Patten Genealogy)

On Nov. 2, 1637, the General Court made a grant of land in the following language: "The Deputy, Mr. Dudley hath a thousand acres granted him wheare it may not pjudice any plantation granted, nor any plantation to bee granted wth out limiting to time of impo[t]." (*Hazen's History of Billerica*, p. 3.) On May 2, 1638, this grant was enlarged and located "& the Deputie Governo[r] to have his thousand acres on the northerly side of the said two great stones (w[ch] stones were lately named the Two Brothers) * * * about 6 miles from Concord northwards, * * * close by the ryver-side that comes fro Concord." "The Deputie Governo[r] is to run a line easterly from the said stones so that hee may take in a meadowe on the other side of a hill [Indian Hill] & so to extend his thousand acres as farr northerly as hee will," etc. About 1639 the General Court increased Mr. Dudley's Farm by the addition of 500 acres. Some time before June 14, 1642, there was erected about two and one half miles from the "Two Brothers" the Shawshin house. After having been granted several times upon conditions, this territory of "Shaweshin" was granted to Cambridge, March 7, 1643/4, "p[r]ovided the church & p[r]sent elders continue at Cambridge." Thus we see why the proprietors of Cambridge had a right to convey their interests in the township of Billerica, and why they did not settle it themselves. On Feb. 28, 1651/2, Thomas Dudley, the Deputy Governor, conveyed "1500 acres" "lying and being about 6 miles northerly from Concord," for £110, unto Thomas Chamberline, Isacke Learned and James Parker all of Woburne in New England and all his right which he "hath therein by virtue of the said grants of the general Courts or by any purchase from any Indian", provided the grantees pay £55 of money, oxen, steers, cowes, heifers or calves at his dwelling house in Roxbury upon April 28, 1653, and the "like summe" in "cattaile or in corne" at the same place as follows: "£15 in wheate & £35 in Rye, pease or Indian corne" on April 28, 1654 and annually until the full sum was paid. One of the proprietors of the Dudley Grant, James Parker, settled in Billerica and it is fair to assume that the twelve original settlers on the Dudley Grant as proprietors of Billerica delivered their products to Governor Thomas Dudley in payment for their lands. The deed was recorded Sept. 19, 1656, showing that the Governor, or his heirs, had been paid in full before that date. William Chamberlain became interested in Billerica as early as June 9, 1652, and I conjecture that in that year he commenced to fell the primeval forests on the Dudley Grant. Presumably his family remained in Woburn until the next year when doubtless they removed to their log-cabin home in the forest-girdled settlement of ancient Billerica. After 1652 there is no further record of the family in Woburn.

For thirteen years, 1652–1665 the settlers on the Dudley Grant held their title by possession or by some unrecorded agreement. Thomas Dudley's heirs permitted the proprietors to record their title Sept. 19, 1656. On March 6, 1656, "Mary Chamberline of Chelmsford the wife of Thomas Chamberline" quitclaimed all her interest in the Dudley Grant unto William Chamberline, Edm: Chamberline and eight other settlers. About one month after Gov. Dudley's deed was recorded in Middlesex County, on Oct. 22, 1656, Edmund "Chamberline" of Chelmsford, planter, deeded one dwelling house and about 50 acres in Billerica to William Baker, "bounded on the northeast with William Chamberline," etc., "which land I * * * * purchased both meadow and upland of Isack Lerned, Thomas Chamberline and James Parker, the whole being one twelfth of all that farme of 1500 acres by them purchased of the Worshipfull Thomas Dudley, Esq. deceased." (*Middlesex Deeds*, I. 197)

About 1656 James Parker, one of the proprietors of the Dudley Grant, removed from Billerica to Chelmsford, leaving the original settlers William French, George Farley, Benjamin Butterfield, Joseph Parker, Jacob Parker, John Stearns, Henry Jefts and William Chamberlain with later purchasers in possession of the Dudley Farm. Of the Cambridge grantees Goodman Hammond owned lot No. 50, containing 15 acres. This passed into possession of William Chamberlain March 25, 1654. From this time until Nov. 24, 1665, it is to be inferred that he acted as agent for the proprietors of the Dudley Grant and at the expiration of that time received his title to 125 acres including his homestead therefor and that his services constituted "a valluable consideration to us well and truly payd by Wm Chamberline of Billerica, planter." By their deeds of the same date the other settlers paid a "valuable consideration of *money*" for their shares of the Dudley Farm.

On Nov. 24, 1665, the surviving proprietors of the Dudley Grant, "James Parker and Thomas Chamberline of Chelmsford, Planters, for a valluable consideration to be well and truly payd by Wm Chamberline of Billerica, planter," deeded him 125 acres "of that farme by us purchased of Thomas Dudley, Esq. deceased, both upland and swamp * * the upland bounded with Lt. W^m ffrench on the south, Ralph Hill, Senr west, Mr. Richard Champney north and the farme line east." (*Middx Deeds*, 3: 152). This was the homestead of William Chamberlain. It was located a little north of Bare Hill just southeast of the present village of Billerica, near where the Woburn road and the Concord road diverge. There is an old cellar there, from which has been obtained an old brick and a pewter spoon—relics of the bygone centuries, but the old house was removed before 1835, and perhaps long before that date. He received eleven grants of land from the town and must have owned at least 200 acres there. In 1664 the highway was built through his land "by his house upon y^e farme" and he was granted four and one-half

To the Constable of Billerica:

In his Maties name
you are required to warne ye
freemen to meet, & choose two able & meete
men to serve at the Court to be held at Cambr
the 1st of the next mo. the one of them on the Grand
Jury. & the other on the Jury of tryalls. and hereof
you are to make a true returne under yr hand &
not to faile at yr perill. Dat. 10. 1. 167 2/3.

Thomas Danforth R.

According to this warrant.
Job Laine is chosen to serve on ye grand jury,
& John French, on ye Jury of tryalls: and both
warned accordingly. 24: 1mo 1673:
William Chamberlin. Constable.

AUTOGRAPH OF WILLIAM CHAMBERLIN OF BILLERICA, MASS.

acres for damages (*Billerica Land Grants*). Grants were made to him of land at "Treeble Cove", "on the Plaine north of Heeth Brooke", on "the Pine Plaine", "on the northeast side of Prospect Hill", "in Heeth Meadow", "on the west side of Concord River", "in Heeth Swamp", "west of the Great Pond called the Mill Pond", in "Pond Meadow", in "River meadow" and at "French's Hill Meadow."

"April 20, 1663, The Townsmen doe order that for the repayring the High way Ledinge from the Cuntry Rode that Leads from our Town to Concord to ye Cuntry Rode y^t^ Leads to Shawshin: through the Land of Henry Jefts and Willi Chamberlin: and Leftent Willi frenches land that: John Stern Henry Jefts and Willi Chamberlin and Willi french shall mend the way and make it passable and they shall set of there chrge on ye account of publiq chrge in high way worke." July 3, 1663, he drew a lot on the west side of Concord River. His rate for the maintenance of Rev. Samuel Whiting for the year 1663 was £01 : 00 : 08. Jan. 29, 1667, at a "publich towne" meeting, he was one to consent "that any proposition shall be determined by a major vote of the town."

In 1673, he was chosen constable of the town, serving for one year. At that time the New England town constables served warrants upon all freemen and freeholders for town meetings, warrants upon the selectmen for choice of jurors, warrants upon offenders against the laws; collected the country rates and the minister's rates and paid the latter to the settled minister of the township, who was for many years the only person in the township who received a compensation for his services at public expense. The accounts which William Chamberlain and other early constables rendered to the town of Billerica show that the rates were paid in rye, wheat, Indian corn and other New England farm products. Oct. 8, 1677, the town of Billerica appointed tithing-men and placed under each the care of a half dozen families. William Chamberlain's family was under the care of George Farley. In May 1677 he was behind in his last year's rates to the amount of £04 : 02 : 05. This was on account of King Philip's War which ruined the property of many families all over New England. He was one of the forty inhabitants of Billerica who were in arrears for their rates due the Rev. Samuel Whiting Jan. 4, 1685, his rate being £01 : 03 : 04.

Capt. Daniel Gookin and John Eliot, the Apostle to the Indians, visited the Wamesit Indians on the Merrimack river about five miles north of the Billerica settlement May 5 and 6, 1674, and heard the chief Numphow declare that he would become a Christian. In Gookin's narrative (*Hazen*, 105, 106) he gives full details of this visit. In that account Capt. Gookin said, "In this town [Billerica] they observe the same civil and religious orders as in other towns and have a constable and other officers." The "constable" to whom he here referred was Samuel Manning for 1674 and William Chamberlain for 1673, whose duties had been so performed that Numphow and his tribe refused to join King Philip one year later, and so the inhabitants of Billerica, although living in constant fear, escaped the cruel tomahawk and the loss of their homes, although they were domiciled in garrisons as the inhabitants of other towns were.

SARAH SHELLEY.

From its genealogical significance the will of Sarah Shelley of Boston is reproduced verbatim et literatim :

"I Sarah Shelley of Boston in New England Spinster, being Sick in body, but through mercy of sound disposing minde Knowing the uncertainty of this present Life do hereby revoke all former and make and declare this my last will and Testament.

First and principally I commit my Spirit into the hands of Almighty God my Creato^r^ hopeing to receive full pardon and forgiveness of all my Sines and eternal Life and Salvation through the alone Merits of the Lord Jesus Christ my ever blessed Redeemer. My body I commit unto the dust to be decently interred at the discretion of my Executo^r^ hereafter named in faith of a glorious Resurrection.

And for my temporal Estate I will that it be imployed and bestowed as in and by this my will is exprest.

Impr^s^ I will that all my just debts and funeral Expences be paid and discharged by my Executo^r^ in convenient time after my decease.

Item. I give and bequeath unto my Rev^d^ and much Respected Friends Mr Samuel Nowell Mr James Allen and Mr Joshua Moody all of Boston Forty Shillings apeice in money.

It. I give and bequeath unto my Cousens Captn Penn Townsend and Sarah his wife Five pounds apiece in money and to my Cousen Ann Peirce Five pounds in money and to each of my Cousen Townsends and Cousen Peirse:^s^ Children now Liveing Forty Shillings apeice in money to be paid by my Execto^r^ into the hands of their parents for their use. Also I give unto my Cousen Rebecca Davenports two Children Forty Shillings apeice in money Viz^t^: Addington Davenport and Rebecca Davenport: Further I give unto the s^d^ Rebecca Davenport and Rebecca Townsend my two Silver Spoons Rebecca Townsend to have that I comonly use More to my Cousen Rebecca Davenport one new pewter pot and a Silver Bookin. [sic]

It. I give unto my Cousen Isaac Addington Ten pounds in money and to his wife Twenty Shillings in money to buy a Ring.

It. I give unto my good Friend Mrs Dorothy Hawkins widow Twenty Shillings in money to buy her a Ring.

It. I Release unto my Brother William Chamberlin a debt of Six pounds which he oweth me and I give and bequeath unto my Sister his wife and unto her three daughters Twenty Shillings apeice in money: Farther I give unto my s[d] Sister and her three daughters and my Cousen John Chamberlin's wife all my wearing Apparrell and Household goods of all sorts to be equally divided among them Excepting three small pewter dishes marked S: S: which I give unto my Cousen Sarah Sheds Children now liveing.

It. I give and bequeath all the rest and residue of my Estate whatsoever unto my Sister Chamberlins Eight Sons to be equally divided to and among them onely my two Cousens John and Clement Chamberlin to have the value of Twenty Shillings apeice over and above an equal Share with their other Bretheren.

It. upon farther consideration I do give and bequeath unto M[r] Roberts Sanderson M[r] Henry Alline and Mr Joseph Bridgham Deacons of the first Church of Christ in Boston whereof I am an unworthy member to and for the use of the s[d] Church and poor thereof Ten pounds in money which Sume I hereby reserve out of the residue of my Estate willed to be divided as aboves[d]. And of this my Last will and Testament I do nominate ordein and appoint my Kinsman Isaac Addington to be the sole and whole Executo[r]. In Testimony whereof I have hereunto Set my hand and affixed my Seale. Dated in Boston the Second day of February Ann[o] Dom[i] 1686/7 Annoqz R:R[s] Jacobi Angliæ &c[a]: Secundi: Secundo.

Further I give unto each of my Cousen John & Thomas Chamberlins and my Cousen Sarah Shed[s] Child[n]: now liveing Ten Shillings for ye raysing of wch I have some small Remnants of Goods by me wch my Executo[r] may dispose of

Signu
Sarah s Shelley [Seal]

Signed Sealed and what is conteined in these two pages was published by Sarah Shelley to be her last will and Testament in the presence of us.

William Griggs
John Ballantine
Martha Collings

Coram Viro Honorabili Josepho Dudleo Armiger o: Apr[ll] 21, 1686. [1687]

This Instrument being Presented by Is[a]: Addington Executor W[m] Griggs and John Ballantine made oath that they were Present and Saw Sarah Shelly Signe Seale & Publish the same as her last will and testam[t] and that when she so did she was of sound mind and memory to their best understanding and y[t] they saw Martha Collin Signe wth them as witness. Jurat at Supra
Attest[r] Tho Dudley Cler."

The foregoing will appears to have been drawn by Isaac Addington, the distinguished colonial magistrate of Suffolk County, whom the testatrix called her "kinsman" and her "cousin." The paper was folded together so that the contents were on the two inside pages of the paper. The person who drew up the will also wrote on the outside page in its middle part: "M[rs] Sarah Shelley her Last Will 1686." On the same outside page of the original will at least two other persons wrote: "Sarah Shelley Will April 21, 1686" and "Sarah Shelleys Will 21 Apr[l] 1687" and "Sarah Shelleys Last Will Proved 21 Apr[ll] 1687."

The testatrix was admitted to the First Church of Boston, Aug. 14, 1670, and continued to live in Boston until her death, which occurred between Feb. 2 and Feb. 22, 1686/7. During these sixteen years Sarah Shelley frequently loaned money to various persons. She, or another person of the same name, received a gift of five shillings by the will of Mrs. Anne (Fisher) Leverett, widow of Elder Thomas Leverett of Boston, on Oct. 15, 1656. Elder Thomas Leverett made a nuncupative will bequeathing all his property to his "wiffe" Ann Leverett with no mention of other kindred. Elder James Penn of Boston made his will, Sept. 29, 1671, in which he bequeathed to his wife Katharine (who subsequently returned to England) to his kinsmen Mr. James Allen and Penn Townsend, to his sister Mary Miner and to Sarah "Sheally." In these instances no kinship to either testator is expressed.

From the will of Sarah Shelley it is apparent that Rebecca, the wife of William Chamberlain, was her "sister." In legal usage the word "sister" sometimes meant own sister, sometimes half sister and not infrequently sister-in-law, but the phraseology of this will excludes the latter interpretation as the words are here used. Our present knowledge fails to enable us to determine whether the word "sister" was intended to denote own sister or half sister. The testatrix called the eleven children of her sister Chamberlain her "cousins," by which it is plain that she meant her nephews and nieces. The word "cousin" was, of course, an indefinite term used as we now use kinsman.

In the same document she called the children of Capt. Isaac and Anne (Leverett) Addington of Boston her "cousins." Did the word "cousin" applied to the Addington children have the same or another meaning from what it had in its application to the Chamberlain children?

In 1672 Gov. John Leverett sent to Old Boston in Lincolnshire for a transcript of the baptisms of his father's family which was sent him that year. On March 15, 1678/9, while Governor of the Massachusetts Bay Colony, he made his will mentioning all of the children of his sister Anne (Leverett) Addington but neither Sarah Shelley nor Rebecca Chamberlain. His transcripts show that he was baptized in St. Botolph's in Old Boston July 7, 1616, and that the family consisted of thirteen children baptized between 1612 and 1632. These transcripts show that John Leverett had a sister Sarah Leverett bapt. there Sept. 26, 1622. She does not appear to be accounted for but the transcripts fail to show any sister named Rebecca Leverett. (Mass. Hist. Coll. Fourth Series, 2:225.) The widow of Elder Thomas Leverett in her will bequeathed to her son "John Capt. Leverett", to her "daughter Leverett" by which she meant daughter-in-law and to her "daughter Anne Addington", Oct. 15, 1656—from which it is inferred that only two of her children were then living. The parish register of St. Botolph shows that Mr. Thomas Leverett and Anne Fisher were married there Oct. 29, 1610, and since Sarah Shelley and Rebecca Chamberlain were one generation younger than Thomas Leverett and his wife, it is apparent that they could not be sisters to either. Therefore, the kinship of Capt. Isaac Addington's children to Sarah Shelley and Rebecca Chamberlain did not originate in the Leverett family and must have come from the Addington family.

It is evident that neither the author of the Addington Genealogy—Thaddeus William Harris, M. D., nor the authors of the Leverett Memorials indicated any relationship of either family with Sarah Shelley and Rebecca Chamberlain. The Memorial stated that Elder Thomas Leverett was reputed to be the father of sixteen children—the transcripts from St. Botolph's show only fourteen and of that number only three have been identified in Boston in New England. Is it likely that Elder Thomas Leverett left beyond the seas eight or ten living children from fourteen years to six months of age and came in 1633 bringing only three children? Only two of these are mentioned in Mrs. Anne Leverett's will in 1656. Either death removed these children early or else there was intentional neglect to recognize family ties in Mrs. Anne (Fisher) Leverett's will.

Mrs. Anne (Leverett) Addington was living in Boston in New England Jan. 29, 1656/7, when she appeared in court and made oath to the inventory of her mother's estate. Her subsequent career appears to be a mystery as I have found no further record of her; neither has Savage nor Pope published a later record of her.

Rebecca Chamberlain was marriageable in 1648 and became the mother of thirteen children between Aug. 13, 1649, and Sept. 27, 1671. She was, therefore, probably born between the years of 1625 and 1634. She and her sister Sarah Shelley were of the same generation as Capt. Isaac Addington and his wife Anne (Leverett) Addington, and since they were not sisters of the latter, they were likely to have been either own sisters or half sisters to Capt. Isaac Addington who appeared in Boston in New England as a "singleman" before June 6, 1640, and lived here until his death in 1652.

But the will of Sarah Shelley described her as a "spinster" as did the inventory of her estate—both in the handwriting of Isaac Addington, Jr. Across the outside page of the will the scrivener wrote: "Mrs Sarah Shelley her Last Will 1686". If "spinster" and "M^rs^" as legally used by Isaac Addington were intended to imply that she was a maiden then the family name of Rebecca Chamberlain was probably Rebecca Shelley, which is the point in question. Granting that to be true, then they were, I believe, half sisters to Capt. Isaac Addington of Boston, 1640–1652. At the time this will was drawn the title "Mrs." was used as a title of respect to any gentlewoman —that is to one who belonged to the gentry and not to the yeomanry. It was also a title applied to married women and widows to distinguish them from singlewomen. In New England previous to the administration of Sir Edmund Andros as Governor marriages were performed by civil magistrates excepting those solemnized by clergymen of the Church of England. At a later period the ceremony was performed by both the civil magistrates and the Puritan clergy. In many localities the latter most carelessly wrote the title "Mrs." indiscriminately before the name of every woman whose marriage they recorded. As to the legal usage of the word "spinster" in New England before the American Revolution, it appears to have been applied to both maidens and widows, both were free from the marriage contract, both were single, both were unmarried and both were therefore "spinsters". Rarely this discrimination appears in legal documents in New England and in Old England. Sarah Osgood, a widow, and the mother of three children came in the *Confidence* in 1635 and was called a "spinster"; Martha Wilder, a widow, and the mother of Mary Wilder of Hingham was called a "spinster"; Rebecca Binney, the widow of Samuel Binney of Hull, in her deed to James Dawson of Boston was styled a "spinster"; "Susannah Satchwell of Haverhill spinster-widow and executrix of the will of Theophilus Satchwell of Haverhill deceased" deeded Stephen Kent, Sr. land in Haverhill (Essex Antiquarian 10:11). Administration on the estate of Jane Bryan [sic] of Teddington, County of Middlesex, England, "*spinstex*", deceased, was granted for the benefit of Elizabeth Bryant [sic] *legitimate daughter* of the deceased on June 23, 1674. (Prerogative Court of Canterbury 1674).

The estate of Sarah Shelley amounting to £234 : 13 : 4½ was not an insignificant property for a singlewoman to possess in the town of Boston between 1670 and 1687. Her home was well furnished and it may be assumed that this property did not represent her earnings either in Boston-town or elsewhere but that the larger portion of it was an inheritance. Had she received this from her parents, her sister Rebecca Chamberlain would have been likely to have received a considerable portion of which there is not the slightest evidence.

For these reasons I *believe* that Sarah Shelley was a "spinster-widow" whose estate had fallen to her by the death of a husband and she, being left alone in the world, decided to pass her last years in Boston near her nephews and nieces but I do not *know* that she was a widow. Whether she was an own sister or a half-sister to Capt. Isaac Addington or a more distant kinswoman my researches have failed to disclose. The time will doubtless come when this puzzle will be solved—probably from sources of information from beyond the seas.

"Inventory of the Goods and chattles of Sarah Shelly late of Boston Spinst^{r} dec^{d} apprized 22^{ond} ffebruary 168$\frac{9}{0}$ by us the Subscribers:

Item	£	s	d
Imp^{rs} One Flock Bed 2 ffeather Boulst^{rs} 3 pillows and pillow beers Two paire of blanketts and Coverlett - - -	05	00	00
It. one Bedsted and Cord	£00	10	00
One Trunk containeing Linnen	£00	05	00
It. Ten white aprons 24 handkerchers 24 caps 10 p^{r} of cuffs 6 underneck-cloths and other Small weareing Linnen 4 p^{r} thred Gloves 3 p^{r} Leath ditto	£03	10	00
It. 14 Sheets and a Cotton blankett	£08	08	00
It. 48 Pillow beers 16^{s} one Table cloth 14 napkins 15^{s} - - - -	£01	11	00
It. 5 Shifts 20^{s} ffive blew aprons 2 course towells 6/	£01	06	00
It. 1 pillow beer course Towell and old blew apron	£00	02	00
It. Woollen weareing apparrel of all Sorts muff and Gloves	£08	07	00
It. Silke hoods and Scarfes 30^{s} one Trunk 7^{s} one bible 3/	£02	00	00
It. one Trunk 3/ Rye meale 2/	£00	05	00
It. 6 flagg bottom Chaires 1 wainscott Chaire & Stoole	£00	15	00
It. one Cupboard and Counter	£00	07	00
It. 5 Small Low Formes 2^{s} 4 p^{r} old Shooes & 1 p^{r} pattens 5^{s}	£00	07	00
It. 7 Small pewter dishes 14^{s} one Chamber pott, pint pott, small cupp, one Porringer 2 Spoones and grater 8^{s}	£01	02	00
It. one new pewter quart pott or three pint	£00	03	00
It. 2 Small Brass Kettles, Skillett, Iron pott and hookes 8/	£00	08	00
It. Earthen ware and Glass bottles 4^{s} Straw hatt and baskett 1/	£00	05	00
It. ffire shovell, Tongs, Tramil and broken doggs	£00	05	00
It. Smoothing Box and heaters 2/6 Spinning wheel 3/ - - -	£00	05	06
It. one Reete and Iron Lamp	£00	01	00
It. Lumber 4^{s} one Cord and halfe of wood 15^{s}	£00	19	00
It. one Small box for Linnen	£00	02	06
It. 2 Silver Spoones and one Silver bodkin	£00	17	00
It. Cash	£00	18	08
It. $\frac{1}{2}$ y^{d} Course Holland 2^{s} 1 yd $\frac{1}{2}$ finer Holland att 5^{s} - - - - -	£00	09	06
It. 14 yds $\frac{1}{2}$ Scotch cloth att 18^{d} ℘ yd	£01	01	09
It. 7 yds $\frac{1}{4}$ Dowlaix att 2/2 ℘ yd $\frac{1}{2}$ Ell course dowlax 1	£00	16	08$\frac{1}{2}$
It. 5 yds course Shirting Holland att 2/ ℘ yd - - - - - -	£00	10	00
It. 1 ℘^{r} $\frac{1}{2}$ of ribbon 12/ Tape and ffilliting 2/ - - - - - - -	£00	14	00

It. Flax 10s 2 yds blew Linnen att 9d ℔ yd	£00 11 06
It. 2 yds ½ alamode att 4s	£00 10 00
It. Provisions 6/	£00 06 00
Apprized by us Ephraim Savage, Arthur Mason.	£42 : 19 : 01½

In Debts Oweing and Standing out at the time of the decease of sd Sarah Shelley Vizt

From Nathl Johnson of Roxbury since Recd	£ 4 : 3 06
From Obadiah Sale by Obligacon For wch also there is a mortgage	£62 : 19 : 00
From Thomas Skinner, Phillip Squire &c. by obligacon since Rcd	£52 : 16 : 09
From Samuel Boighton by Bill besides Interest	£05 00 00
Cash recd since of the late wife of Hugh Baboll	£01 04 00
From Hugh Baboll due by bond and mortgage	£16 04 00
From Captn Townsend by bill £40 with Interest att 6 5s ℔ Ct from 9 June ult to the time of her death neer 8 months	£41 : 13 : 00
Due upon a Pledge £6 : 6 : 0 whereof 25s is since Recd	£ 6 : 6 : 00
She affirmed { From George Woodward of Watertowne for money Lent	£ 1 : 00 : 00
She affirmed { From John Shed of Bilerica for ditto	£ 0 08 00
Errors Excepted	£234 13 4½

℔ Isa : Addington Exector

Whereof I Crave allowance

For Funerall Charges and other disbursments pd	£17 : 04 : 09
For Probate of will and Inventory	£00 : 07 : 00

Mr Isa Addington Execr made oath that this accot Containes a just and true Inventory of the Estate of Sarah Shelly of what hath come to his knowledge and that when more appeares he will Cause it to be added

Jurat Coram J Dudley Esqr Aprll 21 : 1687.

Attestr Tho : Dudley Cler."

(Suffolk Probate. 9 : 350)

William Chamberlain probably belonged to the great middle class of Englishmen—the yeomanry, pronounced by Wendell Phillips to be "the best blood in Europe." He and his wife were both able to write and they probably possessed such general education as the English yeomanry could acquire. In settling in Billerica they were in a wilderness eighteen miles from Boston and within five miles of the Wamesit Indians on the Merrimack. Of their thirteen children only one could write. What was true concerning the lack of education in their children was likewise true of three-fourths of the children of the pioneers of New England who lived before the days of King Philip's war.

How William Chamberlain disposed of his estate does not appear in the county records, but a critical study of his land-grants and of the deeds given by his sons convinces me that they shared in his estate. The title to the 125 acres conveyed to him by the proprietors of the Dudley Farm I have failed to trace after attempting to do so.

William Chamberlain m. about 1648. This marriage may have occurred in England as no record of it has been found in New England. His wife Rebecca was the mother of thirteen children, twelve of whom reached maturity and ten of whom left descendants. In 1692 the witchcraft delusion spread from Salem Village to Andover, Haverhill, Reading, Lexington, Chelmsford, Billerica and other towns. In 1816, John Farmer, the pioneer antiquary of New England, in his article on the *Early History of Billerica* in referring to the death of Rebecca Chamberlain on Sept. 26, 1692, said that she was probably "a victim of the infatuation which prevailed at that time." An examination of every paper in the Middlesex Co. Court Files from 1670 to 1700 has revealed many witchcraft cases but nothing relating to Rebecca Chamberlain. The town records of Billerica state that she "died in ye prison at Cambridge." I have the documentary record of several of whom it was recorded that they died there on the charge of witchcraft. Both she and her husband were probably buried in the Old South Cemetery in Billerica. Here she spent forty years of her life and William Chamberlain about fifty-four years. He was the last of the original settlers of ancient Billerica to enter "into that peace that passeth understanding."

Children last nine born in Billerica:

i TIMOTHY[2] CHAMBERLAIN, b. at Woburn 13th 6 mo, 1649 (Aug. 13, 1649). Savage stated in his *Genealogical Dictionary* that he was born at Concord, but his birth is recorded at Woburn where his parents were then living. He probably d. young as no further reference to him has been found in many years of searching.

ii ISAAC[2] CHAMBERLAIN, b. at Woburn Oct. 1, 1650; probably named for his uncle Capt. Isaac Addington; assigned to Sergt. Ralph Hill's garrison with his father's family, Oct. 8, 1675 (*Hazen*, 110); d. at Billerica, July 20, 1681, aged 30 years.

2 iii WILLIAM[2] CHAMBERLAIN, JR., b. about 1652.

3 iv JOHN[2] CHAMBERLAIN, b. about 1654.

4 v SARAH[2] CHAMBERLAIN, b. Jan. 18, 1655/6 (18 d. 11 mo. 1655).

5 vi JACOB[2] CHAMBERLAIN, b. Jan. 18, 1657/8. (18 d. 11 mo. 1657).

6 vii THOMAS[2] CHAMBERLAIN, b. Feb. 20, 1658/9. (20 d. 12 mo. 1658).

7 viii EDMUND[2] CHAMBERLAIN, b. July 15, 1660.

8 ix REBECCA[2] CHAMBERLAIN, b. Feb. 25, 1662/3.

9 x ABRAHAM[2] CHAMBERLAIN, b. Jan. 6, 1664/5.

xi ANN[2] CHAMBERLAIN, b. Jan. 6, 1665/6; alive Feb. 2, 1686/7. The town of Billerica paid Clement Chamberlain £08: 03 for "keeping" her and Dr. How 12s. for "doctering" her, Dec. 12, 1726, from which it is inferred that in her old age she became a town charge.

10 xii CLEMENT[2] CHAMBERLAIN, b. May 30, 1669.

11 xiii DANIEL[2] CHAMBERLAIN, b. Sept. 27, 1671.

SECOND GENERATION

2 WILLIAM[2] CHAMBERLAIN, JR. (*William*[1]) born about 1652; d. at Lexington, Mass., Jan. 20, 1734. He was assigned to Jacob French's garrison in Billerica, Oct. 14, 1675, at which time he had no family. (*Hazen*, 111). He was credited £1 1s. 4d. in the ledger account of Treasurer John Hull for military services during King Philip's war, the account being dated Feb. 24, 1676/7. (Bodge's *Soldiers of King Philip's War* (*1897*), 447.) He took the oath of fidelity 4 d. 12 mo. 1677. On Dec. 22, 1684, "William Chamberlaine, Junr is ordered forthwith to provide himself a service or els ye Selectmen will place him out according to law." (*Billerica Town Records*). On Jan. 4, 1685/6, he and 39 other inhabitants of Billerica were in arrears for Rev. Samuel Whiting's salary, his rate amounting to £01 01 03. Again his arrears in 1697 amounted to £01 01 10. (*Ibid.*) His name does not appear on the Billerica Town Records after 1698. He m. at Watertown, Mass. Dec. 20, 1698, Deliverance Fergerson (Bond's *Watertown*, I, 152) who was bapt. and owned the Church covenant at Cambridge Feb. 28, 1696/7. He appears to have removed to the part of ancient Cambridge called Menotomy.

"At a Meeting of the Select men [of Cambridge] 11 Nov^r: 1700. "Whereas there hath been of late a publick Contribution In this Town for y^e: Reliefe of W^m: Chamberlin his Substance having been of late Consumed by fire the Selectmen have Ordered £03 : 00 : 00 of S^d Money to be disposed of for W^m: Chamberlins use". Feb. 14, 1703/4, the selectman again ordered "that M^r: Jason Russel take care of W^m: Chamberlin's *youngest* Child & provide Nesscesseary clothing for her & that he bring an acc^t: of his Disburstments on s^d: Child to the Select Men on ye Second Monday in March next." March 13, 1703/4. they gave an order "to pay Mr Jason Russel twelve shillings for ye keeping W^m: Chamberlins Child to this day & Agreed s^d Russel to keep s^d Child untill ye Second Monday in May Next for which he is to Receive of ye Town 18^d pr. week (*Town Records of Cambridge*, 349). July 10, 1704, the selectmen ordered that Mr. Jason Russel be paid twelve shillings for keeping W^m: Chamberlins child, viz. Sarah Chamberlin to this day. Also agreed with said Jason Russel to keep said child until she is eighteen years of age for which he is to be paid out of the Town Treasury four pounds." Jason Russell lived in the part of Cambridge which is now Arlington. William Chamberlain Jr. lost what little personal property he had and spent his last years in Lexington. He probably owned no real estate and d. in poverty. "Wm Chamberlain from Lexington was warned to depart the Town [of Boston] as the Law Directs" Sept. 3, 1726. (*Boston Record Commissioners Report*, 1700–1728, 153)

Children probably born in Cambridge:

i ———[3], CHAMBERLAIN, b. about 1699, d. at Lexington, in 1703.

ii SARAH[3], CHAMBERLAIN, b. about 1701; living in the home of Jason Russell of Menotomy (Arlington) July 10, 1704.

3 JOHN[2] CHAMBERLAIN (*William*[1]) b. at Billerica about 1654; d. there April 1, 1712. He m. (1) at Billerica, Dec. 6, 1681, Deborah Jaco, who d. there Feb. 24, 1703/4. In 1679, he was taxed for one poll and on property 1s. 8d. (*Hazen*, 193). He took the oath of fidelity "Aprill 23, 1666". (*Billerica Town Records*). On Dec. 9, 1673, it appears that he furnished two bushels of Indian Corn at 06s: towards the support of Mr. Whiting. In 1677, he lived in the southeast part of the town. In May 1677, he was reported behind in his rates to Mr. Whiting 12s. He was no exception, as all the inhabitants were struggling with the expenses of King Philip's war. On Jan. 8, 1682, his family was under the care of George Farley. On Jan. 4, 1685, he was one of forty persons in arrears to Rev. Samuel Whiting, his unpaid rate being £00: 16: 07. He had ammunition distributed to him in 1703. (*Hazen*, 200). On Feb. 2, 1686/7, he was bequeathed by his "cousin" Sarah Shelley of Boston, twenty shillings over and above what was given him as one of the eight sons of her sister Rebecca Chamberlain. To her cousin John Chamberlin's wife she bequeathed a portion of her wearing apparel. He married a second time a woman whose name is unknown to me, as appears from his will here reproduced in full:

"The last will and Testament of John Chamberlain of Billerica febre: 22: 1711/12."

"In the name of God amen, the twenty second day of febrewary Annoque Domini one thousand seven hundred and Eleven twelve I John Chamberlain of Billerica in the County of Midd^x. in her Maj^ts Province of the Massachusets Bay in New England, being weak in body, but of sound Judgment and memory do make and ordain this my last will and testament after the following manner and forme, that is to say principally and first of all I give and Recommend my Immortal soul into the hands of god that gave it, and my body to the Earth with a decent christian burial; and for such worldly Estate wherewith it hath pleased god to bless me in this life I give; demise and dispose of the same as in manner following:

1. (five pounds in money I do give unto my son John Chamberlain & my lot of twenty two acres and one hundred poles of upland and swamp lying on the south side of Nuttens Pond; allso I do give unto him my lot of forty one acres and Eighty poles of land Eastward of the great swamp.

2. I do give unto my Son Abraham Chamberlain my homestead or house lott, allso I do give unto him my lot of twenty acres on the west side of Concord River only the said Abraham shall pay unto his three sisters five pounds a piece and to his mother twenty shillings a year beside her thirds, and after her deceas the moveables that are left I do give unto my daughters to be equally divided among them,

I do constitute and appoint my two sons John and Abraham, to be my lawfull Executors of this my will Rattefying and Confirming this and no other to be my last will & testament.

In Witness whereof I have hereunto set my hand and seal the day and year abovewritten. In the tenth year of the Reign of our sovereign Lady Anne of great Britain France and Ireland Queen, &c.

John Chamberlain [Seal]
his ʒ marke

Signed, sealed published pronounced and declared by the said John Chamberlain to be his last will and testament before us the subscribers Henry Jefts, John Needham, Edmond Chamberlain his v marke.

[Upon the other side of this will the Judge of Probate wrote and erased the following :]

Midd[x] at Camb[e] 28th April 1712.

John Needham of Billerica p[e]sent one of the Witnesses to this Will & who took the Minutes of this Will & Carryed them to Capt. Whiting to put them in forme sayes upon his oath y[t] the S[d] decd spake of the widow's thirds to be only in the homestead P[er] F. F.

[On the same sheet below he wrote :]

Middlesex Camb Aprill 28, 1712. This Will was this Day Exhibited for probate, by John Chamberlain Son of John Chamberlain late of Billerica in y[e] County of Midd[x] Decd and Execut[r] therein named, And the Three Witnesses Thereto were psent & they Made Oath That They Saw the Testator Sign Seal & publish & Declare y[e] Same to be his last Will & Testam[t] And that at Same time he was of Sound & Disposing Mind And y[e] s[d] John Chamberlain took upon him y[e] s[d] Trust & room is left for Abraham another Son of y[e] Testator, Execut also therein nominated, a minor ab[t] 19 Years Old, if he se cause to Accept w[n] he comes of Age & in the mean time Samuel Hill of Billerica aforesd is Appointed & Chosen Guardian to & by y[e] s[d] Abraham & This Will is proved and Allowed & the Adm[n]: thereof Comitted to John Chamberlain Aforesd well to adm[r] the Same according to the true intent thereof w[h] is something dark but being of small value & haveing directed the Kindred now p[e]sent (all Exept Abram a Son of the s[d] Decd) to agree w[th] my Explanation thereof I have allow[d] this Will as aforesd. F[rancis] F.[oxcroft] J. Prob. Exam[d] ꝑ Dan Foxcroft Reg[r]:

His inventory, taken April 24, 1712, included only a part of his personal estate valued at £16 : 16 : 11 : also "two old swords 4s" etc. It stated that he had disposed of his bedding and given away his real estate, both of which were not inventoried.

Children all born in Billerica:

i Deborah[3] Chamberlain, b. Nov. 17, 1682; became the mother of Samuel Farley, b. at Billerica, April 14, 1708; the father being Caleb Farley, Jr.

12 ii John[3] Chamberlain, b. Jan. 22, 1684/5

iii Sarah[3] Chamberlain, b. Sept. 29, 1687.

13 iv Lydia[3] Chamberlain, b. Oct. 6, 1689.

14 v Abraham[3] Chamberlain, b. April 17, 1693.

4. SARAH[2] CHAMBERLAIN (*William*[1]) b. at Billerica, Jan. 18, 1655/6; d. there Jan. 17, 1735/6. She m. at Billerica, Jan. 9, 1676/7, John Shed, who was b. there March 2, 1655, and d. there Jan 31, 1736/7. He was an ensign.

Children all born at Billerica:

i SARAH[3] SHED, b. Nov. 3, 1678; m. Nathan Crosby.
ii ELIZABETH[3] SHED, b. Jan. 7, 1681/2; m. Ebenezer Farley.
iii BENONI[3] SHED, b. June 11, 1684; d. June 26, 1684.
iv REBECCA[3] SHED, b. May 21, 1685; m. Joshua Abbot.
v JOHN[3] SHED, Jr. b. July 6, 1687.
vi MARY[3] SHED, b. Dec. 7, 1689; she did not marry her cousin Abraham Chamberlain as Hazen stated.
vii DOROTHY[3] SHED, b. Jan. 11 or 14, 1691/2; m. Samuel Danforth.
viii HANNAH[3] SHED, b. March 23, 1693/4; m. her cousin Nathan Shed of Billerica.
ix BENJAMIN[3] SHED, b. Aug. 5, 1696.
x JEMIMA[3] SHED, b. Jan. 18, 1698/9; m. John Wilson of Billerica; d. there Sept. 14, 1740.

5. JACOB[2] CHAMBERLAIN (*William*[1]) b. at Billerica, Jan. 18, 1657/8; d. at Newton, Mass. April 11, 1712; one of the eight sons of Rebecca Chamberlain referred to in Sarah Shelley's will, Feb. 2, 1686/7. Jacob Chamberlain aged 23 years or thereabouts deposed in the case of Hall vs. Prout June 21, 1681 and "saith that Mr. Ebenezer Prout this last fishing-time past improved y[e] fishing at y[e] mill & y[e] wars [weirs] above y[e] mill 21 : 4 : 81" (*Middlesex Co. Court Files*, June 1681). The case shows that the parties concerned were Medford people. His name appeared on the tax lists of Medford, Mass. Jan. 31, 1686; Jan. 20, 1686/7; Oct. 1, 1687, and on May 18, 1691, when his tax amounted to £01 : 06 : 03. "Att a publick meeting of the Inhabitants of Cambridge for the Choice of Town Officers, March 11, 1694/5 Jacob Chamberline" was chosen "a Howard for Horses"; (*Cambridge Town Records*, 310). He was chosen to inspect the swine for "Menottomie" (now Arlington) March 27, 1695. (*Ibid.* 311). At a "Publick Town Meeting" there he was chosen "Hog Constable," "ffor Minottomie," March 9, 1695/6. He was one of the jurors at the inquest of John Bull who was drowned at Cambridge April 4, 1698 (*Suffolk Co. Court Files*, 3690) and served with Jason Russell and others. The wife of Jacob Chamberlain contributed a "pig wth Toes" valued at 1s. 8d. towards the support of Rev. William Brattle, pastor of the First Church of Cambridge who recorded it Jan. 15, 1697/8, under contributions from "my good neighbors." Again he recorded, Jan. 9, 1699/1700, that "Goody" Chamberlain had sent a pig since Nov. 20, 1699.

In the year 1699 Jacob Chamberlain removed from Cambridge to Newton as the following abstract shows:

"Jonathan Hide, Jun[r]: of Newton in the County of Middlesex in y[e]

Maj[s] Prov[c] of the Massach: Bay in N: England, yeoman," for £90 deeded "Jacob Chamberlin of Cambridge in the County afores[d], Yeoman," "all that my Messuage or Tenement being within the Limits of Newton afores[d] consisting of a Dwelling house and one hundred and twenty acres of Land thereto adjoining" bounded "with an highway to Dedham Easterly; with the land of John Ward Sen[r] southerly; with meadows of Elijah Marrick decd lying upon Charles River westerly and with my own land northerly (Excepting and reserving a Drift-way at the westerly end of s[d] Land where they now pass to the meadow)." Signed by Jonathan Hide, Jun[r]. in the presence of Richard Truesdel and Jonathan Remington, May 11, 1699, and acknowledged on the same day but recorded Sept. 14, 1721. (*Middlesex County Deeds*, 21: 430). This farm located at Oak Hill in Ward V in the present city of Newton remained in the Chamberlain family until Dec. 4, 1778, when Jacob Chamberlain's grandson, Simon Chamberlain, deeded it to Daniel Richards of Newton. (87:12) It was owned by Jacob Chamberlain, Sr., 1699–1712; by Jacob Chamberlain Jr. 1715–1771; by Simon Chamberlain 1771–1778; and by Daniel Richards 1778–1830.

The present house, owned by Mr. Charles Esty, was built during the time that the property was owned by the Chamberlains. It was originally constructed as a two story leanto and stood facing the road leading from Newton to Dedham (Baker street). The frame was of oak and in remodeling the house the frame is the only original part preserved. When the house was turned to face the lane, the old chimney which occupied the center and contained the fireplaces was removed and two small chimneys put in the ends. The walls of the house were filled with brick, the laths were split with an ax and the nails were hand-made. Standing back from the buildings is an old oak, the only living landmark which remains unchanged since Jacob Chamberlain purchased the farm. It is the only living witness of the passing of six generations. Under date of April 1, 1902, Rev. Daniel Richards, then of Somerville, Mass., who was born in the Oak Hill house, wrote: "I remember when my grandmother lived in the old house and the marriage of her daughter in 1825 when I was seven years old. The house was old then with an immense kitchen and an old barn and well between the house and street. I am now in my 84th year—the last of a great family—and have been away from Newton since 1837," etc. Charles Esty, the owner in 1902, wrote: "The house as it was when my father bought the place had one chimney, two large rooms, one either side the front door, which was located then in what is now the end of the house facing the street. The room used for a kitchen had a brick floor, a large brick oven and a large fireplace. The house has an oak frame and I found in putting in new windows that the outside walls are filled with brick & clay." The house was remodeled and renovated about 1833.

CHAMBERLAIN HOMESTEAD, OAK HILL, NEWTON, MASS.

"Inventory of the estate of Jacob Chamberlaine late of Newtown, decesed: as it was vallued by us the subscribers upon May the: 14: 1712:

	£	s	d
Wearing Clothes	07	00	00
Fether bed bedsted and furnitur	08	00	00
Flock bed bedsted and bedding	03	00	00
Trundle bedsted and bedding	02	10	00
12 yeard Cersie Cloath	03	00	00
12 pound of wooll	00	12	00
7 pound flax: 7^s: 1 pound cotton 1:6	00	08	06
2 chists and a box	00	12	00
2 spinning whells	00	09	00
Pannell and pillion cloath	00	06	00
Craddell: 4^s: 2 moall Sives 1-6	00	05	06
9 bushells Malt	01	07	00
In Ry[e] and indian meall	00	08	00
Meall secks and wallets	00	03	00
Wooll and hops	00	03	00
Meall trough and other lumber	00	05	00
Arms and amanition	02	00	00
In brass	01	01	00
In putter	01	13	00
Erthen ware: 3^s in tine 3^s	00	06	00
Glass bottels morter and other lumber	00	03	00
Books at	00	10	00
Looking glass and specktels	00	02	00
In yearn	00	10	00
Podring tube and meat	01	00	00
Churn barrells and other kask	00	13	06
Pails and other lumber	00	05	00
Iron pott and Kittell	00	16	00
Tramell and tonges	00	05	00
Chafing dish, greidiron and spitt box iron, heaters lampe & candelstick	00	09	00
Table and Joynt stooll	00	05	00
Chairs	00	06	00
Axes and other husbandrie tools	01	00	00
Siths and hoose	00	12	00
Plow chain and horse harnish	01	00	00
Fetters yoake shakell and pin	00	05	06
Cart and whells	03	03	00
On[e] bridle	00	02	00
Two oagers and warrow hoe	00	04	00
On[e] plow	00	09	00
Horse kind at	08	10	00
On[e] pair of oxen	08	00	00
4 cows and a calf	13	15	00
On[e] Sow and 4 pigs	02	00	00
6 Sheep and 4 lambs	03	00	00
Sheets 2 pillow bears & a towell	01	15	06
Half a dozen napkins 2 table cloaths	00	14	00

The homestead with the buildings	160	00	00
11 ackers of meddow	28	00	00
Tottall	£271	00	06

Camb. May 19, 1712

NATH: HEALY
PHILLIP WHITE
ROBERT MURDOCK

Invy: Exhd: May 19, 1712	£270— 0— 0
real estate	188— 0— 0
personal	83— 0— 0
Tottall debts	25—12— 2
	£57 7 10

"An account of debts payed by Experience Chamberlan which was dew from her late husband Jacob Chamberlan's Estat that is deceased with his ffunerall Charges:

	£	s	d
Payed to Nathaniel Hollis	00	07	06
to Phillip Whitt	00	08	00
to Doctor Shadick	00	07	04
to Nathaniell Hollie	00	02	06
to Robert Murdock	00	05	00
to Robert Murdock	00	06	00
In Small debts	02	03	05
In Rats [rates]	02	04	00
In funerall Charges	07	11	08
To John Stapels	06	00	00
Daniell Chamberlan	00	08	00
to John Ward	00	03	00
The tottall Sum is	20	07	02
payed mor to doctor Wheett	1	15	00
	22	2	2

An Account of what debts apeared to be dew from the Estate of Jacob Chamberlaine who deceased: Aprill the: 11: 1712

Funerall Charges	05	11	02
In other depts	08	18	04
tottall	14	9	06

After 1715 the widow Experience Chamberlain m. (2) one of the Jonathan Dykes (Dike) of Newton. Her grave-stone standing on the west side of the old Central Cemetery at Newton Center reads as follows: "Here Lyes ye Body of Mrs. Experience Dyke wife to Mr Jonathan Dyke who Died May 24 1749 Aged 83 years 2 months & 2 Ds. She was Formerly wife to Mr Jacob Chamberlain who Died April 11 1712 By Whome she had 5 Sons All living at her Death." In the settlement of Jacob Chamberlain's estate the Judge of

Headstone

Footstone

GRAVESTONES OF EXPERIENCE CHAMBERLAIN DYKE, 1666-1746, NEWTON

Probate wrote May 16, 1715, a memorandum of these children's names as follows: "Jacob, John, William, Jason, Ebenezer" and this tomb stone shows that they were all living in 1749. The stone also shows with exactness that Experience was b. presumably March 22, 1666, or thereabouts. She was admitted to the First Church of Cambridge March 26; 1699, as "Goody" Chamberlain. After years of search no evidence has been found showing who her parents were, but I conjecture that she was the daughter of Joseph and Experience (Foster) French who were married at Billerica, Nov. 4, 1663, and whose first recorded child Elizabeth was b. there July 16, 1668. It is assumed by me that Experience was an elder daughter b. two years earlier and perhaps not in the Billerica settlement, at least not recorded on the Billerica town records with the children of Joseph French.

It may be of interest to state that Jonathan Hyde Jr. of Newton, from whom Jacob Chamberlain purchased his homestead in 1699, was the son of Mary French and the grandson of Lieut. William French, one of the nearest neighbors to, and earliest settlers with, William Chamberlain in Billerica. These people were not strangers to each other by any means.

Children, all by wife Experience:

15 i JACOB[3] CHAMBERLAIN, JR., b. at Medford, Feb. 19, 1691/2.

16 ii JOHN[3] CHAMBERLAIN, b. probably in Cambridge about 1694; bapt. there at the First Church July 18, 1697.

17 iii WILLIAM[3] CHAMBERLAIN, b. about 1697; bapt. in the First Church of Cambridge, July 9, 1699.

18 iv JASON[3] CHAMBERLAIN, b. at Newton, Feb. 26, 1701.

19 v EBENEZER[3] CHAMBERLAIN, b. at Newton, July 31, 1704.

6 THOMAS[2] CHAMBERLAIN (*William*[1]) b. at Billerica, Feb. 20, 1658/9; d. at Newton, before Nov. 2, 1724. He m. at Cambridge, April 18, 1682, Elizabeth, daughter of Thomas and Elizabeth (Stedman) Hammond of Newton. She was b. Nov. 3, 1664, and d. at Newton Feb. 1, 1733. Nathaniel Hammond of New Cambridge (Newton) for "a valuable price"—deeded Thomas Chamberlain of the same place a wood-lot in New Cambridge, whereon "he hath erected a barn and house, bounded north by the highway leading from New Cambridge to Muddy River (Brookline) July 6, 1688. (*Middx Deeds*, 12: 666). Tho: Chamberlain was taxed on one person and estate at New Cambridge alias Little Cambridge (Newton) Sept. 5, 1688. (*New England Historical Genealogical Register*, 31: 306) In 1693 and 1694 he purchased land in Newton of Isaac and Ann (Kenrick) Hammond. In 1695 he was executor of the will of John Clark of Newton. He was surveyor

Thomas Chamberlin Constable

of Newton 1689, 1690, and constable 1698 and 1699. He was a fence viewer there 1712, 1715 and 1716. On March 3, 1698/9, he paid £21 : 12 : 07 in full of his part of the Meeting house rate. Elizabeth Chamberlain the widow, was appointed administratrix of her husband's estate, Nov. 2, 1724, and John Greenwood, weaver, and Eleazer Hammond, yeoman, all of Newton were her sureties. Her first account was allowed June 2, 1726. The inventory was taken Oct. 23, 1724, including his house and barn and about three-fourths of an acre on which the barn stands valued at £50; 12 acres of orchard and pasture land £150; 15 acres of woodland and swamp £40; and personal estate £141 : 04 : 06. Before the estate was settled the administratrix died, and Sept. 23, 1734, the Judge of Probate appointed a commission to appraise the real estate of Thomas Chamberlain late of Newton dec'd and the real estate of Elizabeth Chamberlain (late widow of Thomas) who is now also dec'd and to distribute the estate among the heirs. The last valuation was as follows:

One dwelling house and 17 acres adjoining being the estate of Elizabeth Chamberlain	£492—00—00		
Old barn and one half acre being the estate of Thomas Chamberlain	£35	10	00
Sawmill meadow in Brookline—3 acres—the estate of Elizabeth Chamberlain	£45	00	00
Woodlot—16 acres—the estate of Thomas Chamberlain valued at	£54	05	00
Total	£622	15	00

Division.

To Phillip Chamberlain and Elizabeth Chamberlain (heirs of Thomas Chamberlain late of Boston, decd) eldest son of Thomas Chamberlain late of Newton the south part of the house lately built with three acres £149—07—00, which with £40 advanced to Thomas Chamberlain of Boston by his father makes his double share £189—7—00

To Sarah Chamberlain wife to Eleazer Chamberlain, dec'd's youngest daughter the back part of the house with three acres £94—13—06

To the heirs of Mary Chamberlain deced's third daughter, who is deceased since we received this Commission, 8 acres of woodland being westerly half (easterly half set off to Elizabeth Ireland) £27—02—06

Also 2 acres in the home lot 67 11 00

To Elizabeth Ireland wife of William Ireland ye decd eldest daughter £27 02—06

Also 3 acres in the home lot 67 11 00

To Rebecca Adams wife of Daniel Adams ye decd's second daughter saw mill meadow £45 00 00

Also 2 acres in the home lot £49—13—06

To John and Elizabeth Chamberlain heirs to John Chamberlain decd the youngest son to the decd the barn and barn lot £31 10 00

Also 2½ acres of the home lot £63 03 06

Dated at Newton Jan. 7, 1734/5 (*Middx Probate Files*, 4206)

Children all born at Newton:

20 i THOMAS³ CHAMBERLAIN, JR., b. Sept 10, 1683.

21 ii ELIZABETH³ CHAMBERLAIN, b. Aug. 1, 1686.

iii REBECCA³ CHAMBERLAIN, b. March 11, 1689; m. Daniel Adams of Cambridge, who rented the Thomas Chamberlain meadow in Brookline May 4, 1737. (*Brookline Records*, 648)

iv MARY³ CHAMBERLAIN, b. Feb. 11, 1693; d. there Dec. 10, 1734. She did not marry Isaac Hammond as Jackson stated in his *Hist. of Newton*, but died a "single-woman".

22 v SARAH³ CHAMBERLAIN, b. Oct. 18, 1695.

23 vi JOHN³ CHAMBERLAIN, b. Sept. 26, 1698.

7 EDMUND² CHAMBERLAIN (*William*¹) b. at Billerica, July 15, 1660; d. there after July 28, 1740. On Jan. 8, 1682, the selectmen of Billerica "at the same time did order that whereas Edmond Chamberlain by order of yᵉ County Court was ordered to submitt himselfe to yᵉ government of yᵉ select[men] of this town they do order him yᵉ said Edmond Chamberlain to live with his master Joseph Walker for yᵉ space of six moneths next ensuing after the manner of a journey man to attend family orders and government therein acording to law. Also not to make any bargain with any man without his masters approbation and at the end of six moneths as aforesaid to declare to the selectmen where he intends to reside and what course of life he intends to lead and his master engageth to have speciall inspection unto his said servant in yᵉ said interim and to inform yᵉ selectmen in case he cannot Keep him to good order and diligence" (*Hazen*, 195). It is evident that a young man in colonial times had no rights whatever but to obey superiors. Sergt. Foster, surveyor in the south east part of the town, was ordered "to warne to cut bushes two days Edman Chamberlaine" Nov. 19, 1677. (*Billerica Town Records*). He took the oath of fidelity Feb. 4, 1677. On Jan. 4, 1685, he was one of the forty persons in arrears for their rates due Rev. Samuel Whiting, his arrearage being £00: 04: 06. Aug 14, 1688, he was taxed on one person and one cow 1s. 11d. (*Hazen*, 194).

He m. at Billerica or Woburn Aug. 26, 1691, Mrs. Mercy Abbott, widow, of Woburn. (*Woburn Marriages*, 33). She d. at Billerica Feb. 27, 1697/8. He lived in Groton from 1705 to 1707, and on July 9, 1707, was about to remove from that town on account of the Indians. He m. (2) Abigail ——. He, or another man of the same name, m. at Reading, Jan. 17, 1717, Sarah Furbush of Reading. He was living in Billerica Sept. 15, 1718, at which time he was a witness in court.

Clement Chamberlain of Billerica, for £7 deeded Edmund Chamberlin of Groton 21 acres in Billerica on the west side of Concord River, Nov. 28, 1709, but the deed was not acknowledged till April 11, 1716. (*Middx Deeds*, 22: 439) He was in Capt. Joseph Blanchard's Co. Aug. 30 to Oct. 29, 1725, when he resided in Reading. (*Mass. Archives*, 91; 169) In Capt. William

Chandler's Co. posted at Rutland in 1724. (91 : 126[a]) Abraham Chamberlain of Brookline for £5 deeded Edmund Chamberlain of Groton land in Billerica containing 17½ acres upon the Pine Plain between the Mill Pond and John Trull's meadow; also 4¾ acres on the west side of the Great Pond called the Mill Pond, Nov. 4, 1706. This deed was acknowledged by Abraham Chamberlain June 28, 1728. (*Middx Deeds*, 28 : 154) In 1664 the town of Billerica granted "seaventeen acres of land be it more or less lying upon a pine plaine betwene y[e] mill pond and Jo[n] Trulls meadow called Jeiffs Cove" unto William Chamberlain, and in 1685 there was granted unto him "four acres and three quarters of land lying on the west side of our great pond called y[e] mill pond." Thus two of the grants to William Chamberlain were sold within six months of his death by Abraham Chamberlain of Brookline to his brother Edmund Chamberlain of Groton and Billerica. Edmund Chamberlain of Billerica, husbandman, for £50, deeded Timothy Fletcher of Concord, husbandman, the same property which Clement Chamberlain deeded him, "with a dwelling house and barn standing thereon," Feb. 5, 1729/30 (*Ibid.* 31 : 143), and Timothy Fletcher of Billerica deeded this back again Jan. 6, 1730/1 (*Ibid.* 32 : 438). Edmund Chamberlain of Billerica, husbandman, for £60 deeded Clement Chamberlain of Billerica, husbandman, the identical property on the west side of the Concord river in the first range containing 21 acres and five poles July 19, 1740, which had been originally deeded to him by Clement Chamberlain, Sr. Nov. 4, 1706. Clement Chamberlain, the grantee, was his nephew and he acknowledged this deed, July 28, 1740, at Billerica. This is the last mention of him on record and he probably died soon after this date, as he was then a little more than 80 years of age. In all these transfers his wife is not mentioned and there was no settlement of his estate. As he sold his property when he was eighty years of age to his nephew, I conjecture that his children were not then surviving.

Children by wife Mercy born in Billerica:

i HANNAH[3] CHAMBERLAIN, b. June 10, 1692.

ii EBENEZER[3] CHAMBERLAIN, twin, b. Feb. 17, 1697/8; d. there March 5, 1698/9.

iii MARAH[3] CHAMBERLAIN, twin, b. Feb. 17, 1697/8;

Child by wife Abigail:

iv ELIZABETH[3] CHAMBERLAIN, b. at Groton, Aug. 18, 1705.

Perhaps there were other children whom I have not identified as such.

8. REBECCA[2] CHAMBERLAIN (*William*[1]) b. at Billerica Feb. 25, 1662/3; death not recorded at Billerica. She m. (1) at Watertown, June 20, 1688, Thomas Stearns son of John Stearns of Billerica. He was b. at Billerica Dec. 6, 1665, and d. there Feb. 9, 1696/7. She m. (2) at Billerica, July 14, 1699, George Farley son of Caleb and Rebecca (Hill) Farley of Billerica. He was b. there July 30, 1677, and d. there before Aug. 17, 1733, when his inventory was taken. John Stearns and Sergt. John Shed, executors of the

will of Thomas Stearns late of Billerica, deeded Rebecca Stearns now the wife of George Farley of Billerica in consideration of a covenant with them to bring up and educate the young children of the deceased, the mansion or dwelling house of Thomas Stearns with 4 acres of orcharding, March 2, 1701. This deed was acknowledged by his brother John Stearns and the other executor, Jan. 11, 1706/7. (*Middx Deeds*, 14: 199) Rebecca Farley, supposed to be the wife of George Farley, was a grantor, May 31, 1727, (*Ibid.* 44: 372) but she did not sign this deed with the other heirs.

Children all born in Billerica by first husband:

i REBECCA[3] STEARNS, b. Apr. 23, 1689.
ii MARY[3] STEARNS, b. June 18, 1692; m. Benj. Frost.
iii SARAH[3] STEARNS, b. Apr. 27, 1694; m. Jan. — 1720/1, Joshua Child of Weston, Mass.
iv HANNAH[3] STEARNS, b. Aug. —, 1696.

Children born in Billerica by second husband:

v LYDIA[3] FARLEY, b. about 1700.
vi ANNA[3] FARLEY, b. Apr. 29, 1702.
vii ENOCH[3] FARLEY, b. July 23, 1704; d. Aug. 17, 1723.
viii ESTHER[3] FARLEY, b. May 31, 1707; m. Jonathan Baldwin.

To these children Hazen added another daughter Rebecca Farley who m. at Billerica, Jan. 8, 1733/4, Daniel Shed. Some doubt exists about the parentage of this Rebecca Farley and I do not wish to assign her to this family without some evidence in the case.

9. ABRAHAM[2] CHAMBERLAIN (*William*[1]) b. at Billerica, Jan. 6, 1664/5; d. after June 28, 1728. "Abraham Chamberlin of Brookline for £5 deeded Edmund Chamberlin of Groton land in Billerica viz. 17½ acres upon the Pine Plain between the Mill Pond and John Trull's meadow and 4¾ acres on the west side of the Great Pond called the Mill Pond, Nov. 4, 1706. He acknowledged this deed June 28, 1728" (*Middx Deeds*, 28: 154) The witnesses were Oliver Whiting, George Farley and John Chamberlain and a comparison of the bounds shows that these were two of the identical lots which the town of Billerica had granted to William Chamberlain in 1664 and in 1685 (*Billerica Land Grants*). "Abraham Chamberlain of Newtown, planter, and Elizabeth his wife for £15 deeded Thomas Hammond of Newtown, husbandman, all that our piece or parcell of woodland in Cambridge on the south side of Charles River [Newton] Jan. 23, 1692/3. Acknowledged by him Oct. 15, 1718. (*Middx Deeds*, 21: 148). In the account of Constable Chamberlain, reported to the town of Billerica in a "publick towne" meeting Oct. 9, 1673, Abraham Chamberlain contributed one bushel of Indian corn valued at 03^{s} towards ye last year rates. He took the oath of fidelity at Billerica Sept. 8, 1681. "Abraham Chamberlain and Elizabeth his wife were married at New Town March 9, 1691/2", by James Trowbridge, Clerk of ye Writts for New Town. He m. (2) at Watertown, Feb. 24, 1697/8, Mary

Randall of Watertown. He was one of the petitioners to have Muddy River (Brookline) set off from Boston, Aug. 13, 1704. He removed from Newton to Brookline about 1695. He was a surveyor of "highwayes" for "ye District of Muddy River" for 1704/5. (*Boston Record Commissioners Report*, 1700–1728, 33) He d. probably before May 17, 1734, on which day the town of Brookline "voted to abate the rates of Abraham Chamberlain for the last year and two years past".

Children, the first born in Newton and the second in Brookline:

24 i ABRAHAM[3] CHAMBERLAIN, b. Oct. 16, 1693.

25 ii ELIZABETH[3] CHAMBERLAIN, b. Feb. 11, 1697.

It seems probable that there were other children especially by the second wife but my analysis fails to identify them positively.

iii ELEAZER[3] CHAMBERLAIN, bapt. at Brookline, Dec. 10, 1721; perhaps a son of this union. (See p. 117)

10. CLEMENT[2] CHAMBERLAIN (*William*[1]) b. at Billerica, May 30, 1669; d. there after May 22, 1732 and before Dec. 23, 1741. Clement Chamberlain of Billerica for £200 deeded his son William Chamberlain of Billerica 40 acres on the west side of Concord river in Billerica "it being one half of my homestead where I now dwell, April 25, 1732 (*Middx Deeds*, 35: 610). Clement Chamberlain of Billerica "for love that I have for my son William Chamberlain of Billerica and other good causes" deeded him 35 acres on the west side of Concord river in Billerica bounded on the west by the said William Chamberlain's land with all buildings thereon standing, but "the said William Chamberlain is not to be in the possession of the above said land and premises till after my decease and my wife's". This deed he signed May 1, 1732, and acknowledged both May 22, 1732. (*Ibid.* 35: 612) He mortgaged this farm March 2, 1714, and again Feb. 13, 1720, and the mortgage was released by the hands of his son William Chamberlain April 12, 1732. (*Ibid.* 21: 267) His other transfers of small lots were made between 1709 and 1725. These data show that he and his wife were living on May 1, 1732, at which time he was about 63 years of age. He m. about 1692 Mary ——— who was the mother of all his children. She m. as his third wife Dr Roger Toothaker who d. Mch 9, 1745/6.

Children all born in Billerica of wife Mary:

i MARY[3] CHAMBERLAIN, b. Jan 20, 1692/3; probably m. at Newton, Feb. 11, 1716, Isaac son of Isaac and Ann (Kenrick) Hammond of Newton. He was b. there July 31, 1698, and removed to Lebanon, Conn. where they lived 1721 to 1727: she left distinguished descendants.

26 ii CLEMENT[3] CHAMBERLAIN, JR, b. in 1694.

27 iii JOSEPH[3] CHAMBERLAIN, b. in Nov. 1696; removed to Conn.

iv JOHN[3] CHAMBERLAIN, b. June 8, 1699; d. in June 1716.

v PEGE (PEGGE)[3] CHAMBERLAIN, b. March 12, 1701/2. Her correct name was probably Margaret.

28 vi WILLIAM[3] CHAMBERLAIN, b. March 23, 1703/4.

vii REBECCA[3] CHAMBERLAIN, b. April 14, 1705; m. at Lebanon, Conn., Dec. 12, 1727, Samuel Gridley. She and her husband were living Oct. 14, 1754, when her brother Joseph Chamberlain as her attorney signed a receipt for her interest in her father's estate, which her brother William Chamberlain had not settled in his life time. (*Middx Probate*, 4207)

viii ANNA[3] CHAMBERLAIN, b. May 29, 1708.

ix ELIZABETH[3] CHAMBERLAIN, m. about 1724 Joseph Kemp of Billerica and they were living, there Mch 6, 1754.

William Chamberlain's Estate (1738).

"Billerica, March ye 6, 1754.

Then Received our full share out of our Honored mother Mary Toothacre's movable estate and the Twenty Pounds which our Honored father Clement Chamberlin ordered our brother William Chamberlin deceased to pay to us and do hearby discharge our sd Brother William Chamberlin's Heirs in full of all Dues or Demands as witness our hands

Joseph Kemp
Elizabeth Kemp, her mark"

11. DANIEL[2] CHAMBERLAIN (*William*[1]) b. at Billerica, Sept. 27, 1671; living there as late as Nov. 22, 1725. The town of Billerica granted him six acres of land on the west side of Fox's Hill *during his natural life* on May 15, 1704. He also had four acres more granted on the same day, "but he is not to dispose of this land." Hence upon his death it reverted to the town. He was evidently not possessed of property, for Dec. 17, 1701, the record shows "loss in ye Town rate by Daniell Chamberlin 00 01 06." The town treasurer was ordered to pay to him Sept. 1708, £01 08: 06; Nov. 25, 1709, £01: 03: 00; 1710, £01: 07: 00; Nov. 10, 1712, £01: 10: 00; and Dec. 19, 1716, £01: 10: 00. In later years he appears to have been sexton of the Meeting House, as the town paid him for sweeping it Nov. 9, 1722, £01 05 00; 1723 £01: 05: 00 and Nov. 22, 1725, £00: 12: 06, which is the latest reference that I found to his name in the town records. He had no deeds recorded, and there was no settlement of his estate in Middlesex County. In the account of debts paid by Experience Chamberlain which were due from her late husband Jacob Chamberlain of Newton, "Daniell Chamberlain" received £00: 08: 00. He m. about 1694, Mary —— who was living in 1713.

Children born in Billerica excepting Mary who was born in Wilmington:

29 i ISAAC[3] CHAMBERLAIN, b. Aug. 3, 1695; Hazen incorrectly gave Daniel for Isaac.

30 ii EBENEZER[3] CHAMBERLAIN, b. Sept. 5, 1698; if the town clerk of Billerica recorded his name correctly I have failed to trace him. In his stead I find Eleazer Chamberlain who may, or may not, be identical. (See p. 116).

31 iii EPHRAIM[3] CHAMBERLAIN, b. Jan. 16, 1700/1.

32 iv THOMAS[3] CHAMBERLAIN, b. Aug. —, 1703.

v MARY[3] CHAMBERLAIN, b. Feb. 25, 1706; m. at Billerica, Dec. 1, 1732, Jonathan Cram, son of John and Sarah Cram of Wilmington, Mass. Their daughter Elizabeth Cram was b. at Wilmington Nov. 4, 1741. About 1742 they removed to Lyneborough, N. H. Her tombstone indicates that she was born in 1706. Hazen stated that Jonathan Cram m. Mary the daughter of Clement Chamberlain of Billerica but the latter was born thirteen years earlier than this Mary Chamberlain was.

vi DOROTHY[3] CHAMBERLAIN, b. Dec. 25, 1713; perhaps she was the Dorothy Chamberlain whose marriage intention to Samuel Newhall was recorded April 1, 1736. (*Essex Inst. Coll.* 18: 240)

THIRD GENERATION

12. JOHN[3] CHAMBERLAIN (*John*[2], *William*[1]) b. at Billerica, Jan. 22, 1684/5; d. there March 3, 1722/3. He m. at Concord, "march y[e] 13: 1709/10", Margaret "*Gould*" of Billerica, daughter of Samuel and Mehitable (Barrett) "*Goole*" of Dunstable, Mass. She was b. May 26, 1687, and was living at Billerica as late as March 8, 1725/6. The *Gould* Genealogy (1895) p. 315 is in error in stating that she m. as above stated "Joseph" Chamberlain. The original records of both Concord and Billerica show that she married *John* Chamberlain. On April 2, 1723, Margaret Chamberlain, widow, with Nathaniel Hudson as surety, gave bond to administer upon the estate of her late husband John Chamberlain late of Billerica, deceased. The inventory was taken, April 22, 1723, and among the items are mentioned: "About 22 acres of upland with a small dwelling house upon it £46: 00: 00"; "One old Bible and three other Books 00: 06: 00", etc. (*Middlesex Probate*, 4165).

Children all born in Billerica:

i JOSIAH[4] CHAMBERLAIN, b. Aug. 27, and d. Sept. 6, 1710.

ii JOHN[4] CHAMBERLAIN, b. and d. May 26, 1711.

iii ANNA[4] CHAMBERLAIN, b. April 3, 1712; m. at Billerica, March 27, 1735, John Willoughby, who was b. Dec. 25, 1707; lived in Billerica southeast of Nutting's Pond till 1743 when they moved to Hollis, N. H. where he d. Feb. 2, 1793. Their descendants are numerous.

33 iv JOHN[4] CHAMBERLAIN, JR., b. March 28, 1714.

v DEBORAH[4] CHAMBERLAIN, b. Aug. 9, 1716.

34 vi SAMUEL[4] CHAMBERLAIN, b. April 22, 1719; removed to Union, Conn. and later to Petersham, Mass.

vii MEHITABLE[4] CHAMBERLAIN, b. Nov. 12, 1721; m. as second wife, May 1, 1740, William, son of Jonathan and Rachel (Stone) Butterfield; lived in Arlington, Mass. Her husband's step-mother was Elizabeth daughter of Thomas, Jr., and Sarah (Proctor) Chamberlain of Chelmsford. (*One Branch of Descendants of Thomas Chamberlain*, p. 9.) She m. (2) June 6, 1770, Samuel Locke. (*Locke Genealogy*).

13. LYDIA[3] CHAMBERLAIN (*John*[2], *William*[1]) b. at Billerica, Oct.

6, 1689; m. at Concord, Mass., "Oct ye 22: 1711", Benjamin Parker son of Benjamin and Mary (Trull) Parker of Billerica. He was b. at Billerica, Oct. 26, 1689. They removed from Billerica about 1735.

Children all born in Billerica:

i LYDIA[4] PARKER, b. March 12, 1712.
ii BENJAMIN[4] PARKER, b. Sept. 17, 1720.
iii SARAH[4] PARKER, b. May 12, 1724.
iv MARY[4] PARKER, b. Oct. 12, 1726; m. Simeon Jefts.
v ROBERT[4] PARKER, b. July 13, 1730.

14. ABRAHAM[3] CHAMBERLAIN (*John*[2], *William*[1]) b. at Billerica, April 17, 1693; d. there before Dec. 25, 1739. He m. at Woburn, July 23, 1718, Mary daughter of Nathan and Mary (French) Shed of Billerica. She was b. there June 22, 1697, and m. second as his second wife June —, 1742, John Wilson son of John and Elizabeth (Foster) Wilson of Billerica. John Wilson was b. there Dec. 26, 1695 and m. (1) Jemima daughter of John and Sarah (Chamberlain) Shed of Billerica. She d. Sept. 14, 1740, and John Wilson m. as above the widow of Abraham Chamberlain, who was a cousin to his first wife and not her sister as Hazen stated on p. 130. Abraham Chamberlain's wife was not his cousin. Abraham Chamberlain of Billerica for £125 deeded his honored father-in-law Nathan Shed of Billerica land in Billerica bounded east by the highway, west by the land of Dea. Samuel Hill, north by land of Samuel Hill, Jr., and partly by the Burying place and south by the land of John Needham, Henry Jefts and highway. He and his wife Mary signed this deed, April 11, 1732. (*Middx Deeds*, 37 : 645) Therefore, he m. Mary daughter of Nathan and not Mary daughter of John Shed as Hazen stated. In the settlement of Abraham Chamberlain's estate (*Middx Probate*, 4132) by his widow Mary two inventories were taken, the first Dec. 25, 1739, and the second Dec. 23, 1741. By the inventory his homestead consisted of 100 acres lying on the west side of Concord river in Billerica bounded on the south by the land of Benjamin Shed, east on the Concord river, north on the land of Jonathan Hill and Samuel Hill and partly by the land of Clement Chamberlain's Heirs, (*sic*) north by the land of Henry Jefts and Jefts Pond so called, west and south by the land of Edward Farmer, with the buildings thereon standing valued at £260. The heirs agreed upon the division of the estate June 15, 1742—The estate was divided Aug. 17, 1747, between the widow, now the wife of John Wilson, and six children, Abraham the eldest son having a double portion and Benjamin, John, Tabitha, Mary and Nathan, the youngest son, having equal shares. On Nov. 16, 1747, John Chamberlain was ordered to pay to the assignee of his brother Abraham deceased and to the assignee of the widow deceased the portions which had been set off for them. Thus the homestead passed into the possession of John Chamberlain.

Children all born in Billerica:

i MARY[4] CHAMBERLAIN, b. Dec. 28, 1718; d. young.

ii ABRAHAM[4] CHAMBERLAIN, b. Aug. 25, 1720; d. between Dec 27, 1742 and Nov. 16, 1747.

iii BENJAMIN[4] CHAMBERLAIN, b. Oct. 18, 1722; d. between Dec 27, 1742 and Jan. 20, 1745/6.

35 iv JOHN[4] CHAMBERLAIN, b. March 19, 1724/5.

v NATHAN[4] CHAMBERLAIN, b. March 18, 1726/7; d. between Dec 27, 1742 and Jan. 25, 1747.

vi ZACCHEUS[4] CHAMBERLAIN, b. Sept. 19, 1729; d. before Dec. 27, 1742.

vii TABITHA[4] CHAMBERLAIN, twin, b. Sept. 19, 1729.

viii MARY[4] CHAMBERLAIN, b. Oct. 16, 1734.

15 JACOB[3] CHAMBERLAIN (*Jacob*[2], *William*[1]) b. at Medford, Feb. 19, 1691/2; d. at Newton, Mass. July 28, 1771. He was the purchaser of the Chamberlain homestead of 120 acres at Oak Hill, Newton, of his mother and his brothers May 16, 1715, at which time he gave bond for £300 for the settlement of the estate. On Jan. 25, 1720, he deeded Ebenezer Woodward five acres of land in Newton "at a place commonly called the River Meadows," bounded on the south by the Charles River. In this deed his wife Susannah joined with him (*Middx Deeds* 21 : 239). May 11, 1720, he with others entered their dissent "aginst this voate of having but one schoole house in this towne" of Newton. (Smith's *Hist. Newton*, 243). On June 15, 1725, he was one of the witnesses at Newtown to the deed from David Stowell of Newtown to William Chamberlain "of Dover within the province of Main or Newhampshire." (*Middx Deeds*, 25 : 510). He was chosen surveyor of highways Mch 4, 1722/3; tythingman, March 1, 1724/5; constable March 1, 1731; constable March 1, 1735/6 and March 7, 1736/7; surveyor March 6, 1737/8; tythingman March 1, 1740/1: school constable March 5, 1743/4 and March 4, 1744/5; selectman March 3, 1745/6; fenceviewer March 2, 1746/7 and March 7, 1747/8. (*Town Records of Newton*) He m. about 1718, Susannah daughter of Dea. Simon and Sarah (Farnsworth) Stone of Groton, Mass. She was b. there Oct. 23, 1694, and d. at Newton, July 26, 1774. He deeded his son Simon Chamberlain of Newton for £160 one half of the homestead of 120 acres situated "at a place called Oak Hill" including "one half of the buildings and land where I now live" bounded by the road leading from Watertown to Dedham June 22, 1762. (*Middx Deeds*, 68 : 54). A few years later he made his will as follows:

IN THE NAME OF GOD AMEN this Tenth Day of March Anno Domini one thousand Seven Hundred and Seventy I Jacob Chamberlain of Newton in the County of Middlesex and Province of the Massachusetts Bay in New England Being far Advanced in Years and Knowing the Uncertainty of this Life here on Earth am Desirous While My Memory is Sound and Perfect to Settle My affairs and Therefore Have and by these Presents Do, Renouncing all Other and former Will or Wills by me Made Do Make and Declare this My Last Will and testament in Manner and form following: (that is to Say) first and Principally I Recommend My Soul to Almighty God who Gave it and My Body to the Earth to be Buried in Such Decent and Christian Manner as my Youngest Son Simon Chamberlain Whom I Name Constitute and Ordain Sole Executor of this my Last will and testament Shall Judge Meet and Convenant, and touching Such Worldly Goods as the Lord in his Great Mercy hath Lent me My Will and Meaning is that the Same be Imployed and Disposed of in Manner and form following:

Imprimus: I will that all my Just Debts and funeral Charges be paid by my Executor out of my Estate Within Twelve Months after my Decease, and all Debts that May be Due or Owing to me from any Person or Persons Whomsoever be Demanded by my Executor.

I give to my Well Beloved Wife Susannah Chamberlain all the Income of all my Estate Both Real and Personal together with the one half of My Buildings During her Natural Life that I have not Conveyed to My Youngest Son Simon Chamberlain her fire wood Like Wise to be Cut and Brought home to the Door fit to Lay on to the fire by My Youngest Son Simon Chamberlain without his having any Consideration therefor and after her Decease the Same to be Disposed of in Manner and form following:

My Will and Meaning is that my Eldest Son Jacob Chamberlain have out of my Estate the Sum of One Hundred and Six Pounds Thirteen Shillings and four Pence, Besides what he May have Received of me in times past. The Remaining Part of my Estate both Real and Personal to be to my two Daughters Sarah and Margaret Chamberlain to be Divided Equally Between them together with my In Door Movables.

My Will and Meaning further is that after my Wifes Decease my two Daughters Sarah and Margaret Chamberlain have the Improvement of the Chamber in that part of the House I now Dwell in as Long as they Shall Remain unmarried or the house Shall Remain un-Sold.

My Will further is that my Grand Son Josiah Chamberlain have a Lot of my Land in the Last Division in the town Ship of New Marlbrough.

I Likewise Give to his Brother John Chamberlain and to his Sisters Mary Simpson and Susannah Chamberlain the Sum of Six Shillings Each to be paid to them Within twelve Months after my Wifes Decease.

My Will further is that my Grand Children Isaac and Mary Chamberlain have Paid unto them the Sum of Six Shillings Each, Within twelve Months after my Wifes Decease.

My Will further is that my five Cows and One Horse be Improved by my Wife Susannah Chamberlain During her Natural Life and at her Decease to Dispose of the Same as She Shall think Best.

My Will further is that all my Out Door Movables be to my Youngest Son Simon Chamberlain Without his Rendering any Accompt therefor. I Like Wise Give to my two Sons my Wearing apparrel and Arms.

Signed Sealed Pronounced and Declared By the testator to be his Last Will and Testament In Presence of us

JOHN WILSON
SAMUEL RICHARDSON JACOB CHAMBERLAIN [SEAL]
ANNA WILSON

Simon Chamberlain presented this will for probate Sept. 10, 1771. (*Middlesex Probate*, 2776)

Inventory taken July 1, 1772, by Jonas Stone, John Palmer and Jeremiah Wiswell as follows:

	£	s	d
"Part of a Dwelling House and part of Barn and Well	20	00	00
Sixty Acres of Land part Orchard part plow land part Medow and part Woodland	240	00	00
Nine pair of Sheets 21/ Seven Napkins 6/	01	07	00
Four pillow cases 3/8 One table Cloth 8d ——	00	04	04
Best Bed and furniture in the Chamber	03	15	00
Sarah's Bed (so called) and furniture	02	10	00
Bed in the Chamber 1/10 Chest of Drawers 7/ old chest 2/8 - - - -	01	19	08
Oval Table 6/ Square Table 1/ Eight Chairs 16/ Andirons and tongs 6/	01	09	00
Two Looking glasses 7/ little Wheel 4/ Small Box 1/	00	12	00
Bed in the lower Room and furniture £3 Chest of Drawers 8/	03	08	00
Small Chest of Drawers 4/ Six Chairs 4/ Settle 4/ Warming pan 4/	00	16	00
Mettle pot and Dish Kittle frying pan 10 Andirons and tongs	01	00	00
Two Trammels and Lamp and fire Shovels 9/8 Iron Scellet 2/	00	11	08
Toasting Iron 1/6 Bellows 4/ Spit 3/ Seven Pewter Dishes £1:1:4	01	09	10
Eleven pewter plates 7/4 two basons 4/ Two small Ditto 1/4	00	12	08
Two pewter porrangers 1/ Tankard 1/ Pewter Quart 2/	00	04	00
Old Tubs and Earthern Ware 7/ Two Brass Kettles £1—12	01	19	00
Bible 12/ Large Books 6/ Sundrie Small Books 7/	01	05	00
Two Silver Spoons 10/ Box iron and heater 5/	00	15	00
Quick Stock	15	04	00
	£299	02	02

Exhibited by Simon Chamberlain, the executor, to Samuel Danforth Judge of Probate, July 7, 1772.

Children all born in Newton:

36 i JACOB[4] CHAMBERLAIN, JR., b. Nov. 28, 1719.

37 ii JOSIAH[4] CHAMBERLAIN, b. Nov. 13, 1721.

iii SUSANNAH[4] CHAMBERLAIN, b Sept. 27, 1724; d. Feb. 23, 1748/9, "in ye 25th Year of her Age"; buried by the side of her grandmother Experience Chamberlain-Dyke in the old Central Cemetery at Newton Center.

38 iv ISAAC[4] CHAMBERLAIN, b. April 6, 1728.

v WILLIAM[4] CHAMBERLAIN, b. Sept. 22, 1730; m. at Newton, June 20, 1754, Anna Hyde; d. there of the small pox Dec. 9, 1760. He was corporal in Capt Jonathan Brown's Co., Col. William Williams's Regt. Apr. 14 to May 24, 1758 (*Mass. Arch.* 96: 409)

vi SARAH[4] CHAMBERLAIN, b Sept. 19, 1733; m. at Newton, March 28, 1786, Richard Sanders.

vii MARGARET[4] CHAMBERLAIN, b. Sept. 20, 1736; m. at Newton, June 6, 1771, James Ryan of Roxbury.

39 viii SIMON[4] CHAMBERLAIN, Sept. 5, 1739.

16. JOHN[3] CHAMBERLAIN (*Jacob*[2], *William*[1]) [b. about 1694] bapt. at Cambridge, July 18, 1697; d at Weston, Mass., May 19, 1781, aged 87 years. He was a "cordwainer", and settled in Charlestown before 1719. On Dec. 10, 1734, he was appointed keeper of the "Goal" in Charlestown, and Dec. 9, 1735. the treasurer of the Province of Massachusetts paid him for keeping the Goal. Jn° Chamberlain was paid for keeping French prisoners in Middlesex Goal £13 : 11 : 06 between May 30, 1744 and May 29, 1745. He was also paid for keeping French prisoners in the Goal at Charlestown £115 : 04 : 11 between May 28, 1746 and May 27, 1747. He also received £38 : 08 : 03 in June 1748. (*Province Treasurer's Account—Mass. Archives* 124: 14, 193, 317) Clement Chamberlain, Jr., of Billerica deeded him a pasture in Billerica June 2, 1741 (*Middx Deeds* 41 : 520). In 1736 he joined with the other heirs of Nathaniel Wilson in deeding a house on Fish Street in Charlestown. In 1741/2 he bought a lot on Main Street, Charlestown, of the executors of Thomas Call, and at the same time purchased land adjoining to Jonathan Call and others. Here was his home until Charlestown and his home were burned June 17, 1775. About 1802 or 1803 one of his grandsons wrote in his family record as follows: "At the time of the Battle of Bunker Hill and the burning of Charlestown I together with my mother, sister and younger brother Joseph forsook the town never more to return; crossed over to Malden in scow-loads and was left destitute on the shore with neighbors, women and children. . . . A good old lady, the widow of a former minister of the town took us in and was very kind to us. . . . In a few days a man, a relative of mine from Hopkinton came by my father's request and carried the family to Holliston. I was put to a relation in that town and my brother Joseph to another relative at Westborough—ten or twelve miles from me." He did not name his relatives in Holliston and in Westborough, but to one who has studied all the migrations of the Chamberlain families the statements are of great historical value as they identify John Chamberlain of Charlestown as the son of Jacob Chamberlain of Newton.

He m. about 1718, Thankful daughter of Nathaniel and Thankful (Beaumont) Wilson of Charlestown. She was b. Dec. 20, 1693, and was admitted to the First Church of Charlestown, April 28, 1717. She d. Aug. 26, 1764, being in the 71st year of her age. He m. (2) at Charlestown, Dec. 4, 1764, Milicent Rand, who was living at Charlestown, Oct. 1, 1783. The inventory of his estate shows that he was poor—made so by the Revolution. His son Willson Chamberlain came over from Holliston to Cambridge to administer upon his estate, and the inventory mentions for real estate one house lot in Charlestown. His kindred were scattered—Charlestown was in ruins—and at the age of 87 years he went over to Weston, where death relieved him of his poverty and misery.

In the Name of God Amen I John Chamberlain of Charlestown in the County of Middlesex & Province of the Massachusets Bay in New England Cordwainer being now advanced in Years, yet throh the Goodness of God in Health of Body & in the free exercise of my Understanding and considering the uncertainty of this Life after having committed my Spirit into the Hands of my dear Redeemer hopeing to obtain Mercy only throh Him & my Body to the Dust to be buried in a decent and frugal Manner at the Discretion of my Executors hereafter named in Hopes of a Resurrection to immortal Life & Glory Do (in order that my Estate may be disposed of agreeable to my Mind) make & ordain this my Last Will & Testament

Imprs My Will is that my just Debts & funeral Charges be paid by my Executors as soon as conveniently can be done after my Death out of such a part of my Estate as I have not in this Will particularly disposed of.

Item I Give unto my beloved Wife Melecent Chamberlain for ever all the House hold Stuff & every thing she brought with her at our Marriage & what ever may be due or belonging to her on the account of her late Husband Jonathan Rand's Estate, & if the above should not be sufficient to make a full Third of my personal Estate Then my Will is that the Deficiency be made up out of what was mine before our Marriage. Also I Give my said Wife over & above what I have already will'd her my best Silver Spoon, three of my best pewter plates & one pewter Dish. Further I give my said Wife during her Life the use and Improvement of the South Easterly lower Room in my mansion House & the Shop & the Liberty of using the Well & the necessary House as Occasion may require & the privilege of putting half a Cord of Wood at a Time in my Wood House.

Item. I Give to my Son Willson Chamberlain his Heirs & Assigns forever, the two North Westerly lower Rooms in my House above-mentioned with the Cellar under the back Room & the privilege of going thro the back Entry & the little back Shed, Also the North Westerly part of my Garden running back thirty seven Feet from the House just so as to take in a Damasen Tree, and said Land is twenty two Feet wide next the House & Twenty one Feet wide at the Bottom. Also I give my said Son his Heirs & Assigns the privilege of carrying any thing through the Yard & using the Well & puttinge half a Cord of Wood at a Time into my above mentioned Wood House. Also I give my said Son all my wearing Apparel.

Item I Give the Children of my Son John Chamberlain deceased, to be equally divided as much of the Remainder of my Real Estate as five Men, four chosen by them & the fifth by the four shall judge to be equal in value to what Real Estate I have given my Son Willson—The Garret over the Room given to my said Son Willson is to belong to the other End of my House.

Item My Will is that all the Remainder of my Real & personal Estate not before given away be equally divided between my Children or their Heirs in the following manner viz[t] my Son John's Children one quarter, Son Willson one quarter, the Children of my Daughter Thankful Larkin deceased one quarter, my Daughter Anne Phillips one quarter, my grand Children to be equal in the part of their Father or Mother.

Item My Will is that the part of my Real Estate I have given my Wife during Life be after her Death divided in the same manner as above mention'd That is to say one quarter to my son John's Children one quarter to my Son Willson one quarter to my Daughter Thankful's Children one quarter to my Daughter Anne Phillips.

Item My Will is That if the Real Estate I have given to my Children and Grand Children can[t] be divided That in that Case the same be Sold & the Neat proceeds divided among them in the abovesaid proportion. The Reason why I have not made my Daughter Thankful's Children & my Daughter Anne equal with my other Children is because of what I did for them at their Marriage.

Item My Will is That if any of my Son John's Children or the Children of my Daughter Thankful should be under Age at my Death or the Death of my Wife That my son in law Nathaniel Phillips Husband of my above named Daughter Anne take the whole Care of their part of my Estate & Improve it for their Use till they come of Age.

Lastly I Constitute & appoint my Son Willson Chamberlain & Son in Law Nathaniel Phillips above named to be the Executors of this my Last Will & Testament, hereby Revoking all former & Confirming this only to be my Last Will & Testament. In Witness whereof I the said John Chamberlain have hereunto set my Hand & Seal this eighteenth Day of May in the Twelfth Year of His Majesty's Reign & in the Year of our Lord Christ One thousand Seven hundred & Seventy two

Signed Sealed & Delivered by the Testator John Chamberlain to be his Last Will and Testament in Presence of us who in

John Chamberlain

his Sight & at his Desire
Signed our Names as Witnesses

Nehemiah Rand — Lodged Sept 3, 1783
Thos Rand — Proved Oct. 1, 1783."
Seth Sweetser — (*Middx Wills* 4171)

Oct 1, 1783 By virtue of the within citation I have notified the Heirs of Mr. John Chamberlain Deceased to appear at Cambridge the 1st of October
Viz the widow of the Deceased at Charlestown
Nathll Phillips & wife at Marlborough
John & Nathll Chamberlain & Thankful Smith at Salem
Mary Steel & Mary Groves at Boston
The widow Chamberlain at Boston
Joanna Larkin at Westborough
Thomas Rand Witness of the will of the Deceased at Charlestown
Cambridge October 1st 1783.

[Signed] WILLSON CHAMBERLAIN

Children all born in Charlestown:

i THANKFUL[4] CHAMBERLAIN, b. July 20 bapt July 26, 1719; d. there Oct. 13, 1724.
40 ii JOHN[4] CHAMBERLAIN, b. May 8 bapt May 14, 1721.
41 iii WILLSON[4] CHAMBERLAIN, b. Sept. 24, 1724.
iv THANKFUL[4] CHAMBERLAIN, b. Oct. 12 bapt. Oct. 15, 1727; m. at Charlestown, Jan. 12, 1748, Joseph Larkin; she d. before 1783.
v ANN[4] CHAMBERLAIN, b. Nov. 8, bapt. Nov. 22, 1730; d. young.
vi ANN[4] CHAMBERLAIN, b. Jan. 21, bapt. Jan. 23, 1731/2; admitted to the First Church in Charlestown, Dec. 7, 1755; m. at Charlestown, June 21, 1757, Nathaniel son of John and Alice (Brigden) Phillips. He removed to Marlborough; she d. at Barre, Mass., Aug. 1815, aged 82 years.
vii MARGARET[4] CHAMBERLAIN, b. Sept. 4, bapt. Sept. 8, 1734.

17 WILLIAM[3] CHAMBERLAIN (*Jacob*[2], *William*[1]) was born in the part of old Cambridge which is now Arlington, about 1697, and was bapt. at the First Church of Cambridge, July 9, 1699; d. at Rochester, N. H. between April 23 and May 30, 1753; learned the carpenter's trade in Boston; was admitted to the First Church of Boston, April 29, 1716. He removed to Dover, N. H., as early as 1718 or 1719. Here let the Dover Land Grants tell the story:

"Wharas Capt. Samuell Tebbets of Dover had three Score Acres of Land Laid outt to him on the north side of ye path yt Leades to barbadus in the year 1713 and the Sd Samll: Tebbets hath and doth quit his Clame to 40 Acres of that Laiing out and Clames but twenty acres thereof which his Sone In Law William Chamberline is Setteled upon and wee ye Subscribers by and Att the Request of ye above Sd Tebbets and Chamberline to measuer and Lay Out the Said 20 acres of Land wee begun as folloeth att a beach tree markt S. T. And from Thence west nor west north wardly 60 Rods to another beach markt S T Standing on the north Side of ye path that Leads to barbadus Leauing about 8 or 10 rods Betwen y^t^ bound mark and John Cukes(?) fence for a highway from Thence north an[d] by East 55 Rods to an Aspe tree Standing in a Swamp markt S T and from thence East South East 60 Rods to a hemlock tree marked S T and So on a Straight Line To the tree whare we first begun all which 20 Acres of Land is Laid out and bounded the 7 day of Februarey 1720/1 by us

THOMAS TEBBETS
JOSEPH ROBERTS
(*Dover Book of Land Grants* 131) ISRAEL HOGDON

Nov. 16, 1724, William Chamberlin of Dover, N. H., "Joyner," deeded Joseph Twombly of Dover, cooper, for £150 thirty-two acres at a place called Littleworth in Dover, 20 acres of it bounded by a highway that leads to a place called Barbados, west by Jno. Cookes land, together with "all ye Edifices & Houses" whatsoever. This deed was acknowledged Mch 30, 1725 (*N. H. Colonial Deeds* 22 : 443). At "Littleworth" William Chamberlain lived from 1719 to 1724—about five miles west of the compact part of the settlement of Dover and when Lovewell's war was on he returned to Newton, Mass. "Daniel Stowell of Newtown within his Majesty's Province of Massachusetts Bay in New England" for £190 deeded "William Chamberlain of Dover within the province of Main or Newhampshire", "Joyner", a tenement with 39 acres in Newton, June 15, 1725. (*Middx Deeds* 25 : 510). William Chamberlain was dismissed from the First Church of Boston to "ye chh in Newton" Apr. 20, 1727. (*Transcribed First Chh Records of Boston*, 196). At a town meeting in Newton he was chosen tithingman, March 4, 1727/8 (*Newton Town Records*). March 1, 1728/9, he deeded his Newton home to Thomas Brown of the same town (*Middx Deeds* 32 : 356). March 13, 1728/9, William Chamberlin "of ye Town of Newtown, In ye Prov^e^ : of ye Mass^ts^ Bay In N-Engl^d^ Joyner" purchased for £88 of Samuel Canney of Dover 10 acres "on Dover Neck joyning to ye fore River Comonly so Called being part of my homes^d^ or tenement where I now dwell." (*N. H. Colonial Deeds*, 20 : 282)

William Chamberlain of Dover, "joyner", for £100 deeded John Bickford Jr. of Dover land "toward ye uper End of Dover Neck being part of that lott of land on which my Dwelling house Now Stands." This deed he signed Nov. 7, 1732, and acknowledged it May 20, 1734. On the former date John Bickford of Dover, husbandman, for a like consideration deeded William Chamberlain of Dover, "joyner", land in Rochester—one whole share granted unto said Bickford "Being ye 1st division 15th lot & 2d Division ye 104th lot as also ye just proportion of ye undivided land in s^d^ Rochester Belonging to ye s[d] Share." This was evidently an exchange, as both deeds were signed and acknowledged on the same date. (*Ibid.* 20: 219). He moved to Rochester before July 30, 1733, and on that date Pomfret Whitehouse of Rochester sold him 60 acres "being ye 47th lot In ye first Division of said Rochester which I purchased of Nath[l] Hanson of Dover." (*Ibid.* 20: 218) He "preferred" a petition for the support of the gospel at Rochester to the General Assembly of New Hampshire Jan. 9, 1733/4 (*N. H. Provincial Papers*, 4: 798) He petitioned for the gospel ministry of Rochester to be aided by the proprietors of the township, April 26, 1736 (*Ibid.* 9: 722). He and John Jenness both inhabitants of Rochester petitioned for further relief from the non-resident proprietors Feb. 13, 1741. When the St. Francis Indians attacked the town June 27, 1746, they passed near his home, and on July 1, 1746, he joined with the entire settlement in a petition for a guard of soldiers (*Ibid.* 9: 725). He was chosen constable of the town March 20, 1738/9; and selectman 1743, 1745, 1750 and 1751. He was town clerk in 1745, and the records for that year are well written. On July 9, 1751, the town left with "Lieut. William Chamberlain" a sum of money for safe keeping. Rev. Amos Main in his account book as physician, charged "Lieut. William Chamberlain" for medical attendance. No military record of him has been found but it is assumed that he was a Lieut. of some company engaged in scouting and guarding the town. He was admitted to communion in the First Church of Rochester Feb. 12, 1741. In 1745 he "desired forgiveness for all offences past that he had given and the church by a great majority voted him forgiveness."

He m. about 1719 Mary daughter of Capt. Samuel and Dorothy (Tuttle) Tebbetts of Dover. She was admitted to the First Church of Dover Mch 3, 1723. She was born about 1700 and was living at Rochester in 1760. She was admitted to membership in the First Church of Rochester Jan. 7, 1741; and after withdrawing from the communion she was restored May 11, 1744. William Chamberlain and his wife were buried in the old Cemetery on Meeting House Hill in Rochester. The inscriptions on their stones have become illegible. He built two houses on his farm, both on the west side of the main road leading from Meeting House Hill to Central Square. Both houses had disappeared before 1830. An old well and two cellars are the only witnesses to one of the original settlers of Rochester who cleared up and occupied from 1733 to 1753, a large farm there.

WILL

In the Name of God Amen this 23d day of April Anno Domini 1753 I Willaim Chamberlin of Rochester In the Province of New Hampshire In New England Husbandman being exercised with Bodyly Infirmities but of a Sound & Perfect mind and Memory Knowing it is appointed for all Men once to Die do make this my Last Will & Testament that is to Say Principally & first of all I Recommend my Spirit into the hands of God that gave it & my Body I recommend to the Earth to be buried in a Decent Christian Manner at the Discretion of my Executor hereafter mentioned & as Touching such worldly Estate as it hath Pleased God to Bestow upon me I Give Demise & dispose of the Same in the following manner Viz[t]—

Imprimis My Will is that my just Debts & funeral charges Shall be Paid & Discharged by my said Executor.

Item I Give to my Beloved Wife Mary Chamberlin the free full & Sole use & Improvement of the easterly half Part of my Dwelling house & the use of such a Part of the Cellar under said house as She Shall have occasion of for her own Service and the westerly half Part of my Barn for her own use together with Such a Privilege of the floor in said Barn as She Shall have occasion of to thresh her Grain During the Term of her Continuing my widow. I also Give to my said wife the free full & Sole use & Improvement Profit & Income of thirty acres of my homestead Land viz—Beginning at the North Easterly End of my said homestead Land from thence Running Southwesterly as my said Land Runs adjoyning to the South Easterly side Line of my said Land Seventy one Rods & Twenty Seven Rods in Weadth & from that extent of Seventy one Rods Running North Westerly on a Square with the side Lines of my said homestead Lot of Land to the North west side Line of my said Lot & from thence Running South Westerly as said Lot Runs holding the whole weadth of said Lot Untill the said thirty acres Shall be Compleated my Will that my said Wife Shall have the free use & Improvement Profit & Income of the Aforesaid thirty acres of Land Yearly & Every Year until my Youngest Son Ephraim Shall arrive at the age of twenty one years & from that Term my will is that my said Wife Shall have the Improvement Profit & Income of But twenty acres of the aforesaid Land Viz. which Twenty acres of it She Shall Chuse During the Term of her Continuing my widow. But in as much as my said Dwelling & Barn & my orchard are Comprehended within the Limits of the aforesaid thirty acres of Land my Will is that my son William Chamberlin Shall have the free Liberty of Passing & Repassing over said thirty acres of Land to & from my said Dwelling & Barn to and from my other Land when and so Often as he Shall have accation So to do & also that he my said son William Shall have the fruit of the Southwesterly third part of my said Orchard Yearly & every Year. I also Give to my wife to her own Disposal all my household Goods & Utensils Beds Beding & furniture & all my Live Stock of Cattle Sheep & Swine & my Riding horse except one Yoke of Stears now about two Years old which I give to my Son Samuel when he Shall arrive at the age of twenty one Years & also one Yoak of Stears for each of my Sons Viz Jacob & Ephraim Chamberlin to be Raised from the Stock of Cows which I have Given my said Wife & to be Delivered

To my said Sons Jacob & Ephraim when they arrive at the age of twenty one years. My Will also is that my said Sons Samuel, Jacob & Ephraim Shall have one Cow or Cowkind each Delivered them by my said Wife when they Shall arrive at the said age of Twenty one Years.

I also Give to my said Wife all my farming Tackling & Utensils as Yokes Chains Plows Sleads &c. I also Give my said Wife the free Liberty of fetching firewood Sufficient to support her own fire from off my Lot of Land which I have herein Given to my Son Eben^r: Chamberlin during her Natural Life.

Item I Give to my Son William Chamberlin & to his heirs and assigns forever all my homestead Land Dwelling house Barn & all Other Buildings & Orchards Stand^g: & Being upon said Land except such Part of said Land Buildings & Orchards as I have herein & hereby Given the free use & Improvement of to my wife for a Certain Term of Time & at the Decease of my said Wife I give the aforesaid Land Buildings & Orchards wholly free & Clear of all Incumberances to him my said son William & to his heirs & assigns forever. I also Give to my son William the free and full Liberty of Halling Timber or Logs off that Part of my Lot In the Second division in said Rochester which Lyeth on the South West Side of Cochecho River with one Team for the term of two Years next after my Decease.

Item I Give unto my Son Ebenezer Chamberlin & to his heirs & assigns forever my Lot of Land Lying & Being in the first Division in said Rochester which I Purchased of Pomfret Whitehouse which Lyeth Between Samuel Richards Lot & the Lot on which the Widow Rebecca Heard now Lives being the Lot of Land on which my said Son William Chamberlin hath built a Dwelling house & made Considerable Improvement together with the said Dwelling house & all other Buildings & Privileges Belonging to the said Lot of Land except the Liberty & Privilege which I have herein given to my Wife of fetching firewood for her own fire from said Lot. I also Give to my said son Ebenezer the Liberty of halling Timber or Logs off that Part of my Lot of Land in the Second Division In said Rochester which Lyeth on the South West Side of Cochecho River with a Team for the Term of one Year next after my Decease.

Item I Give unto my Son Samuel Chamberlin & to his heirs and assigns forever all that Part of my said Lot of Land in the Second Division in said Rochester which Lyeth on the North Easterly Side of Cochecho River & also one Yoke of Stears & a Cow or Cow-kind as is Before herein Mentioned.

Item I Give unto my Sons Jacob & Ephraim Chamberlin & to their heirs & assigns forever all that Part of my said Lot of Land in the Second Division in said Rochester which Lyeth on the South West side of Cochecho River with all the Privileges to the Same Belonging except the Privilege I have herein Given to my Sons William & Ebenezer of halling Logs off that Part of said Lot for a Certain term of time. I also Give to my said Sons

Jacob & Ephraim Viz. to each of them a yoak of Stears & a Cow or Cow-kind when they shall arrive at the age of twenty one Years as is Before herein mentioned. I also Give unto my said Sons Jacob and Ephraim & to their heirs & assigns forever all my Land Lying & Being in the third Division In said Rochester & all my Rights and Title in & unto all the undivided Lands in said Rochester to be equally Divided Between them as is also all the Land which I have herein Given them jointly or Together.

Item I give unto my Daughters Mary Door, Rebecca Trickey Experience Knowls, Dorothy Emerson & Anna Leighton forty Pounds old Tenor a Piece or forty Pounds to each of them to be paid to them or their Heirs by my said Executor at the following Periods, Viz. Twenty Pounds to each of them or their heirs within the Term of one Year after the Decease of my said Wife & the other twenty Pounds to each of them or their heirs within the Term of two years after the Decease of my said Wife.

And I do hereby nominate Constitute & Ordain my said Son William Chamberlin to be my Sole Exec[r]: of this my Last Will & Testament & I do also hereby utterly Revoke Disallow & Disannul all & every Other Will or Wills Testament or Testaments by me in any way heretofore made Ratifying & Confirming this & no other to be my Last Will & Testam[t]:

In Testimony whereof I do hereunto Set my hand & Seal the day & Year first above Written.

Signed Sealed pronounced & Declared by the said William Chamberlin to be his Last Will & Testament in Presence of us Witnesses
Thomas Brown
John Mighell
Samuel Whitehouse

N. B the word *house* was interlined Before Signing and also the word *my*.

William Chamberlin [Seal]

At a Probate Court held at Portsmouth, May 30, 1753, William Chamberlin Jr. presented this will which was probated.

(*Colonial Probate Records of New Hampshire* 12 : 445)

Children all by wife Mary:

i MARY[4] CHAMBERLAIN, b. at Dover Oct. 26, 1720; bapt. there Feb. 12, 1721; received into the church at Rochester by dismissal from Dover Oct. 25, 1750. She m. before April 23, 1753, as second wife Henry Door of Rochester who removed to Lebanon, Maine, where he d. Jan. 25, 1792, aged 78 years.

ii REBECCA[4] CHAMBERLAIN, b. at Dover, Dec. 28, 1722; bapt. there Feb. 10, 1723; m. before Oct. 3, 1742, John Trickey Sr. of Rochester. She d. there about 1815, aged 93 years.

42 iii WILLIAM[4] CHAMBERLAIN, b. at Newton, Mass. July 6, 1725; d. at Lebanon, Maine, Dec. 15, 1815, aged 90.

iv EXPERIENCE[4] CHAMBERLAIN, b. at Newton, July 26, 1727; m. at Rochester as third wife, May 30, 1751, Dea. James Knowles, paymaster in the Revolutionary war. She was the mother of eleven children.

43 v EBENEZER[4] CHAMBERLAIN, bapt. at Dover, May 25, 1729; living in New Hampton, N. H., Nov. 6, 1790.

vi DOROTHY[4] CHAMBERLAIN b. at Dover March 7, 1731; bapt. there Mch 21, 1731; m. (1) at Rochester, Nov. 17, 1748, Samuel Emerson of Dover. She m. (2) at Rochester, Sept. 20, 1801, Jeremiah Berry of Rye, N. H. She d. Feb. 18, 1825.

vii ANNA[4] CHAMBERLAIN, b. about 1733; m. at Rochester, Dec. 19, 1751, David Leighton of Rochester.

44 viii SAMUEL[4] CHAMBERLAIN, b. at Rochester Nov. 3, 1735; bapt. there Jan. 13, 1736; remained there till death.

45 ix JACOB[4] CHAMBERLAIN, b. at Rochester May 18, 1738; settled at Alton, N. H.

46 x EPHRAIM[4] CHAMBERLAIN bapt. at Rochester Feb. 14, 1742; The New Hampshire Patriot reads as follows: "Died at Alton, Feb. 14, [1814], Capt. Ephraim Chamberlain, aged 72. A philanthropist and a Christian."

The author of this genealogy is descended from both the eldest and the youngest sons of this family.

18. JASON[3] CHAMBERLAIN (*Jacob*[2], *William*[1]) born at Newton, Mass. Feb. 26, 1701; d. at Holliston, Mass. May 30, 1770. He was a "joyner", "housewright" and "husbandman" and about 1730 removed from Newton to Holliston where he was a large land-owner having 1800 acres in Holliston. He m. (1) at Newton, May 5, 1725, Hannah daughter of Samuel and Elizabeth (Crafts) Clarke of Brookline (*Crafts Genealogy*, 47). He m. (2) Elizabeth —— who was living when he made his will June 18, 1768. She entered her int. of m. at Shrewsbury, May 16, 1776, with Daniel Drury of Shrewsbury who d. there June 5, 1786. Her death has not been found. He contributed towards finishing the public Meeting House in Holliston Jan. 5, 1728. (*Suffolk Co. Court Files*, 28988) At the time of his death he was called "Lieut. Jason Chamberlin". He named his two eldest sons for his old schoolmaster at Newton, Dea. John Staples who bequeathed to each £100 when they became of age (*Crafts Family*, 47). Mr Staples was their great uncle and left no children. He was ensign in Capt. Samuel Bullard's Holliston Foot Co. in 1757. (*Mass. Archives*, 95 : 306)

In the Name of God Amen I Jason Chamberlin of Holliston in the County of Middlesex and within his Majesties Province of the Massachusetts Bay in New England yeoman being favored with some degree of health of Body and of a Sound mind and memory praised be god therfor Calling to mind the mortality of my Body and being apprehensive that the time of my departure is at hand and being willing that the little that god has pleasd to bestow upon me of Temporals not yet desposed of might be setled Do make and ordain this my preasant last will and Testiment on this the Eighteenth

Day of June ano: domini 1768 and in the ninth yeare of his Majesty Reign Georg the third of Great Briton King &c

1st that is to say principaly and first of all I give and Recomend my Soul into the hands of the Lord Jesus that Gave it and my Body to be buried in desent Criston Buriall at the Descresion of my Executor Nothing Doubting but that at the General Reserection I shall Receive the Same again by the mighty power of god and as touching fore mentioned Temporals I give demise and dispose of the same in the following maner and form

First I will that my funaral charges and debts should be paid

Secondly I give and bequeath my well beloved wif the improvement of the East end of my Dwelling hous except in the Rome where the oven is my son Enoch is to injoy the lik priveledge with her farther mor all my improved lands South of my Dwelling Hous upon the East Side of the Roade Leding by my Dwelling hous to Mendon begining at s[d] Enoch's shop So Runing by the fence before the dore to the Barn then following the fence Easterly; to the bridg that leads onto the island in the *Seader* Swamp all my improvements southerly hereof with one half of the Barn to wit the North half with Conveniancy of pasing and Repasing too and from it as allso Convency about the s[d] house for a wood pile and to the well likewise six acres in my wod lot Adjoining westerly To the land[s] of thomas Goold Late Dec[sd] viz the South part of it all and Singerly that I have above bequeathed to my wife is to continue dureing her Naturall Lif and imeadatly after her decease is to Come into the poseson of my Son Enoch. Item I also give to my s[d] wif Eliz Two Cows and one Swine the one half of my indore movables and forty pounds oald teno out of my nots of hand or mony Due to me after my lawful Debts and Funarl Charges are all paid furthermore it is my will that my Son Enoch find her a hors and the free liberty of the Cheare when she is Disposed and abel to goo to meting or upon any other Nesseccary ocasion. Item I give to my said wif a fre pass and repass to above s[d] wod lot bequeathed

Item I give to my Son John the following peice of land To him and his Heirs forever above that I have heretofore Given him viz a peace in the Seder Swamp bounded westerly upon the northeasterly Corner of the bridg leading from my hous on to the Islands in s[d] Swamp begining at s[d] bridg's Corner and thence Runing to a white oak marked thence as far as my land Extends Northeast then begining again at sd Corner of s[d] bridg and Runing Easterly By ceas way Till It Come to an Island thence till it Come to the senter Line in s[d] Swamp by the North side of sd Island To wit all my Lands East and North of sd Bounds likewise five acor of my wod lot lying westerly of my Hous To wit on the North Side of s[d] Lot ajoining To sd Johns own Lands To him and his heirs for Ever furthermore My will is that after my Debts and funaral Chargs are paid and my a Bove s[d] wife has Received her Doury out of the money or Nots of hand due to wit the forty pounds oald tenor my will is then that the Remainder if any there be Should be devided Equaly between my three Sons to wit John and Staples and Samuel

Item I give all the Remainder of my Lands hereto fore not yet mentioned with the buildings to my Son Enoch and to his Heirs and asigns forever furthermore I will that my Sone Enoch have the Riding Chare and harness In order for my Said wife's Bennefete or priveeledg: moreover I Call to mind that it is my will that my wife have free Recors to the above bequeathed wod lot furthermore I will that the Remainder of my live Stock and other movabels together with my wairing Aparil be Equaly Divided amongst my four Sons Item furthermore I give to my Sone Enoch and his heirs and asigns forever after my wif's Decease that part of my Reall Estate above bequeathed to her to him and his heirs forever furthermore it is my will that my Son Enoch pay unto his three bretheren to wit John and Staples and Samuel Tene pounds Lawful money apeace within one year after my wifes Deceace.

Item I constitute make and ordain my son Enoch my sole Executor of this my Last Will and Testement and I Do hereby utterly Disalow revoke and disanul all and Every other Former Will and Testement Confirming this and no other to be my Last Will and Testement Lastly I order all my lawful Debts and funaral Charges to be paid by my Executor. In witness whereof I have hereunto Set my hand and Seal the Day and year above first Ritten

Signed Sealed Published pronounced declared by me the Said Jason Chamberlin As his Last Will and Testement in the presence of us the Subscribers

JOSEPH LOVERING
THOMAS TENNEY
CRAFT LOVERING

Lodged June 25, 1770 by ye Executor (*Middx Probate*, 4154)

Children by wife Hannah:

47 i JOHN^{4} CHAMBERLAIN, b. at Newton, Sept 6, 1728.
48 ii STAPLES^{4} CHAMBERLAIN, b. at Newton or Holliston, Sept. 1 or 2, 1730.
49 iii JASON^{4} CHAMBERLAIN, JR., b. at Holliston, March 8, 1732; d. there, Jan. —, 1754.
50 iv SAMUEL^{4} CHAMBERLAIN, b. at Holliston, July 18, 1734.
51 v ENOCH^{4} CHAMBERLAIN, b. at Holliston, Nov. 18, 1737.
vi ELIZABETH^{4} CHAMBERLAIN, b. at Holliston, Feb. 26, 1739/40; d. there March 13, 1739/40.
vii EBENEZER^{4} CHAMBERLAIN, b. at Holliston, Aug. 19, 1741; d. without issue.

19. EBENEZER^{3} CHAMBERLAIN (*Jacob*^{2}, *William*^{1}) b. at Newton, Mass. July 31, 1704; d. at Westborough, Mass. after May 7, 1779. William Johnson of Southborough, yeoman, for £250 deeded Ebenezer Chamberlain of Westborough, husbandman, 100 acres in Westborough July 26, 1735.

(*Worcester Co. Deeds*, 7 : 420). The church records of Westborough under date June 3, 1736, read : "Ebenezer Chamberlain dismissed from the chh of Ch[t] in Newton was admitted to our communion." He m. (1) at Newton, Nov. 28, 1733, Mary daughter of Thomas and Mary (Goffe) Trowbridge of Newton. She was b. in Newton in 1712 and d. at Westborough, Feb. 1, 1756. (She was a sister to Edmund Trowbridge, a graduate of Harvard College 1728 ; attorney-general of Massachusetts 1749 to 1767 ; justice of the Superior Court of Judicature 1767 to 1775 ; loyalist 1775 to 1783 ; retired citizen of Cambridge 1783 to 1793 ; in his will dated Nov. 1791, he bequeathed five-sixths of his land in Sutton "to the children of my late sister Chamberlain.")

Ebenezer Chamberlain m. (2) at Southborough Dec. 23, 1756, Joanna Morse. Ebenezer Chamberlain, Sr. of Westborough for £200 deeded "my son" Daniel Chamberlain of Westborough, husbandman, 90 acres in Westborough "with the dwelling house and other buildings" bounded east on John Belknap, west on land of Jotham Bellows, south on land of Edmund Chamberlain. "It is to be understood that this deed is not fully to take place till after the decease of me the said Ebenezer Chamberlain." Signed by Ebenezer Chamberlain and Joanna Chamberlain, who surrendered her rights and dower of thirds, Jan. 9, 1778, and acknowledged Jan. 15, 1778. (*Worcester Co. Deeds* 76 : 253). He left no will on record and there was no probate of his estate as this deed disposed of his property. Rev. Ebenezer Parkman in his Diary (260) wrote Aug 8, 1780, "at eve Eben[r] Chamberlain Jun[r] full of earnest conversation about Sallery." By implication Ebenezer Chamberlain, Sr. was living on this date as the title Jun[r] (younger) would hardly have been used after the death of the Sr. Ebenezer. He was selectman of Westborough in 1766 and probably held town office in other years. Mr. Parkman wrote in his Diary, May 7, 1779 (126) "visited Mr. Chamberlain ; his son Daniel gave me half a bushel of Indian Corn and lent me a bushel and a half more." He was in Capt. Benj[n] Fay's Co. at Westborough, Apr. 1, 1757. (*Mass. Archives*, 95 : 244)

Children born in Westborough by wife Mary :

i Anna[4] Chamberlain, b. Jan. 13, 1734/5 ; d. there Jan. 18, 1756.
ii Nathaniel[4] Longly Chamberlain, b. July 1, 1736 ; d. Jan. 22, 1756.
iii Mary[4] Chamberlain, b. July 17, 1738 ; d. Jan. 27, 1756.
52 iv Ebenezer[4] Chamberlain Jr. b. Oct. 10, 1740.
53 v Edmund[4] Chamberlain, b. Aug. 20, 1742.
vi Lydia[4] Chamberlain, b. Feb. 21, 1744/5 ; m. William Brigham.
vii Martha[4] Chamberlain, b. Dec. 23, 1747 ; m. David Brigham.
54 viii Joshua[4] Chamberlain, b. March 1, 1749/50.
55 ix Daniel[4] Chamberlain, b. March 12, 1753 ; bapt. March 18, 1753.

Child born there by wife Joanna :

x Jonathan[4] Chamberlain, b. or bapt. there June 10, 1759 ; probably d. young.

20. THOMAS[3] CHAMBERLAIN (*Thomas*[2], *William*[1]) b. at Newton, Sept. 10, 1683; d. in Boston, before Nov. 7, 1721. He was a carpenter and removed from Newton to Boston about 1706. Elizabeth Snow wife of, and attorney for, Thomas Snow of Boston, fellmonger, for £60 deeded Thomas Chamberlain of Newton, housewright, a lot in the south end of Boston June 28, 1706. On June 29, 1706, he mortgaged this to Richard Keates of Boston, which mortgage was released, March 5, 1714 (*Suffolk Deeds* 23: 18). He mortgaged the same property a second time with the consent of his wife Hannah to Samuel Phillips of Boston, Aug. 29, 1717. Thomas Phillips administrator of the estate of Thomas Chamberlain paid the mortgage to the administrator of the estate of Samuel Phillips Dec. 28, 1723 (*Ibid.* 32 : 56). In the division of the estate of Thomas and Elizabeth Chamberlain of Newton Jan. 7, 1734/5, the commissioners apportioned "to Phillips Chamberlin and Elizabeth Chamberlin (the heirs of Thomas Chamberlin late of Boston dec'd) eldest son of Thomas Chamberlin of Newton the whole of the south part of the house lately built with three acres adjoining valued at £149 : 07 which with £40 advanced to Thomas Chamberlin of Boston by his father makes his double share £189 : 07" (*Middx Probate*, 4206).

He m. at Watertown, April 16, or June 22, 1709, Sarah Mason supposed by Bond to be the daughter of Joseph and Mary (Fiske) Mason, b. there Nov. 17, 1691. If so, she did not survive her husband and marry a second time John Bond as stated in *Bond's Watertown Genealogies*, p. 357. Sarah the wife of Thomas Chamberlin d. in Boston June 1, and was buried June 3, 1714. He m. (2) in Boston, Aug. 18, 1715, Hannah Welch widow of John Welch and daughter of Thomas Phillips of Boston. Thomas and Hannah Chamberlain were admitted to the First Church of Boston, Dec. 29, 1717, and three of their children were there baptized. Thomas Phillips of Boston, innholder, was granted administration on the estate of his son-in-law Thomas Chamberlain late of Boston, housewright, decd. Nov. 7, 1721. The inventory amounted to £548 : 01 : 10. (*Suffolk Probate*, 22: 263) The Selectmen of Boston wrote in their records Sept. 20, 1708: "Whereas Thomas Chamberline hath Lately cast the earth w[ch] he hath dugg out of his cellar into the High way before his House on Orange [now Washington] Street he being present hath liberty granted to lett the s[d] earth lie there for the present and is ordered by the Select men to remove the Same hereafter if the Same Shall *be found* hurtfull to y[e] sd High way. (*Boston Record Commissioners Report*, 1701 to 1715, 79) At a meeting of the Set. men April 29, 1714, "Liberty is granted to Thomas Chamberline to digg open the H. way in Orange Street for the Laying a Comon Shore from his house there down as farr as the sea : Provided that he lay the Same with Brick or Stone as the Law directs and that he forthwith make good Such part of the Street where he shall so digg and that in doing thereof he leave sufficient passageway for horse and cart."

(*Ibid.* 204.) "At a Meeting of y[e] Sel. men Feb[r] 4, Anno 1717 * * * Thomas Chamberlyn[s] Petition for Lycence to sell strong drink as an inholder at y[e] House known by y[e] Name of the White Horse allowed by y[e] Set. m." (*Record Commissioners Report of Boston*, 1716–1736, 32). The White Horse Tavern on Washington St. "at the South End" of Boston was nearly opposite where Hayward Place leads into the street. He was chosen a constable of Boston from March 12, 1716/7; and a viewer of shingles, boards, plank and timber Mch 14, 1719/20 and again March 14, 1720/1. He was elected a member of the Ancient and Honorable Artillery Company of Massachusetts in 1714. He was First Sergeant of the Artillery Company in 1721 when his death occurred. (*History of the Ancient and Honorable Artillery Company* I 386)

Children born in Boston by wife Sarah:

i ELIZABETH[4] CHAMBERLAIN, b. May 12, 1710.

ii SARAH[4] CHAMBERLAIN, b. March 13, 1712/3; bur. Sept. 16, 1714.

iii THOMAS[4] CHAMBERLAIN, JR. b. May 14, 1714; bapt. Mch 23, 1717/8; probably d. young.

Children born in Boston by wife Hannah:

iv PHILLIPS[4] CHAMBERLAIN, b. Sept. 28, 1716; bur. Apr. 8, 1718.

56 v PHILLIPS[4] CHAMBERLAIN, b. June 2, 1719; bapt. June 7, 1719.

57 vi THOMAS[4] CHAMBERLAIN, b. May 21, 1721; bapt. April 9, 1722.

21. ELIZABETH[3] CHAMBERLAIN (Thomas[2], William[1]) b. in Newton, Aug. 1, 1686; m. (1) at Newton, Aug. 8, 1717, George son of Daniel Allen. He made his will Oct. 13, 1718, and d. soon after, bequeathing his wife a small farm in Dorchester. She m. (2) July 26, 1722, William Ireland of Boston and d. about 1739. William Ireland m. (2) May 1, 1740, Mary (Wentworth) Scarlett, widow of Humphrey Scarlett. William Ireland made his will July 4, 1751, and it was probated May 23, 1755. In his will he bequeathed "to Brother Thomas Chamberlain Heirs and to Brother John Chamberlain Heirs and to Sister Adams and to Sister Chamberlain, a piece of land in Dorchester lying on the right hand as you go to the Paper Mills containing 19½ acres to be equally divided between them that is one quarter part to Thomas Chamberlin Heirs, one quarter part to John Chamberlain Heirs, one quarter to Rebecca Adams and one quarter to Sarah Chamberlain, to them forever." This property came to William Ireland by the death of his first wife Elizabeth (Chamberlain) Allen, it being the inheritance of her first husband George Allen. (*Suffolk Probate*, 50: 218) He was administrator of the estate of Thomas and Elizabeth Chamberlain of Newton in 1734, at which time his wife Elizabeth was living and received her share of her parents' estate Jan. 7, 1734/5. (*Middx Probate Records*, 2811). No attempt has been made to trace her descendants. She evidently had no descendants living on July 4, 1751, as they would have received William Ireland's bequest.

22. SARAH^{3} CHAMBERLAIN (Thomas^{2}, William^{1}) b. at Newton, Mass. Oct. 18, 1695; d. there April 9, 1754. She m. at Newton, Dec. 17, 1730, Eleazer Chamberlain of Brookline. They occupied the Thomas Chamberlain homestead in Newton which descended to her grandson John Thwing. Her share in the estate of her father and mother was valued at £94 : 13 : 06 which was set off to her Jan. 7, 1734/5. "For nursing and keeping" her sister Mary Chamberlain "in her last sickness" her husband returned to the Judge of Probate a charge of £1 : 12 : 06, March 28, 1737. (*Middx Co. Probate*, 2793)

Sarah Chamberlin

Eleazer Chamberlain, her husband, was bapt. at the First Parish of Brookline, Mass. Dec. 10, 1721, with Isaac Chamberlain called an "adult." To my mind this Isaac Chamberlain was the son of Daniel Chamberlain of Billerica as shown on p. 117. Eleazer Chamberlain's ancestry I do not *know* but I *believe* that he was either the son of Abraham Chamberlain, Sr., of Brookline, or the son of Daniel Chamberlain of Billerica and the grandson of the immigrant William Chamberlain. It is possible that in recording his birth the town clerk of Billerica wrote Ebenezer for Eleazer. (See p. 116 and 117) He m. (2) at Newton, Dec. 28, 1756, Abigail Chadwick who d. there May 25, 1760. He m. there (3) April 30, 1761, Patience daughter of Eleazer and Hannah (Harrington) Hammond of Newton. She was b. Sept. 8, 1717, and d. at Newton, Dec. 2, 1780. His will reads as follows:

IN THE NAME OF GOD AMEN I Eleazar Chamberlain of Newton in the County of Middlesex Yeoman being at the present writing hereof of a Sound and Disposing mind and memory, and desirous while I am so to set my house in order Do therefore make this my last Will & Testament in manner and form as followeth And first of all I Commend my soul into the hands of my Gracious redeemer and my Body I Commit to the Dust by a Decent Christian Funeral; And as to my worldly Estate or goods I will and dispose of them after the following manner Viz^{t}.

Imp^{rs} I Give unto Patience my well beloved Wife all the moveable Estate she brought to me at our Marriage, to be at her Own Disposal. I also give to her the said Patience the use and improvement of the remainder of my Household Utensils During her natural life (Excepting the provissions of all kinds, Cyder, Cyder Casks & Tubs, Gun Sword, Wearing Apparel &c) I also give to her the said Patience the improvements of that part of my Dwelling House I bought of the heirs of Thomas Chamberlain Deceased, During her natural life and in lieu of her Dower or thirds of my lands I give to her the following Articles Annually and to be provided and paid to her every year During her natural life by my Daughter Sarah Thwing Viz[t] two pounds Lawful Money in Cash One hundred and twenty pounds of good merchantable Pork, Sixty pounds of good merchantable Beef, ten Bushels of Indian Corn, three Bushels of Rye, two Bushels of Malt, One Barrel and a Half of Cyder, three Bushels of Apples, two Bushels of Turnips, half a Bushel of Potatoes, Seven Cord of fire wood reduced to Suitable lengths for the fire and laid within two rods of the Front Door of the House aforesaid, Also the Priviledge of passing and repassing from said House to the Road and to the Well and taking water out of the same, and also Convenient yard room near said House for laying fire wood. Also for my said Daughter to procure and keep for the use of my said wife During her natural life, One Cow a horse & Chair.

Item I have already paid so large sums of Money for my Daughter Elizabeth's Husband, Viz[t] Ebenezer Thwing, which amounts to my said Daughter's full Share out of my Estate notwithstanding, I give to her my said Daughter Elizabeth Thwing the sum of two pounds Lawful money to be paid her at the Decease of my said wife aforesaid, by my aforesaid Daughter Sarah Thwing.

Item I give and bequeath to my Daughter Sarah Thwing (the wife of John Thwing) her heirs & assigns forever all my Buildings and lands Lying in Newton aforesaid & in Brookline adjacent (excepting that part thereof that may be sold for the payment of my Just Debts & funeral Charges) but not to come into the Possession of my House aforesaid untill my aforesaid Wife's Decease. I also give to her the said Sarah all that remains of those moveables that I have given the improvement of to my wife aforesaid to come into possession thereof at my said wife's Decease. I also give to her the said Sarah all my other Estate of what kind or denomination Soever that I have not in these presents otherwise disposed off She providing and paying to my wife aforesaid as abovementioned. She also is to new Shingle & Clabboard the House aforesaid when my said wife shall think it needs the same. And if my wife be deprived of the priviledge of passing to the Cellar as has been usual through that part of my house that stands upon the land that came by my first wife, then for her the said Sarah to make a Convenient Stair way to pass Down the Cellar in the other part of the House.

Item I do hereby authorize & impower my Executor hereafter named to sell & alienate by a good Deed or Deeds of sale so much of my lands as shall be Sufficient to pay my Just debts and funeral Charges.

Finally I do hereby Constitute make and ordain Josiah Greenwood of Newton aforesaid Gentleman to be executor of this my last Will & Testament (he paying all my Just Debts & Funeral Charges) and I do hereby utterly revoke & disannul all former Testaments, Wills, Legacies and bequests Ratifying & Confirming this and no other to be my Last Will & Testament. In

WITNESS whereof I hereunto set my hand & Seal this Seventh Day of March A. D. 1769, and in the ninth year of his Majesty's Reign ~

Signed sealed published pronounced & declared by the said Eleazar Chamberlain as his last Will & Testament in the presence of us the subscribers

Eleazar Chamberlin

Abr Fuller
David Stone
John Stone

Probated by Josiah Greenwood adm[r] cum Testamento annexo Mch 6, 1770.

Children born in Newton all by wife Sarah:

i SARAH[4] CHAMBERLAIN, b. about 1734; m. Dec. 27, 1757, (int. Nov. 13, 1757) John Thwing of Cambridge and of Newton. He d. at Newton 1811 and she d. at Brighton, Oct. 18, 1818. They had thirteen children (Thwing Genealogy, 36).

ii ELIZABETH[4] CHAMBERLAIN, b. March 30, 1736; m. at Newton, July 8, 1756, Ebenezer Thwing of Cambridge and Charlestown, brother to her sister's husband.

iii JOHN[4] CHAMBERLAIN, b. Feb. 9, 1738/9; d. there Dec. 24, 1749, "in y[e] 11th year of his age"; buried at the foot of Experience Chamberlain-Dyke's grave.

23. JOHN[3] CHAMBERLAIN (*Thomas*[2], *William*[1]) born at Newton, Sept. 26, 1698; d. between June 25 and Nov. 5, 1722. He was a husbandman and m. about 1720, Elizabeth daughter of Joseph Champney of Cambridge (*Middx Probate*, vol. 17, p. 441). She probably m. (2) at Cambridge, June 22, 1726, Benjamin Winchester. His inventory was appraised Nov. 5, 1722, and Elizabeth his widow was appointed administratrix Dec. 17, 1722. Samuel Mirick of Newton, chairmaker, with Joseph Champney of Cambridge as surety was appointed guardian to their two children April 26, 1726. (*Ibid* 17: 441). This estate was finally settled June 2, 1742. The heirs of Thomas Hammond, late of Cambridge Village, deeded him four acres bounded by the land of Thomas Chamberlain, April 6, 1720. (*Middx Deeds* 21: 168). John Chamberlain of Newton, husbandman, was appointed guardian unto his niece, Elizabeth Chamberlain about 12 years of age, daughter of Thomas Chamberlain late of Boston, carpenter, deceased, June 25, 1722. (*Suffolk Probate*, 22: 576)

Children born in Newton:

58 i JOHN[4] CHAMBERLAIN, b. March 28, 1721.

ii ELIZABETH[4] CHAMBERLAIN, b. Oct. 15, 1722.

24. ABRAHAM[3] CHAMBERLAIN (*Abraham*[2], *William*[1]) born at Newton, Oct. 16, 1693; d. at Dedham, Mass., between Apr. 7 and the first Tuesday of July 1747. He was a "housewright" and lived in Brookline, West Roxbury and Dedham. He occupied a seat in the West Meeting House in Roxbury in 1725 (*Suffolk Court Files*, 27771). He m. at Watertown Oct. 26, 1716, Mary Whitney of Watertown. She was the daughter of Eleazer

and Dorothy (Ross) Whitney and was bapt. at Watertown Jan. 28, 1699/00. (*New England Historical Genealogical Register*, 11: 120). Jan. 15, 1744/5, Abraham Chamberlain of Dedham, housewright, for £37 : 10 deeded Samuel White, Esq., of Brookline land in "Brookline Marshes" bounded "west upon the Great Creek leading to Boston Bay" and one of the witnesses was Elizabeth Chamberlain (*Suffolk Deeds*, 80: 258). He and his wife Mary for £232 : 10 deeded Abraham Woodward of Brookline three lots in Brookline, the first containing four acres with a house and barn thereon. He signed this April 7, 1747, but John Harris a witness declared he saw the grantor "now deceased" sign the deed, which was thus acknowledged on the first Tuesday in July 1747. (*Ibid.* 75: 243). Aug. 25, 1747, administration on the estate of Abraham Chamberlain late of Dedham, housewright, was granted to his sons Nathaniel Chamberlain and Abraham Chamberlain both of Dedham, yeomen, and his inventory amounting to £846.00: 06 was presented to Probate court, Jan. 26, 1747/8. (*Suffolk Probate* 40: 102, 387) Mary wife of Abraham Chamberlain was received into the First Church of Dedham, May 30, 1742. April 19, 1748, Elizabeth aged about 19 and Dorothy aged 15, daughters of Abraham Chamberlain, late of Dedham, chose John Andrews of Dorchester, cordwainer, for guardian (*Ibid.* 41; 96, 97)

Children by wife Mary:

59 i NATHANIEL[4] CHAMBERLAIN, b. at Roxbury, Aug. 2, 1718; bapt. at the West Meeting House there, Aug. 3, 1718.

ii HANNAH[4] CHAMBERLAIN, b. at Dedham, March 31, 1720; bapt. at West Roxbury, April 3, 1720.

60 iii ABRAHAM[4] CHAMBERLAIN, 3d, b. at Dedham, Dec. 20, 1721.

61 iv MOSES[4] CHAMBERLAIN, b. at Dedham May 26, 1723; bapt. there Nov. 22, 1724.

62 v AARON[4] CHAMBERLAIN, b. at Dedham Jan. 12, 1724/5; bapt. there Jan. 24, 1724/5.

63 vi DAVID[4] CHAMBERLAIN, b. at West Roxbury, Dec. 18, 1726.

vii ELIZABETH[4] CHAMBERLAIN, bapt. at West Roxbury, March 16, 1728.

viii SARAH[4] CHAMBERLAIN, b. at Dedham, May 19, 1731; bapt. there May 23, 1731; d. Oct. 9, 1734.

ix DOROTHY[4] CHAMBERLAIN, b. at Dedham, May 24, 1733; bapt. there May 27, 1733.

25. ELIZABETH[3] CHAMBERLAIN (*Abraham*[2], *William*[1]) born at Brookline, Feb. 11, 1697; d. there, a "maiden", Dec. 26, 1778, aged 80 years. (*First Parish Church Records, Brookline, Historical Publications, No.* 6, p. 124) "Elizabeth Chamberlain of Dorchester, spinster, for £210 deeded Samuel White of Brookline, Esq. land in Brookline, one-third "that was my mother's land that my father Abraham Chamberlain now possesses," about 17 acres bounded south on the land of Abraham Woodward; also a piece of saltmarsh "that was my mother's and Aunt Herring's" bounded south upon the Great Creek leading to Boston Bay, March 4, 1744/5" (*Suffolk Deeds*, 80: 259). By reference to Abraham Chamberlain (24) it will be observed that he deeded land in Brookline Marshes bounded north on the marsh of James

Herring dec'd to this Samuel White Jan. 15, 1744/5, and that his wife Mary signed and Elizabeth Chamberlain witnessed the deed. Abraham Chamberlain had a daughter Elizabeth b. early in the year 1728. If she granted this deed she did so when she was about 17 years of age. If Elizabeth Chamberlain b. in 1697 gave the deed then Abraham Chamberlain, her brother, was living in 1745, and was the Abraham Chamberlain who d. in Dedham in 1747. James Herring m. at Roxbury June 14, 1722, Sarah Curtis at which time both were of Roxbury and he d. there March 1732, aged 76—old enough to have been an uncle to the elder Elizabeth Chamberlain. Elizabeth Chamberlain living in the house of William Weeks in Dorchester was warned from town May 6, 1731. (*New England Historical Genealogical Register*, 50: 69).

26. CLEMENT[3] CHAMBERLAIN JR. (*Clement*[2], *William*[1]) born at Billerica in 1694; d. there Jan. 21, 1754. He m. before 1718, Elizabeth —— who d. at Billerica, Jan 7, 1767. Clement Chamberlain Jr. of Billerica, husbandman, was plaintiff against Samuel Bull of Cambridge, brickmaker, April 29, 1740 (*Middx Court Files*). He and his family were warned out of Tewksbury in April 1738. He was active as a military man and was commissioned at Louisburg by Gov. William Shirley as Lieutenant of the Tenth Company of the Second Massachusetts Regiment under the command of General Samuel Waldo, Feb. 8, 1744. He also served in Gen. William Pepperell's Regiment in October 1745. (*New England Historical Genealogical Register*, 24: 370; 25: 257) His petition to the General Court after his return reads as follows:

"To His Excellancy William Sherley Esqr. Captain General and Governour in Cheiff in and over his Majesties Province of the Massachusetts Bay in New England and to the Honourable the Council and house of Representatives in General Court Assembled June 16th 1747

The Humble petition of Clement Chamberlain of Billerica in the County of Middlesex and Province Afores^{d}. Humbly Seweth, that whereas your petitioner hath been in the Expedition to Cape Britton under the Command of Capt. Joseph Richardson, Serving as his Lieu^{t}. from the beginning of the Said Expedition, until the last Day of October A. D: 1745; and being in Healthfull Circumstances when I your petitioner went there; and using my uttmost Endeavour to Serve my King, my Country & my Superiour Officers in Said Expedition, untill that I your Humble petitioner through the providence of Almighty God was Deprived of my health, and obtained Liberty of his Excellancy Governour Sherley to Return home to my Native Country and my people in a poor, weak and unhealthfull Condition; and hath Remained So ever Since my Arrival here as by many Evidences may Appear, and hath been under the Doctors Hands ever Since, which is very expensive to your Humble petitioner and not being of Ability to pay the Same and Mentain my

Family, which are in poor Circumstances; These are therefore to Inform your Excellancy and Honours of my Circumstances, as to Health and Other Accounts, hoping and Earnestly praying your Excellancy and Honours that in your Wisdoms you would be pleased to make me your Humble petitioner Such Allowances as you in your Great wisdom Shall think proper, and your Humble petitioner as in Duty bound Shall ever pray

In the House of Rep[ives] Oct[r] 27. 1747 Read and Ordered that the Comm[r] of War Allow the Pet[r] five pounds in consideration of the Charge respecting Doctors and Nurses within mentioned. Sent up for concurrence

T. Hutchinson Spkr"

On the reverse side of that petition one reads: "Billerica, August y[e] 17: 1747: We the Subscribers are knowing to the Truth of the facts within mentioned. [Signed] Joshua Abbott, Benj. Tompson, Enoch Kidder Jr., Will[m] Stickney, Ralphe Hill, Selectmen of Billerica. In Council Oct. 27, 1747, read and concurred, J. Willard, Secy, Consented to W. Shirley" (*Mass. Archives* 72: 742, 743).

Probably Clement Chamberlain removed to Preston, Conn., for a short time, as Elizabeth the daughter of Clement Chamberlain was bapt. at the First Church in Preston, Feb. 2, 1718.

Child born at Billerica:

i ELIZABETH[4] CHAMBERLAIN, b. Dec. 27, 1717; perhaps the mother of Joseph Harris, b. at Billerica, Dec. 19, 1739, and who d. at Fort Edward July 15, 1758.

27. JOSEPH[3] CHAMBERLAIN (*Clement*[2], *William*[1]) born at Billerica, Nov. —, 1696; d. probably at Amenia, N. Y. about 1765. He m. about 1719, Mary Johnson according to the town records of Billerica which do not give the date. Joseph Chamberlain of Mansfield, Conn. was plaintiff against Thomas Stimpson, physician, of Reading, Mass. Nov. 25, 1737. He recovered a debt of £9 May 29, 1738 (*Middx Court Files*). Joseph Chamberlain of Tolland, Conn., was plaintiff against Daniel Champney Jr. of Cambridge, husbandman, July 28, 1742. Champney gave a promissory note to Chamberlain dated at "Brookline Feb. 1, 1741/2," for £9. (*Ibid.* 1742). These data together with a wide survey of all the New England Chamberlain families indicate that this Joseph Chamberlain removed to Connecticut about 1725. He first moved to Lebanon, 1727 to 1732; later went to Mansfield and from Mansfield to Tolland and thence to Amenia, Duchess Co. New York in 1755.

Children by wife Mary first three born in Billerica, Mass.; fourth and fifth in Lebanon, Conn.; sixth to ninth in Mansfield, Conn. and last four in Tolland, Conn.

i ELIZABETH[4] CHAMBERLAIN, b. April 5, 1720; m. at Mansfield, Conn. March 30, 1738, Peter Dimmock of Mansfield, Ct.

64 ii JOSEPH[4] CHAMBERLAIN JR. b. Feb. 24, 1721/2.

iii MARY[4] CHAMBERLAIN, b. Jan. 27, 1723/4.

iv MEHITABLE[4] CHAMBERLAIN, bapt. at the First Church of Lebanon, Conn. Sept. 3, 1727; probably d. soon.

v MEHITABLE[4] CHAMBERLAIN, b. at Lebanon, Aug. 29, 1729.

65 vi JOHN[4] CHAMBERLAIN, bapt. June 21, 1730.

vii ABIAL[4] CHAMBERLAIN, bapt. March 12, 1732.

66 viii JAMES[4] CHAMBERLAIN, b. Feb. 11, 1734; bapt. March 31, 1734.

ix PHEBE[4] CHAMBERLAIN, bapt. Aug. 7, 1737.

67 x COLBEE[4] CHAMBERLAIN, b. Jan. 2, 1738.

68 xi JACOB[4] CHAMBERLAIN, b. Jan. 21, 1740/1.

69 xii WILLIAM[4] CHAMBERLAIN, twin, b. Jan. 25, 1744/5.

xiii REBECCA[4] CHAMBERLAIN, twin, b. Jan. 25, 1744/5.

28. WILLIAM[3] CHAMBERLAIN (*Clement*[2], *William*[1]) born at Billerica, March 23, 1703/4; d. there before Nov. 20, 1738. He m. about 1728 Esther —— who m. (2) at Billerica, Dec. 21, 1743, Benoni Spaulding of Billerica. He was b. Feb. 6, 1691, and d. Dec. 17, 1752. She was Spaulding's second wife. Esther Chamberlain, widow, was appointed administratrix of the estate of William Chamberlain late of Billerica, deceased, Nov. 20, 1738. His personal estate, including a "gun and sword" was valued at £133 : 07 : 00. The "account of Esther Spaulding formerly Esther Chamberlain" was returned Jan. 12, 1746, and an inventory of his homestead of 70 acres on the west side of Concord river in Billerica and also of 40 acres "being the westerly part of the homestead that was Clement Chamberlain's deceased" was inventoried. The widow appearing before the Judge of Probate declared that she would not have her thirds of the real estate and quitclaimed to her children. By agreement with John, the eldest son, William Chamberlain, the second son, was to have the homestead. This was signed by Esther Spaulding, John Chamberlain, William Chamberlain and Andrew Farmer, guardian for the two minors July 10, 1753. (*Ibid.* 4207) Furthermore it was agreed that William Chamberlain was to pay Joseph Chamberlain for his interest in the estate of Clement Chamberlain £50; Samuel and Rebecca Gridley for their interest in the estate of Clement Chamberlain £30; a legacy to Joseph and Elizabeth Kemp of £20 and to Elizabeth Chamberlain "for boarding and nursing the deceased's mother" £300. Furthermore the son William was to pay his brother John £104 : 08 : 08 and his sisters Esther and Mary each £52 : 04 : 04. Joseph Chamberlain gave a receipt for £6 : 13 : 04 in right of his father Clement Chamberlain's estate, Oct. 14, 1754; and at the same time as attorney receipted for Samuel and

Rebecca Gridley. Joseph Kemp and Elizabeth Kemp gave receipt for their share out of our mother Mary Toothacre's personal estate and for their share of our father Clement and our brother William Chamberlain's estate, March 6, 1754. The final inventory was taken Sept. 18, 1754, and 38 acres valued at £470 lying on the west side of Concord river was settled upon William Chamberlain. (*Ibid.* 4207) He was in Col. Eleazer Tyng's Co. from Aug. 21 to Nov. 29, 1722. (*Mass. Archives*, 91 : 66)

Children all born at Billerica :

70 i JOHN[4] CHAMBERLAIN, b. March 15, 1729/30.
71 ii WILLIAM[4] CHAMBERLAIN, b. March 13, 1731/2.
iii ESTHER[4] CHAMBERLAIN, b. Sept. 18, 1734.
iv MARY[4] CHAMBERLAIN, b. about 1738. She made choice of Andrew Farmer of Billerica for her guardian June 18, 1753, stating that she was the daughter of William Chamberlain late of Billerica and that she was "in her 15th year" (?) (*Middlx Probate*, 4210) Esther Chamberlain "upwards of 14 years" daughter of same made choice of same guardian same day (4208)

29. ISAAC[3] CHAMBERLAIN (Daniel[2], William[1]) b. at Billerica, Aug. 3, 1695. As an "adult" he was bapt. at the First Parish of Brookline, Dec. 10, 1721, and at the same time Eleazer Chamberlain was baptized. (*Brookline Hist. Publication Society*, No. 8 : 70). He was a "centinal" in Capt. —— Williams's Co. from Nov. 1724 to Nov. 1725. (*New England Historical Genealogical Register*, 49: 190). Isaac Chamberlain of Watertown gave a bond to serve as a servant one Anthony Caverly of Watertown in May 1733. (*Middx Court Files*). "Anthony Caverly of Watertown, gentleman, was plaintiff against Isaac Chamberlain of Brookline, husbandman, alias Isaac Chamberlain of Watertown, husbandman, June 19, 1733." (*Ibid.*) Isaac Chamberlain, a resident of Boston was mentioned in the account of Mrs. Caleb Eddy Dec. 27, 1751. (*New England Historical Genealogical Register* 42: 256). No further trace of this man has been found nor does it appear that he left descendants unless he were identical with Isaac Chamberlain of Westmoreland, N. H.

31. EPHRAIM[3] CHAMBERLAIN (Daniel[2], William[1]) b. at Billerica, Jan. 16, 1700/1; d. at Northfield, Mass. before 1750. He removed from Billerica to Newton where he was living in 1723. He m. (1) at Watertown, Oct. 31, 1723, Mary Sawin of Watertown. She was the daughter of Munning and Sarah (Stone) Sawin of Watertown where she was b. Feb. 14, 1694/5. She probably died within a few years of her marriage. He undoubtedly removed to Northfield as early as 1730 and m. (2) there in 1733, Anna daughter of Theophilus and Mary Merriam. Her father was killed by the Indians Aug. 21, 1723. She was b. at Wallingford, Conn. Sept. 6, 1715, m. (2) about 1755, Benjamin Rice and d. July 7, 1778.

Children all born in Northfield by wife Anna:

i LYDIA[4] CHAMBERLAIN, b. Feb. 17, 1733/4; m. Alexander Norton.

ii SARAH[4] CHAMBERLAIN, b. Dec. 17, 1735; m. Ambrose Ward of New Haven, Conn.

72 iii THEOPHILUS[4] CHAMBERLAIN, b. Oct. 20, 1737; was in Capt. Nathaniel Dwight's Co. Sept. 15 to Dec. 10, 1755, in the expedition to Crown Point (*Mass. Archives*, 95: 168). In Capt. John Burk's Co. March 17, 1757, to March 15, 1758; at the capitulation of Fort William Henry, Aug. 9, 1758; in captivity until Jan. 11, 1759. (*Ibid.* 96: 42); graduated at Yale College, 1765; removed to Preston, N. S. 1792.

iv ANNA[4] CHAMBERLAIN, b. about 1740; m. in 1758, Thomas Stebbins and (2) Reuben Frizzell of Bernardston, Mass.

73 v EPHRAIM[4] CHAMBERLAIN, JR., b. about 1742; settled in Southwick, Mass. in 1785.

74 vi SAMUEL[4] CHAMBERLAIN, b. about 1744; settled in Middletown, Conn.

32. THOMAS[3] CHAMBERLAIN (*Daniel*[2], *William*[1]) b. at Billerica, Aug. —, 1703; d. in Vermont, ——. He was a grantee of Township No. 2 (now Westmoreland, N. H.) under the Massachusetts charter, Nov. 30, 1736. The first settlers there went across the country to Northfield and then in canoes worked up the Connecticut to the Great Meadow where they built a stockaded fort about 1744. Here Thomas Chamberlain and Isaac Chamberlain, perhaps his brother (29), joined the garrison. After the line between Massachusetts and New Hampshire was established the settlers of Number 2 petitioned that "we sometime, viz. about seven years before the last Indian war settled under the Massachusetts at a place called Number Two lying on the east side of Connecticut River about fourteen miles above Fort Dummer," etc. This petition was signed Jan. 30, 1750, by Thos. Chamberlain, Isaac Chamberlain, Josiah Chamberlain, Thomas Chamberlain, Joshua Chamberlain, Jedediah Chamberlain, Job Chamberlain and 36 others. The petitioners stated that several had entered the names of their children in order to obtain two or three rights and their petition was granted by New Hampshire Feb. 12, 1752. (*Hist. of Westmoreland in Hurd's Hist. of Cheshire County*, 460) The first meeting of the proprietors under the New Hampshire charter was held at the house of Thomas Chamberlain, March 31, 1752. They appear to have met there frequently. At his house the proprietors voted "to build a meeting-house and set it on ye hill by Daniel Hows—to build it fifty feet long, forty feet wide and twenty feet post," May 4, 1762. The first church covenant was signed, Sept. 26, 1764, by nine members of other churches, viz. William Goddard pastor-elect, member of the First Church at Newtown, Mass. Thomas Chamberlain member of the church at Newtown and seven others. The destruction by fire of the records of the First Church of Newton, Mass. in 1770 prevents us from making a clear analysis but it is plain that the Thomas Chamberlain born at Billerica in 1703 was the only Thomas Chamberlain who was old enough in 1736 to petition for the grant of Number Two, and fifteen years later his sons, some of whom have been positively identified as such, joined with him in order to secure more land. From the

evidence in hand he appears to have lived in Lynnfield in 1734; in Stoneham in 1737; and in Newton before 1750 from which place he took a letter to the church in Westmoreland. His wife Abigail —— d. at Westmoreland, May 18, 1769, "in her 63d year" as is learned from her tomb stone. Hence she was b. about 1706. He, or his sons, all removed to Vermont about 1784 and settled in Stockbridge, Bethel and perhaps elsewhere, in Vermont.

Children, not in order:

75 i JOSHUA[4] CHAMBERLAIN, bapt. at First Church of Lynnfield, Sept. 22, 1734. (*Essex Inst. Coll.* 34: 118); petitioned for Westmoreland Jan. 30, 1750; in Capt. Jonathan Butterfield's Co. Apr. 6 to Apr. 30, 1759. (*Mass. Archives*, 97: 175)

76 ii JEDEDIAH[4] CHAMBERLAIN, bapt. at Stoneham, June 12, 1737; signer of Westmoreland petition Jan. 30, 1750; removed to Bethel, Vt. after 1776.

77 iii INCREASE[4] CHAMBERLAIN, b. in 1741; removed to Stockbridge, Vt. after 1776.

78 iv ISAAC[4] CHAMBERLAIN, perhaps eldest son or brother, lived in Westmoreland, 1744 to 1783; lieutenant; selectman; moderator; representative.

79 v THOMAS[4] CHAMBERLAIN, grantee of Westmoreland, Jan. 30, 1750; in Capt. John Fry's Co. Col. Timothy Ruggles Reg't. Apr. 1, to May 21, 1758. (*Ibid.* 96: 105)

80 vi JOSIAH[4] CHAMBERLAIN, grantee there, Jan. 30, 1750.

81 vii JOB[4] CHAMBERLAIN, grantee there, Jan. 30, 1750; perhaps a son but not proven to be so.

ERRATUM

Page 127, twenty-second line from bottom, for Daniel Stowell read David Stowell.

INDEX TO NAMES IN GENEALOGY

Abbot Joshua 107 143
Mercy 113
Rebecca 107
Adams Daniel 112 113
Rebecca 112 113 137
Addington Anne 98 99
Isaac 96 97 98 99 100 102 103
Allen Daniel 137
Elizabeth 137
George 137
James 96 98
Alline Henry 97
Andrews John 141
Andros Edmund 100
Baboll Hugh 102
Baker William 94
Baldwin Esther 115
Jonathan 115
Ballantine John 97
Barrett Mehitable 118
Beaumont Thankful 123
Belknap John 135
Bellows Jotham 135
Berkeley Robert 90
Berry Dorothy 132
Jeremiah 132
Bickford John Jr. 127
Binney Rebecca 100
Samuel 100
Blanchard Joseph 113
Bodge George M. 104
Boighton Samuel 102
Bond Henry 104 136
John 136
Brattle William 107
Bridgham Joseph 97
Brigden Alice 126
Brigham David 135
Lydia 135
Martha 135
William 135
Brown Jonathan 123
Thomas 127 131
Bryant Elizabeth 100
Jane 100
Bull John 107
Samuel 142
Bullard Samuel 132
Burk John 146
Butterfield Benjamin 94
Elizabeth 118
Jonathan 118 147
Mehitable 118
Rachel 118
William 118
Call Jonathan 123
Thomas 123
Canney Samuel 127
Carter Richard 91
Caverly Anthony 145
Chadwick Abigail 138
Chamberlain Aaron 141
Abial 144
Abigail 113 114 138 147
Abraham 103 105 106 107 114 115 116 119 120 138 140 141 142
Alice 89
Ann 103 125 126
Anna 117 118 123 131 132 135 145 146
Benjamin 119 120
Clement 89 97 103 113 114 116 117 118 119 123 142 143 144 145
Colbee 144
Daniel 103 110 117 135 138 145 146
David 141
Deborah 105 106 118
Deliverance 104
Chamberlain, cont'd
Dorothy 118 131 132 141
Ebenezer 111 114 117 130 132 134 135 138
Edmund (Edmond) 92 94 103 106 113 114 115 135
Eleazer 112 116 117 138 140 145
Elizabeth 111 112 113 114 115 116 117 118 132 133 134 136 137 139 140 141 142 143 144 145
Enoch 133 134
Ephraim 117 129 130 131 132 145 146
Esther 144 145
Experience 107 110 111 117 122 131 132 140
Francis 89
George Walter 89 132
Hannah 114 132 134 136 137 141
Increase 147
Isaac 92 103 117 121 123 138 145 146 147
Jacob 103 107 108 109 110 111 117 120 121 122 123 126 129 130 131 132 134 144
James 144
Jason 111 132 134
Jedediah 146 147
Joanna 135
Job 146 147
John 89 90 97 103 105 106 111 112 113 115 116 118 119 120 121 123 124 125 126 133 134 137 140 144 145
Jonathan 135
Joseph 116 117 118 123 143 144
Joshua 135 146 147
Josiah 118 121 122 146 147
Lydia 106 118 135 146
Marah 114
Margaret (Pegge) 116 118 121 123 126
Martha 135
Mary 89 94 112 113 116 117 118 119 120 121 128 129 130 131 135 138 140 141 142 143 144 145
Mehitable 118 144
Mercy 113 114
Milicent 124 126
Moses 141
Nathan 119 120
Nathaniel 126 141
Nathaniel L. 135
Patience 138
Phebe 144
Phillips 112 136 137
Rebecca 92 96 97 98 99 100 103 105 107 112 113 114 117 131 137 144
Robert 90
Samuel 118 129 130 132 134 146
Sarah 103 104 106 107 112 113 118 119 121 122 123 136 137 138 139 140 141 146
Simon 108 120 121 122 123
Staples 134
Susannah 120 121 122
Tabitha 119 120
Thankful 123 125 126
Theophilus 146
Thomas 89 90 93 94 97 103 111 112 113 118 136 137 138 140 146 147
Timothy 92 103
—Widow 126
William 89 90 91 92 93 94 95 96 98 102 103 104 105 107 111 113 114 115 116 117 118 119 120 123
Chamberlain, cont'd
126 127 128 129 130 131 132 134 136 137 138 140 141 142 143 144 145 146
Willson 124 125 126
Zaccheus 120
Champney Daniel 143
Elizabeth 140
Joseph 140
Richard 94
Chandler William 113 114
Child Joshua 115
Sarah 115
Clark John 111
Clarke Noah 89
Elizabeth 132
Hannah 132
Samuel 132
Collins Martha 97
Convers Allen 90 92
Cooke John 127
Crafts Elizabeth 132
Cram Elizabeth 118
John 118
Jonathan 118
Mary 118
Sarah 118
Crosby Nathan 107
Sarah 107
Curtis Sarah 142
Danforth Dorothy 107
Samuel 107 122
Davenport Addington 96
Rebecca 96
Dawson James 100
Dimmock Elizabeth 144
Peter 144
Door Henry 131
Mary 131
Drury Daniel 132
Elizabeth 132
Dudley Joseph 97 102
Thomas 93 94 97 102
Dwight Nathaniel 146
Dyke (Dike) Experience 110 122 140
Jonathan 110
Eddy (Mrs.) Caleb 145
Eliot John 95
Emerson Dorothy 131 132
Samuel 132
Esty Charles 108
Farley Anna 115
Caleb Jr. 106
Caleb 114
Ebenezer 107
Elizabeth 107
Enoch 115
Esther 115
George 94 95 105 114 115
Lydia 115
Rebecca 114 115
Samuel 106
Farmer Andrew 144 145
Edward 119
John 103
Farnsworth Sarah 120
Fay Benjamin 135
Felt Joseph B. 91
Fergerson Deliverance 104
Fisher Anne 98 99
Fiske Mary 136
Fletcher Timothy 114
Foster Elizabeth 119
Experience 111
—Sergt. 113
Foxcroft Daniel 106
Francis 106
French Elizabeth 111

French, cont'd
Experience 111
Jacob 104
Joseph 111
Mary 111 119
William 94 95 111
Frizzell Anna 146
Reuben 146
Frost Benjamin 115
Mary 115
Frye John 147
Fuller Abraham 140
Furbish Sarah 113
Goddard William 116
Goffe Mary 135
Gookin Daniel 90 95
Gould Margaret 118
Mehitable 118
Samuel 118
Goold Thomas 133
Greenwood John 112
Josiah 139 140
Gridley Rebecca 117 144 145
Samuel 117 144 145
Griggs William 97
Groves Mary 126
Hall —— 107
Hammond Ann 111 116
Eleazer 112 138
Elizabeth 111
Hannah 138
Isaac 111 113 116
Nathaniel 111
Patience 138
Thomas 93 94 111 115 140
Hanson Nathaniel 128
Harrington Hannah 138
Harris John 141
Joseph 143
Thaddeus W. 99
Hawkins Dorothy 96
Hazen Henry A. 93 95 103 104 105 107 113 115 117 118 119
Healy (Hollie) Nathaniel 110
Heard Rebecca 130
Herring —"Aunt" 141
James 141 142
Sarah 142
Hibbins William 91
Hide (Hyde) Anna 123
Jonathan Jr 107 108 111
Hill Jonathan 119
Ralph 94 103 143
Rebecca 114
Samuel 106 119
Hodgdon Israel 127
How —Dr. 103
Hows Daniel 146
Hudson Nathaniel 118
Hull John 104
Hutchinson Thomas 143
Ireland Elizabeth 112 137
Mary 137
William 112 137
Jackson — 113
Jaco Deborah 105
Jefts Henry 94 95 106 119
Mary 119
Simeon 119
Jenness John 128
Johnson Mary 143
Nathaniel 102
William 134
Keates Richard 136
Kemp Elizabeth 117 144 145
Joseph 117 144 145
Kenrick Ann 111 116
Kent Stephen Sr. 100
Kidder Enoch Jr. 143
Knowles Experience 131 132
James 132
Lambard Richard 90
Larkin Joanna 126
Larkin, cont'd
Joseph 126
Thankful 125 126
Learned Isaac 93 94
Leighton Anna 131 132
David 132
Leverett Anne 98 99
John 98 99
Rebecca 98
Sarah 98
Thomas 98 99
Locke Mehitable 118
Samuel 118
Lovering Craft 134
Joseph 134
Lovewell John 127
Main Amos 128
Manning Samuel 95
Marrick (Myrick) Elijah 108
Mason Arthur 102
Joseph 136
Mary 136
Sarah 136
Merriam Anna 145
Mary 145
Theophilus 145
Mighell John 131
Miner Mary 98
Mirick Samuel 140
Moody Joshua 96
Morse Joanna 135
Murdock Robert 110
Needham John 106 119
Newhall Dorothy 118
Samuel 118
Norton Alexander 146
Lydia 146
Nowell Samuel 96
Numphow (Indian) 95 96
Osgood Sarah 100
Palmer John 122
Parker Benjamin 119
Jacob 94
James 90 93 94
John 92
Joseph 94
Lydia 119
Mary 119
Robert 119
Sarah 119
Parkman Ebenezer 135
Peirce Ann 96
Pierce Thomas 92
Penn James 98
Katharine 98
Pepperell William 142
Philip King 96
Phillips Alice 126
Anne 125 126
Hannah 136
John 126
Nathaniel 125 126
Samuel 136
Thomas 136
Wendell 102
Pope Charles H. 99
Proctor Sarah 118
Prout Ebenezer 107
Rand Jonathan 124
Milicent 124
Nehemiah 126
Thomas 126
Randall Mary 115 116
Remington Jonathan 108
Rice Anna 145
Benjamin 145
Richards Daniel 108
Samuel 130
Richardson Joseph 142
Samuel 122
Roberts John 89
Joseph 127
Ross Dorothy 141
Ruggles Timothy 147
Russell Jason 104 107
Ryan James 123
Margaret 123
Sale Obadiah 102
Sanders Richard 123
Sarah 123
Sanderson Roberts 97
Satchwell Susannah 100
Theophilus 100
Savage Ephraim 102
James 90 92 103
Sawin Mary 145
Munning 145
Sarah 145
Scarlett Humphrey 137
Mary 137
Shattuck Philip 110
Shed Benjamin 107 119
Benoni 107
Daniel 115
Dorothy 107
Elizabeth 107
Hannah 107
Jemima 107 119
John 102 107 114 119
Mary 107 119
Nathan 107 119
Rebecca 107 115
Sarah 97 107 119
Shelley Rebecca 99
Sarah 96 97 98 99 100 101 102 105 107
Shirley William 142 143
Simpson Mary 121
Skinner Thomas 102
Smith Francis 91
Thankful 126
Snow Elizabeth 136
Thomas 136
Spaulding Benoni 144
Esther 144
Squire Phillip 102
Staples John 110 132
Stearns Hannah 115
John 94 95 114 115
Mary 115
Rebecca 114 115
Sarah 115
Thomas 114 115
Stebbins Anna 146
Thomas 146
Stedman Elizabeth 111
Steel Mary 126
Stickney William 143
Stimpson Thomas 143
Stone David 140
John 140
Jonas 122
Rachel 118
Sarah 120 145
Simon 120
Susannah 120
Stowell David 120 127
For Daniel read David 127 147
Sweetser Seth 126
Taverner Henry 90
Tebbetts Dorothy 128
Mary 128
Samuel 126 128
Thomas 127
Tenney Thomas 134
Thwing Ebenezer 139 140
Elizabeth 139 140
John 138 139 140
Sarah 139 140
Tidd Samuel 92
Tompson Benjamin 143
Toothaker Mary 116 117 145
Roger 116
Townsend Penn 96 98 102
Rebecca 96
Sarah 96

Trickey John Sr. 131
Rebecca 131
Trowbridge Edmund 135
James 115
Mary 135
Thomas 135
Truesdel Richard 108
Trull John 114 115
Mary 119
Tuttle Dorothy 128
Twombly Joseph 127
Tyng Eleazer 145
Waldo Samuel 142
Walker Joseph 113
Ward Ambrose 146
John Sr. 108
John 110
Sarah 146
Weeks William 142
Welch Hannah 136
Welch cont'd
John 136
Wentworth Mary 137
Wheat —Dr. 110
White (Whitt) Phillip 110
Samuel 141 142
Whitehouse Pomfret 128 130
Samuel 131
Whiting Oliver 106 115
Samuel 95 104 105 113
Whitney Dorothy 141
Eleazer 140 141
Mary 140
Wilder Martha 100
Mary 100
Willard J. —143
Williams —Capt. 145
William 123
Willoughby Anna 118
John 118
Wilson Anna 122
Elizabeth 119
Jemima 107
John 107 119 122
Mary 119
Nathaniel 123
Richard 91
Thankful 123
Winchester Benjamin 140
Elizabeth 140
Winn Edward 92
Winthrop John 90
Wiswell Jeremiah 122
Woodhouse John 89
Mary 89
Woodward Abraham 141
Ebenezer 120
George 102

OFFICERS

President

MAJ.-GEN. JOSHUA L. CHAMBERLAIN, LL.D., Brunswick, Me.

Vice-Presidents

COL. THOMAS CHAMBERLIN, Philadelphia. Pa.
REV. ELNATHAN E. STRONG, D.D, Boston, Mass.
PROF. THOMAS C. CHAMBERLIN, LL.D., Chicago, Ill.
MYRON L. CHAMBERLAIN, M. D., Boston, Mass.
GEORGE M. CHAMBERLIN, M.D, Chicago, Ill.
PRES. MCKENDREE H. CHAMBERLIN, LL.D., Lebanon, Ill.
MR. LEWIS H. CHAMBERLAIN, Detroit, Mich.
SENATOR GEORGE E. CHAMBERLAIN, Portland, Oregon.
REV. LEANDER T. CHAMBERLAIN, D.D., New York City.
MR. RICHARD H. CHAMBERLAIN, Oakland, Cal.
MR. WILLIAM WILSON CHAMBERLAINE, Norfolk, Va.
PROF. PAUL M. CHAMBERLAIN. Chicago, Ill.
MR. EMERSON CHAMBERLIN, N. Y.
MR. PIERSON CHAMBERLAIN, N. J.
JUDGE LOYED E. CHAMBERLAIN, Brockton, Mass.
MR. EUGENE CHAMBERLIN, Brooklyn, N. Y.
MR. MARTIN H. CHAMBERLIN, Rutland, Vt.

Corresponding Secretary

MISS ABBIE MELLEN CHAMBERLAIN, 6 Exeter Park, Cambridge, Mass., and Washington, D. C.

Recording Secretary

MR. MONTAGUE CHAMBERLAIN, 202 Boylston Street, Boston, Mass.

Treasurer

MR. THOMAS CHAMBERLAIN, State National Bank, Boston, Mass.

Assistant Treasurer

MRS. SOPHIA A. C. CASWELL, R. F. D., Route 1, Jefferson, Mass.

Auditor

LEWIS J. BIRD, Boston, Mass.

Executive Committee

JUDGE WM. T. FORBES, *Chairman*, Worcester, Mass.
HON. LOYED E. CHAMBERLAIN, Brockton, Mass.
MISS LAURA B. CHAMBERLAIN, Cambridge, Mass.
The President, Secretaries, and Treasurers, *ex-officio*.

STANDING COMMITTEES

Genealogical Committee

Col. William T. Harding, *Chairman*, 146 Broadway, New York City.
Col. Thomas Chamberlin, Philadelphia, Pa.
Mr. Herbert B. Chamberlain, Brattleboro, Vt.
George M. Chamberlin, M.D., Chicago, Ill.
Miss Jenny Chamberlain Watts, A.M., Cambridge, Mass.
Rev. A. J. Fretz, Milton, N. J.

Committee on English Ancestry

Mr. Samuel D. Chamberlin, Hartford, Conn.
Mr. Roswell W. Chamberlain, Chester, N. Y.
Mr. Elliot C. Kimball, Dubuque, Iowa.
Mrs. Charles B. Platt, Englewood, N. J.
Mr. William C. Chamberlain, Dubuque, Iowa.

Committee on History

Maj.-Gen. Joshua L. Chamberlain, *Chairman*, Portland, Me.
Com. Eugene T. Chamberlain, Commissioner of Navigation, Washington, D. C.
Mr. Montague Chamberlain, Boston, Mass.
Miss Laura B. Chamberlain, Cambridge, Mass.
Miss S. Emma Chamberlin, Cleveland, Ohio.
Prof. Ralph Curtis Ringwalt, New York City.

Committee on Colonial and American Revolutionary Ancestry

J. W. Chamberlin, M.D., *Chairman*, Endicott Building, St. Paul, Minn.
Mr. Wm. S. Boynton, St. Johnsbury, Vt.
Mrs. O. A. Furst, Bellefonte, Pa.
Mrs. Florence C. Moseley, New Haven, Conn.
Mr. Prescott Chamberlain, Boston, Mass.
Miss Isabella S. Chamberlin, Washington, D. C.
Mr. Raymond Chamberlain, Ph.D., Brooklyn, N. Y.

Committee on Recent Wars

Capt. Orville T. Chamberlain, *Chairman*, Elkhart, Ind.
Mr. Justin Morrill Chamberlain, Washington, D. C.
Mr. Rollin S. Chamberlain, Wilkesbarre, Pa.
Capt. Hiram S. Chamberlain, Chattanooga, Tenn.
Mrs. Emily A. Capron, Winchendon, Mass.
Miss Helen C. Chamberlain, Washington, D. C.

LIST OF MEMBERS

Life Members

Mrs. Lucy P. Chamberlain .... Medford, Mass.
†Rev. Leander T. Chamberlain, D. D. .... New York, N. Y.
Mr. William Chamberlain .... West Chesterfield, N. H.
George M. Chamberlin, M. D. .... Chicago, Ill.
*Rev. Jacob Chamberlain, LL. D. (died March 2, 1908) .... Madras, India
Mr. Charles Willis Smith .... Pittsburg, Pa.

Active Members

Mr. Andrew Adams .... Kahuka, Oahu, Hawaii
Mr. G. A. Adams .... Chicago, Ill.
Mrs. George W. Adams .... Dorchester, Mass.
*Col. Henry H. Adams (died June 25, 1905) .... New York, N. Y.
Mrs. Horace G. Allen .... Boston, Mass.
Capt. Abram P. Andrew .... La Porte, Ind.
Mrs. Martha E. Austin .... Roxbury, Mass.
Mrs. Emily S. Bartlett .... Chicago, Ill.
Mrs. Maitland C. Bennett .... Washington, D. C.
Mrs. Luther B. Benton .... Baltimore, Md.
Mr. Henry Chamberlain Bird .... Boston, Mass.
Mr. Lewis J. Bird .... Boston, Mass.
†Mrs. Ellen E. C. Blair .... Dorchester, Mass.
Miss Amy E. Blanchard .... Philadelphia, Pa.
*Mr. D. C. Bloomer (died February 26, 1900) .... Council Bluffs, Iowa
Mrs. Sarah M. C. Bodwell .... Clifton Springs, N. Y.
Mrs. William A. Boyd .... Cambridge, Mass.
†Mr. William S. Boynton .... St. Johnsbury, Vt.
†Mrs. J. M. Brant .... East Weymouth, Mass.
Mrs. Amy Pearson Brooks .... Hartford, Conn.
Mrs. George M. Brown .... Hartford, Conn.
Mrs. Hattie C. D. Brown .... Chicago, Ill.
Mrs. J. S. Brown .... La Grange, Ind.
Mrs. Carrie M. Butts .... Newton Center, Mass.
Mrs. Emily A. Capron .... Winchendon, Mass.
Mrs. Emma A. Carr .... Dorchester, Mass.
†Mrs. Sophia A. C. Caswell .... Holden, Mass.
†Miss Abbie M. Chamberlain .... Cambridge, Mass.
*Hon. Abiram Chamberlain (died May 15, 1911) .... Meriden, Conn.
Mr. Adelbert S. Chamberlain .... Moravia, N. Y.
*Mr. Albert Chamberlin (died April 17, 1909) .... North Abington, Mass.
*Albert H. Chamberlain, M. D. (died Feb. 19, 1909) .... London, Eng.
Mr. Albert S. Chamberlin .... Hartford, Conn.
†Mr. A. C. Allen Chamberlain .... Boston, Mass.
Mr. Alfred L. Chamberlain .... Sandusky, Mich.
Mr. Allen Chamberlin .... New York, N. Y.
Mr. Allen G. Chamberlain .... Denver, Col.
*Mr. Almond W. Chamberlain (died January 30, 1905) .... Harbor Beach, Mich.
Miss Anna P. Chamberlain .... East Orange, N. J.
Mr. Archie S. Chamberlain .... Paterson, N. J.
Mr. Arthur B. Chamberlain .... Rochester, N. Y.
Mr. Arthur Hale Chamberlain .... Plainfield, N. J.
†Mr. Asa W. Chamberlin .... Jamaica Plain, Mass.
Miss Catherine J. Chamberlayne .... Boston, Mass.
Mr. Cecil C. Chamberlain .... Enderlin, N. Dak.

* Deceased.
† Charter Members.

Mr. Charles A. Chamberlin .... Detroit, Mich.
Mr. Charles A. Chamberlain .... Forge Village, Mass.
Mr. Charles Cahoon Chamberlin .... Ann Arbor, Mich.
Mr. Charles E. Chamberlin .... Roxbury, Mass.
Mr. Charles E. Chamberlain .... New Bedford, Mass.
Mr. Charles H. Chamberlin .... Kingston, Pa.
*Mr. Charles K. Chamberlin (died May 14, 1899) .... Pittsburg, Pa.
Mr. Charles T. Chamberlain .... Excelsior, Minn.
*Mr. Charles W. Chamberlain (died Oct. 31, 1908) .... Dayton, Ohio
Mr. Charles W. Chamberlain .... Seattle, Wash.
Mr. Chauncy W. Chamberlin .... Boston, Mass.
Mr. Clarence Abner Chamberlin .... Eau Claire, Wis.
Mr. Clarence M. Chamberlain .... Rochester, N. Y.
*Miss Clarissa A. Chamberlin (died Nov. 9, 1908) .... West Concord, N. H.
Mr. Curtis A. Chamberlain .... Concord, N. H.
*†Cyrus N. Chamberlain, M. D. (died July 18, 1899) .... Andover, Mass.
*†Hon. Daniel H. Chamberlain, LL. D. (died April 13, 1907) .... W. Brookfield, Mass.
*†Hon. Daniel U. Chamberlin (died June 15, 1898) .... Cambridgeport, Mass.
*Davis S. Chamberlain, M. D. .... Des Moines, Iowa
*Mr. Dwight S. Chamberlain (died May 11, 1903) .... Lyons, N. Y.
Mr. E. P. Chamberlin .... Bellefontaine, Ohio
Mr. Earl Chamberlin .... Brookline, Mass.
Miss Edna W. Chamberlin .... Summit, N. J.
Mr. Edward F. Chamberlin .... Scranton, Pa.
*Mr. Edward Wilmot Chamberlain, LL. B. (died January 18, 1908) .... New York, N. Y.
*†Mr. Edward Watts Chamberlain (died December 18, 1905) .... Louisville, Ky.
Mr. Edward W. Chamberlin .... Braintree, Mass.
Mr. Edwin Chamberlain .... Berkeley, Cal.
Mr. Edwin Chamberlain .... San Antonio, Tex.
Mr. Edwin Abiel Chamberlin .... Lima, Ohio
Mr. Edwin M. Chamberlin .... Albany, N. Y.
Miss Elizabeth B. Chamberlin .... Chicago, Ill.
*Miss Elizabeth E. Chamberlain (died November 19, 1909) .... Roxbury, Mass.
Miss Ellen Jeanette Chamberlin .... Spokane, Wash.
Miss Ellora G. Chamberlain .... Norwich, Conn.
Mr. Emerson Chamberlin .... Summit, N. J.
Mr. Ephraim Chamberlain .... Norwood, Mass.
Mr. Erastus H. Chamberlin .... Detroit, Mich.
Miss Etta Susan Chamberlain .... Montpelier, Vt.
Mr. Eugene Chamberlin .... Brooklyn, N. Y.
*Mr. Eugene G. Chamberlin (died September 1, 1905) .... Chicago, Ill.
Hon. Eugene Tyler Chamberlain .... Washington, D. C.
Mr. Eugene V. Chamberlin .... Buffalo, N. Y.
Gen. Frank Chamberlain .... Albany, N. Y.
Mr. Frank Addison Chamberlain .... Albany, Ill.
Mr. Frank D. Chamberlin .... Hartford, Conn.
Mr. Frank E. Chamberlain .... Manistee, Mich.
Mr. Frank Everett Chamberlin .... Chicago, Ill.
Mr. Frank H. Chamberlain .... Dorchester, Mass.
Mr. Frank H. Chamberlain .... Hudson, Mass.
Mr. Fred D. Chamberlin .... Portland, Ore.
Mr. Fred W. Chamberlin .... Detroit, Mich.
Mr. Frederick E. Chamberlin .... Bayonne, N. J.
Mr. Frederic W. Chamberlain .... Three Oaks, Mich.
Mr. George A. Chamberlin .... Yonkers, N. Y.
Mr. George B. Chamberlin .... Chicago, Ill.
Mr. George Clinton Chamberlin .... Indianapolis, Ind.
Mr. George D. Chamberlain .... Springfield, Mass.
George E. Chamberlain, M.D. .... Manilla, P. I.
Hon. George E. Chamberlin .... Portland, Ore.
Mr. George F. Chamberlin .... New York, N. Y.
Mr. G. Howard Chamberlin .... Yonkers, N. Y.
George M. Chamberlain, M. D. .... Brookline, Mass.

George M. Chamberlin, M. D. ....Chicago, Ill.
Mr. George Pierce Chamberlain ....Natchez, Miss.
*Mr. George R. Chamberlain (died February, 1910) ....New Haven, Conn.
Mr. George Thomas Chamberlain ....Columbus, Ohio
Mr. George W. Chamberlin ....Summit, N. J.
*Rev. George W. Chamberlain, D. D. (died July 31, 1902) ....Bahia, Brazil, S. A.
†Mr. George W. Chamberlain ....Malden, Mass.
Miss Gertrude Chamberlin ....Boston, Mass.
Mr. Harlow H. Chamberlain ....Minneapolis, Minn.
Mr. Harold Wyllys Chamberlain ....Brunswick, Me.
Mr. Harry G. Chamberlin ....Chicago, Ill.
Miss Hattie J. Chamberlain ....New Haven, Conn.
Miss Helen Chamberlain ....Hyde Park, Mass.
Miss Helen M. C. Chamberlin ....Washington, D. C.
*Miss Henrietta M. Chamberlaine (died December 13, 1906) ....Baltimore, Md.
*Mr. Henry Chamberlain (died February 9, 1907) ....Three Oaks, Mich.
Mr. Henry H. Chamberlin ....Worcester, Mass.
*Mr. Henry L. Chamberlin (died September 13, 1909) ....Buffalo, N. Y.
Mr. Henry N. Chamberlain ....Chicago, Ill.
*Mr. Henry R. Chamberlain (died February 16, 1911) ....London, Eng.
†Mr. Herbert B. Chamberlain ....Brattleboro, Vt.
Capt. Hiram S. Chamberlain ....Chattanooga, Tenn.
Mr. Horace A. Chamberlin ....Somerville, Mass.
Mr. Horace P. Chamberlain ....Buffalo, N. Y.
Mr. Ira Chamberlain ....Paterson, N. J.
Mr. Isaac C. Chamberlain ....Dubuque, Iowa
*Mr. Isaac W. Chamberlin (died December 15, 1904) ....Lafayette, Ind.
Miss Isabella S. Chamberlin ....Washington, D. C.
*Mr. J. D. Chamberlin (died January 4, 1910) ....Toledo, Ohio
*Mr. Jacob A. Chamberlain (died June 28, 1907) ....Warwick, N. Y.
*†Mr. Jacob Chester Chamberlain (died July 28, 1905) ....New York, N. Y.
Rev. James A. Chamberlin, D. D. ....Berkeley, Cal.
*Mr. James I. Chamberlain (died June 1, 1906) ....Harrisburg, Pa.
James P. Chamberlin, M. D. ....Boston, Mass.
Mr. James Roswell Chamberlin ....Rochester, N. Y.
Mr. James W. Chamberlain ....Akron, Ohio
Mr. Jay Chester Chamberlin ....Port Washington, Wis.
†Jehiel W. Chamberlin, M. D. ....St. Paul, Minn.
†Miss Jessie C. Chamberlin ....Waco, Texas
Mr. John Chamberlin ....Lexington, Mo.
*Mr. John F. Chamberlin (died September 14, 1905) ....Summit, N. J.
Mr. John W. Chamberlain ....Portland, Ore.
*Mr. John Wilson Chamberlin (died August 11, 1901) ....Tiffin, Ohio
*Joseph E. M. Chamberlaine, M. D. (died January 30, 1901) ....Easton, Md.
Joseph E. Chamberlin ....New York, N. Y.
Mrs. Joseph F. Chamberlain ....Boston, Mass.
Mr. Joseph H. Chamberlin ....Chicago, Ill.
*Mr. Joseph L. Chamberlain (died December 30, 1900) ....Cherry Valley, N. Y.
Mr. Joseph R. Chamberlain ....Raleigh, N. C.
†Maj.-Gen. Joshua L. Chamberlain, LL. D. ....Brunswick, Me.
Mr. Justin Morrill Chamberlin ....Washington, D. C.
Miss Kaitryn Chamberlain ....Albany, N. Y.
†Miss Laura B. Chamberlain ....Cambridge, Mass.
Mr. Lee Chamberlain ....Los Angeles, Cal.
Mrs. Lee Chamberlain ....Los Angeles, Cal.
Mr. Leon T. Chamberlain ....St. Paul, Minn.
Mr. Lewis H. Chamberlin ....Detroit, Mich.
†Miss Lizzie F. Chamberlain ....Cambridge, Mass.
Hon. Loyed E. Chamberlain ....Brockton, Mass.
Miss Margaret E. Chamberlain ....New York, N. Y.
Mark Chamberlin, D. D. S. ....Cody, Wyo.
*Mark A. Chamberlain, M. D. (died July 3, 1905) ....Winthrop, Iowa
Mr. Martin H. Chamberlin ....Rutland, Vt.

Miss Maud L. Chamberlain.......................................Dorchester, Mass.
Pres. McKendree H. Chamberlin, LL. D.......................................Lebanon, Ill.
*†Hon. Mellen Chamberlain, LL. D. (died June 25, 1900).................Chelsea, Mass.
†Mr. Montague Chamberlain.......................................Boston, Mass.
*Mr. Moses Chamberlin (died July 29, 1902).................................Milton, Pa.
Miss Myla Chamberlin.......................................W. Concord, N. H.
†Myron L. Chamberlain, M. D.......................................Boston, Mass.
*†Miss N. Augusta Chamberlain (died March 22, 1900)..............Auburndale, Mass.
*Mr. Nahum B. Chamberlain (died January 11, 1905)...............Jamaica Plain, Mass.
*Rev. Nathan H. Chamberlayne (died April 1, 1901).............Monument Beach, Mass.
*†Mr. Newell Chamberlain (died February 10, 1905)...................Cambridge, Mass.
Mr. Norman A. Chamberlain.......................................Charleston, S. C.
Mr. Norman Saxon Chamberlin.......................................Royal Oak, Wis.
*Mr. Orin S. Chamberlain (died February, 1902).........................Chicago, Ill.
Capt. Orville T. Chamberlain.......................................Elkhardt, Ind.
Mr. Orville Walter Chamberlain.......................................New Orleans, La.
Mr. Patrick Chamberlaine.......................................Chicago, Ill.
Prof. Paul Mellen Chamberlain.......................................Chicago, Ill.
Mr. Pierson M. Chamberlain.......................................Netcong, N. J.
Mr. Prescott Chamberlain.......................................Chelsea, Mass.
Mr. Preston S. Chamberlin.......................................Bradford, Vt.
Raymond Chamberlain, Ph.D.......................................Brooklyn, N. Y.
Mr. Remembrance W. Chamberlain.......................................Bradford, Vt.
Mr. Richard H. Chamberlain.......................................Oakland, Cal.
Mr. Riley William Chamberlain.......................................Marshalltown, Iowa
*Gen. Robert H. Chamberlain (died June 28, 1910).....................Worcester, Mass.
Mr. Robert M. Chamberlain.......................................Detroit, Mich.
Mr. Rollin S. Chamberlin.......................................Scranton, Pa.
Mr. Roswell W. Chamberlain.......................................Chester, N. Y.
Miss S. Belle Chamberlain.......................................Boise, Idaho
Mr. Samuel D. Chamberlin.......................................Hartford, Conn.
*†Brig.-Gen. Samuel E. Chamberlain (died November 10, 1908).......Barre Plains, Mass.
Miss Sarah Abigail Chamberlin..............................Cumberland Foreside, Me.
Miss Sarah E. Chamberlain.......................................Oak Ridge, N. J.
*†Miss Sarah P. Chamberlain (died December, 1910).........................Salem, Mass.
*†Col. Simon E. Chamberlin (died April 20, 1908)....................Washington, D. C.
†Miss S. Emma Chamberlin.......................................Cleveland, Ohio
Mr. S. Harrison Chamberlain.......................................Allston, Mass.
Mr. Smith T. Chamberlin.......................................Derby, Conn.
*Mr. Stillman W. Chamberlain (died September 20, 1903)...............Braintree, Mass.
Mr. Stroud N. Chamberlain.......................................Netcong, N. J.
Mr. Sylvester Chamberlain.......................................Buffalo, N. Y.
Mr. Theodore Chamberlain.......................................Hackensack, N. J.
†Col. Thomas Chamberlin.......................................Philadelphia, Pa.
†Mr. Thomas Chamberlain.......................................Hyde Park, Mass.
†Prof. Thomas C. Chamberlin, LL.D.......................................Chicago, Ill.
Mr. Thomas E. Chamberlin.......................................Brookline, Mass.
Mr. Wallace M. Chamberlin.......................................West Detroit, Mich.
Mr. Walter N. Chamberlin.......................................New Carlisle, Ohio
*Mr. Ward B. Chamberlin (died November 14, 1903)....................New York, N. Y.
Mr. Warren Chamberlain.......................................Honolulu, H. I.
Mr. Wesley Chamberlain.......................................Newfoundland, N. J.
Capt. Wilbur F. Chamberlain.......................................Hannibal, Mo.
Mr. Willard C. Chamberlin.......................................Newton Center, Mass.
Mr. Willard DeWitt Chamberlin.......................................Dayton, Ohio
Mr. Willard N. Chamberlain.......................................Brookline, Mass.
Mr. William Chamberlain.......................................Portland, Me.
Mr. William Chamberlain.......................................Ashbourne, Pa.
Capt. William Chamberlaine.......................................Fort Warren, Boston
*Prof. William B. Chamberlain (died March 7, 1903).......................Oak Park, Ill.
Mr. William B. Chamberlin.......................................Torresdale, Pa.
Mr. William C. Chamberlain.......................................Charlottesville, Va.
Mr. William C. Chamberlain.......................................Dubuque, Iowa

†Mr. William Carlton Chamberlain........................ ....Cannelton, Ind.
Mr. William Gilbert Chamberlain....................................Fort Fairfield, Me.
Mr. William H. Chamberlin..Chicago, Ill.
Mr. William H. Chamberlin..Roxabell, Ohio
Mr. William H. H. Chamberlin...Syracuse, N. Y.
Rev. William I. Chamberlain, Ph.D..................................New Brunswick, N. J.
Mr. William Joseph Chamberlain...Denver, Colo.
Mr. William M. Chamberlin..Davenport, Iowa
*Mr. William N. Chamberlin (died August 9, 1901)......................Pittsfield, Mass.
Major William N. Chamberlin...................... ....Washington, D. C.
Mr. William Porter Chamberlain.................. ....Knoxville, Tenn.
Mr. William Reginald Chamberlain................ ....Portland, Me.
Mr. William Roswell Chamberlain..Chicago, Ill.
Mr. William S. Chamberlain..Cleveland, Ohio
Mr. William W. Chamberlaine..Norfolk, Va.
Mr. Woodbury O. Chamberlin...Surfside, Mass.
*†Mrs. Alice G. Chamberlain Clarke (died July 8, 1899)...............Southbridge, Mass.
Mrs. Mary L. C. Clarke...Andover, Mass.
Mrs. George N. Conklin............ ....Marquette, Mich.
Rev. Thomas M. Corson...Salem, Mass.
†Edward Cowles, M.D., LL.D...Plymouth, Mass.
Miss Caroline Crosman..Detroit, Mich.
Mrs. Abigail C. Curtis...Dorchester, Mass.
Miss Cacia Curtiss.............. ....Howell, Mich.
*Mrs. Amie Whiting Damon (died January 26, 1902).......................Reading, Mass.
Mrs. Nathan A. Davis...Concord, Mass.
Mrs. Nestor W. Davis..................... ....Winchester, Mass.
Mrs. A. E. Dick..Andover, Mass.
Mrs. Nelson R. Doe..Bradford, Vt.
Mrs. Annah Kellogg Drew...Minneapolis, Minn.
Mr. John C. Eccleston..Buenos Ayres, S. A.
Mrs. Sarah C. Eccleston..Buenos Ayres, S. A.
Mrs. De Lucia Chamberlin Eddy...Denver, Col.
*Mrs. Eben B. Ellis (died July 5, 1910)..Berkeley, Cal.
Mr. Elbert Eli Farman.. ....Warsaw, N. Y.
Mrs. Mary E. Fellows..New York, N. Y.
Mrs. J. M. Foley...Roxbury, Mass.
Mrs. Denis Follett..Hastings, Minn.
Judge William T. Forbes..Worcester, Mass.
†Mrs. Caroline W. Furst...Bellefonte, Pa.
Miss Adelaide C. Gray.... ....Farmington, N. H.
Miss Mary E. Grover...White River Junction, Vt.
†Mrs. Helen M. Guilford...Minneapolis Minn.
Mrs. Adeline C. Hamilton..London, Ohio
*Mrs. O. H. Harding (died January 30, 1903)...............................Allston, Mass.
Mrs. Wm. J. Harding...Brooklyn, N. Y.
Mrs. George B. Harvey...New York, N. Y.
Mrs. Julia Woodhull Hay..New York City
*Mrs. William Hayes (died January 31, 1908)...............................Winona, Minn.
Mr. Benj. F. Henry..Olathe, Kansas
Mrs. Harriet C. I. Hewitt...Saratoga Springs, N. Y.
Miss Harriet A. Hill..Belmont, Mass.
†Miss Louise H. Hinckley..Cambridge, Mass.
Mr. Roderick W. Hine...Dedham, Mass.
Mrs. Hattie T. C. Hughes..Mobile, Ala.
Mr. Edward P. Hunt...Newton Center, Mass.
Mrs. H. D. Hurley..Seattle, Wash
Mrs. Cleora E. Jefferds...Foxcroft, Me.
*Mr. Charles A. Jewell (died January 25, 1905)...........................Hartford, Conn.
*Miss Charlotte A. Jewell (died October 23, 1903)........................Hartford, Conn.
Mrs A. E. Johnson..So. Newbury, Vt.
Mrs. Annie B. Chamberlain Keene.......................................Schenectady, N. Y.
†Mrs. Etta F. C. Kendall..Auburndale, Mass.

*†Mrs. Eliza M. C. Kennedy (died September 21, 1903)................Watertown, Mass.
Mrs. Agnes Thompson Kent..Montpelier, Vt.
Mr. Elliot C. Kimball..Dubuque, Iowa
†Mrs. Harriet P. Kimball (died February 7, 1909)....................Dubuque, Iowa
Mrs. Israel H. Light...Brooklyn, N. Y.
Mrs. Helen M. C. Lloyd...Chicago, Ill.
Mrs. Archibald G. Loomis...Providence, R. I.
Mrs. Margaret C. MacFadden...Oak Park, Ill.
Mrs. Edwin T. Mander...Elizabeth, N. J.
Mrs. Franklin H. Martin..Chicago, Ill.
*Rev. Moses Mellen Martin, D.D. (died September 25, 1902)...........Ovid, Mich.
Miss Mamie L. McCormick..Sparta, N. J.
Mr. Robert L. McCormick..Tacoma, Wash.
Mrs. Amy C. McGuinness...Chester, N. Y.
Mrs. C. B. McLean..Pittsburg, Pa.
Mrs. A. A. Metcalf...Worcester, Mass.
Rev. Oscar F. Moore..Lee, Mass.
Mrs. Oscar F. Moore..Delhi, Ohio
Mrs. W. E. F. Moore..Summit, N. J.
Mrs. Florence Chamberlain Moseley..................................New Haven, Conn.
Mrs. M. P. Murray..Athens, Pa.
Mrs. Charles C. Nicholls...St. Louis, Mo.
Mrs. Evan Oldfield...Booneville, N. Y.
*Mr. John Chamberlain Ordway (died April 23, 1905)...................Concord, N. H.
Mrs. Alma C. Osincup...Waverly, Iowa
Mrs. Lucy B. Page..Pepperill, Mass.
Mr. Ralph C. Perkins...Salem, Mass.
†Mr. George Herbert Perry..Revere, Mass.
†Mrs. Minnie A. C. Perry...Revere, Mass.
†Mr. Ralph Dana Perry..Cambridge, Mass.
Mrs. Ralph F. Perry..Watertown, Mass.
Mrs. Scott T. Pierce...Worcester, Mass.
Mrs. Charles B. Platt..Englewood, N. J.
Mrs. Arthur H. Pray..Brookline, Mass.
Mrs. Lucinda C. Ragan (died May 29, 1908)...........................London, Ohio
Lieutenant James W. H. Reisinger, Jr...............................Canton, Ohio
Mr. Roe Reisinger..Franklin, Pa.
Mr. John Ringwalt.........................Mount Vernon, Knox County, Ohio
Prof. Ralph Curtis Ringwalt..New York, N. Y.
Mrs. Elisha Risley...West Hartford, Conn.
Mrs. Albert S. Roe...New York, N. Y.
Miss Emma Ten-Broeck Runk..Lambertville, N. J.
†Mrs. Charles W. Seymour...Hingham, Mass.
Mrs. Amy Chamberlain Shanks (died January 23, 1905).................Round Lake, N. Y.
Miss Maria Gove Shanks...Staten Island, N. Y.
Mr. Frank Chamberlain Shipley......................................Seattle, Wash.
Mrs. Anna Eugenia Smiley...Holyoke, Mass.
Mrs. Charles Willis Smith..Pittsburg, Pa.
Miss Cornelia Buxton Smith...Litchfield, Conn.
Miss Madeleine Smith...Bessemer, Alabama
Mrs. Grace Chamberlin Snook..Hartwell, Ohio
Mr. Arthur C. Sprague..Wollaston, Mass.
Mrs. Louisa Steele...Netcong, N. J.
Mrs. Mary L. Stockwell...Watertown, Mass.
Mrs. Mary Baldwin Stoddard...New York City
†Rev. Elnathan E. Strong, D.D......................................Auburndale, Mass.
Mrs. Charles H. Taylor...Louisiana, Mo.
Mrs. Abbie M. Wadsworth..Holden, Mass.
Mr. James H. Walling...Brooklyn, N. Y.
Mrs. Blanche Warner..Baltimore, Md.
Mr. Edward K. Warren...Three Oaks, Mich.
Mrs. Edward K. Warren..Three Oaks, Mich.
Miss Jenny Chamberlain Watts.......................................Cambridge, Mass.

Mrs. Sarah A. Wells .... Hyde Park, Mass.
Mr. James Dale Whitmore .... Toledo, Ohio
Mrs. Martha C. Wilson .... Hartford, Conn.
Mrs. Charles H. Wood .... Seattle, Wash.
Mrs. Clayton Wrighter .... Netcong, N. J.

Associate Members

Mr. George M. Brown .... Hartford, Conn.
†Mr. George B. Caswell .... Holden, Mass.
Mrs. Abiram Chamberlain .... Meriden, Conn.
Mrs. Anna Garland Chamberlain .... Andover, Mass.
†Mrs. Asa W. Chamberlin .... Jamaica Plain, Mass.
Mrs. Catherine W. Chamberlain .... Cambridge, Mass.
Mrs. Charles E. Chamberlin .... Port Washington, Wis.
Mrs. Emerson Chamberlin .... Summit, N. J.
Mrs. Eugene Chamberlin .... Brooklyn, N. Y.
Mrs. Eugene G. Chamberlin .... Brunswick, Me.
Mrs. Fannie E. Chamberlin .... Philadelphia, Pa.
Mrs. George M. Chamberlain .... Brookline, Mass.
Mrs. Henry H. Chamberlin .... Worcester, Mass.
Mrs. Jacob C. Chamberlain .... New York, N. Y.
Mrs. Mary A Chamberlin .... Greenville, N. H.
†Mrs. Newell Chamberlain (died April 15, 1911) .... Cambridge, Mass.
Mrs. Robert H. Chamberlain .... Worcester, Mass.
Mrs. Samuel E. Chamberlain (died February, 11, 1910) .... Barre Plains, Mass.
Mrs. Thomas Chamberlain .... Hyde Park, Mass.
Mrs. Willard N. Chamberlain .... Brookline, Mass.
Mrs. William B. Chamberlin .... Torresdale, Pa.
Mr. Nathan A. Davis .... Concord, Mass.
Col. William J. Harding .... Brooklyn, N. Y.
Mrs. Charles A. Jewell (died October 7, 1909) .... Hartford, Conn.
†Mr. James H. Kendall .... Auburndale, Mass.
Hon. Oscar H. Leland .... McGregor, Tex.
Mrs. Sarah J. Ordway .... Concord, N. H.
*†Mr. Frank W. Perry (died June 20, 1898) .... Cambridge, Mass.

The plates for the half-tones and line-cuts used in this Report are the property of the Association with the following exceptions,—the plate for the portrait of Mrs. Kimball loaned by Mr. Elliot C. Kimball, that of Mrs. Samuel E. Chamberlain loaned by Mrs. George M. Brown, that of the "Veterans of the Arcot Mission" loaned by Prof. William I. Chamberlain, and those for the pictures and autographs in the three articles on Hon. William Chamberlin, Mellen Chamberlain, Esq., and the "Descendants of Jacob Chamberlain," by Miss Abbie M. Chamberlain, Miss Laura B. Chamberlain and Miss Jenny C. Watts.

For the excellent reproduction of the portrait of Mellen Chamberlain (page 69), we are largely indebted to the kindness of one of our members, Mr. Ephraim Chamberlain, of Norwood, Mass., who photographed the oil painting at the home of its owners in Cambridge.

ERRATA.

Page 71, twenty-third line from bottom, for Erasmus read Erastus.

Page 37, seventeenth line from bottom, for Crowinshields read Crowninshields.

www.ingramcontent.com/pod-product-compliance
Lightning Source LLC
Chambersburg PA
CBHW030832270326
41928CB00007B/1011

* 9 7 8 3 7 4 4 7 2 9 6 2 8 *